learning centers

learning centers

opening up the classroom

John I. Thomas

New Mexico State University

Holbrook Press, Inc.   **Boston**

Library of Congress Cataloging in Publication Data

Thomas, John I
Learning centers: see
slip

Bibliography: p.
Includes index.
1. Open plan schools. I. Title.
LB1029.06T48   371.3   75-2044
ISBN 0-205-04807-2
ISBN 0-205-04808-0 pbk.

To Romayne, Wendy, David,
Peter, and Paul
with love

Contents

preface   xi

introductory note   xiii

one

Invitation to Learning:
The Open Classroom   1

The Educational Setting
Creating the Classroom Environment

two

Defining and Clarifying
Learning Centers   39

Purposes and Characteristics of Learning Centers
Using Centers to Motivate, Diagnose,
Prescribe, and Enrich Learning

three

Attracting Pupils
to Learning Centers   81

Putting Ideas to Work in Single-Object Centers
Multi-Level, Multi-Experience Learning Centers

four

*Using Textbooks and Literature
to Personalize Learning*   **131**

Team Learning in Mathematics
Personalizing Individual Reading Experiences

five

*Ingredients Essential
to Getting Underway*   **171**

Establishing the Climate:
Prerequisite to Open Learning
Preparing the Classroom Environment

six

*Getting Underway:
Preparations for Decentralizing the Classroom*   **201**

Organization of the Classroom
Barriers to Implementation

seven

*Approaches to Implementation
of Learning Centers*   **229**

Implementing Learning Centers Gradually
Implementing Learning Centers Moderately
The Total Implementation of Learning Centers

eight

*Evaluating the Effectiveness
of Open Learning in the Classroom*   **265**

Assessment of Classroom Readiness
for Open Learning
Assessment of Pupils' Needs,
Interests, and Performance
Assessment of Teaching Practices
Effectiveness of Open Education

selected references   **309**

index   **317**

Preface

"The times—they are a-changin," sings Bob Dylan. Elementary schools in the United States are also changing. One such change, that of informal or open education in the open-space school, has caught the imagination and interest of an increasing number of teachers. Most elementary school teachers, however, do not or may not ever have the opportunity to teach in an open-space school. Thus, a book such as this is needed. This textbook is directed to prospective teachers who will be teaching in self-contained classrooms and to practicing teachers who wish to institute informal and open-concept programs in their classrooms. It introduces methods, materials, and media that they may find helpful in making the transition from traditional classroom practices to open education experiences.

In this text, I present, describe, illustrate, and explore practical and tested ideas for opening up the traditional elementary school classroom to provide differentiated and rewarding learning experiences for both pupils and teachers. Although other authors have presented considerable thought and information to this subject, very few have directed their attention to specific approaches applicable to the implementation of open-concept programs in the traditional public school classroom. Most authors, in fact, have restricted their attention to the closed, limited learning experiences prevalent in many of our schools and have contrasted these experiences with the more open practices of the British infant schools. Consequently, much of the very fine work being done by teachers in American schools to encourage open learning has been neglected in the literature. Indeed the critics of traditional education are legion. The point of this book is not to cry out against the injustices that exist in many schools, but rather to present alternatives. For dramatic, growing, positive changes are occurring in elementary schools throughout the United States. This book—dealing with learning-centered, open classrooms—reflects some of these changes.

Although this is not strictly a theoretical book and may be considered by some as lacking the experimental referents common to college textbooks, it offers its readers—whether they are beginning students in education, student teachers, or practicing teachers—a theoretical framework within which they are encouraged to probe the various dimensions of learning centers and their application to open learning in the classroom. It is, furthermore, written on the premise that professors of education and graduate students in education will see fit to field test the ideas, strategies, and media illustrated with the view of subsequently communicating to teachers and having them apply those that maximize the learning experiences of the pupils in their classrooms.

This is a teachers' book, for teachers, written by a teacher. I have written it on the basis of what I think students in education and teachers would want to know. I hope that they will find its practicability more meaningful and of more benefit to them than they do theories of open education that, in my judgment, are yet to be tested systematically and thoroughly. Consequently, I have focused on "nuts-and-bolts" approaches to moving from traditional to open classroom practices. Students in education, beginning and experienced teachers, school administrators, and professors of education will, I feel, find the rich variety of approaches, materials, and media described in the book useful in making this transition. My thesis throughout the text is that there are many ways to implement learning centers and to organize the classroom for this purpose. Thus, I present no cookbook formulas or oversimplified answers. Instead, I illustrate some representative ideas, multiple approaches, and actual public school classroom practices, while leaving you to select, modify, or expand those suitable and applicable to your own classroom circumstances.

In writing this book, I stand on the shoulders of many. I acknowledge, particularly, my former colleagues in the team-teaching schools of Lexington, Massachusetts with whom I spent the most exciting and rewarding years (1957–1966) of my professional career. I acknowledge, also, the numerous student and cooperating teachers in Las Cruces, Anthony, and Alamogordo, New Mexico, who shared their views and work with me over the past eight years. In a very large measure, this is their book. I am indebted, additionally, to those teachers, students, and lay people who critiqued and gave me the incentive to complete this book. In particular, I am grateful to Sandra Abernathy, Dorothy Adcock, Mike Boravica, Paulette Campbell, Betty Dirk, Martha Gray, Laura Lee Harty, Elizabeth Hinkle, Dolores Lucero, Maria Luna, Dolores Minatogawa, Elizabeth Ongley, Judy Runyon, Karen Smith, Tamie Smith, Mike Thayer, David Wier, and teachers and students in my university classes.

Finally, I owe much to my present colleagues who, when I needed them, were always there. To Chuck Bomont, who first planted the idea in my mind, then urged me to write this book, and discussed its development, I am especially grateful. To Dick DeBlassie and Leon Williamson I am similarly grateful for meticulously reading the manuscript and for making valuable suggestions for its improvement. I am also deeply appreciative of the direct and indirect contributions made by Bill Cross, Guillermina Englebrecht, Ed Kugler, Doug Muller, Sherry Engle Robertson, and Bob Wright.

I wish to acknowledge the encouragement and support of Darrell Willey who, through the auspices of the College of Education's Research Center, provided me first with the typing services of Scharilyn Finney and subsequently, with the funds necessary to complete my manuscript.

Finally, I wish to express my appreciation to Holbrook Press, Inc., and its manager, John DeRemigis, for publishing my manuscript and for providing the expert assistance of Pat Torelli as its production editor. Her meticulous editing, pertinent questions, and objective suggestions were invaluable to me.

Introductory Note

One of my purposes in writing this book is to define, clarify, and expand the term "learning center." Professors of education, school administrators, teachers, and students tend to use it synonymously and sometimes erroneously with classroom terms such as "interest centers," "group projects," or "learning stations." Additionally, its interpretation is often confused with specifically designated areas within a school other than classrooms, such as learning resource centers, instructional materials centers, curriculum materials centers, learning systems centers, media centers, and multipurpose libraries.

As cited and illustrated in this text, the learning center consists of any one area within the classroom itself, established temporarily or permanently for the purpose of providing pupils with differentiated learning experiences in the form of individual or group activities, to which pupils may be directed by the teacher or may be given the opportunity to select, manage, and evaluate the experiences of which the center is composed. The learning center may constitute an individual desk, a cluster of desks, an area on the floor, a bulletin board or chalkboard, a table, a file cabinet, or a bookshelf. It may be teacher-constructed, pupil-constructed, or the result of a teacher-pupil effort.

Roland, Age 5

one

Invitation to Learning: the Open Classroom

Deeply intent on a move to be made, two children hunch over a checkerboard. Several youngsters busily measure objects and dimensions as directed on an activity sheet. One pupil at an electric quiz board strives to make appropriate circuit connections in response to questions of interest. Under a table another youngster sprawls on the floor completely absorbed in a book. A boy and girl at a second table argue the merits of a structure being erected with Cuisenaire rods. Conversing animatedly, two pupils explore the movements of fish in an aquarium:

"What are those funny slits on the fishes' heads?"

"Why do the fish swim toward the top of the water?"

"Do fish sleep at night?"

Over a sink still another pair of youngsters pour water into differently shaped vases, debating "is greater than" and "is less than" mathematical concepts. In a make-shift projection booth a group of pupils are engrossed in a filmstrip. Several boys and girls buzz away as they work on a social studies mural along one wall. In a refrigerator carton set off in a nook, a solitary child sits thinking. On one end of a sofa two girls drill each other on selected vocabulary; at the other end two boys behave similarly, each pair using flash cards. And in the "conversation pit," still another group of pupils, legs crossed on a rug, listen to their teacher as she reads of another time and place.

Individual worlds are touching, crossing, and colliding. Each student has the opportunity to test, to contradict, to decide and time to explore and experience.

With their curiosities extended and imaginations stretched, they generate new ideas. Each pupil is finding his own way, in his own time, according to his own needs. The open classroom is a child's world which goes beyond academic thought and action and embraces laughter, song, and movement.

There are various approaches that may be utilized by teachers to provide open educational experiences for their pupils. In this volume, I introduce and develop only one—the learning center approach. The experienced teacher, as well as the student and beginning teacher, who contemplates the use of open-concept activities in his or her classroom will find many ideas to select from in this book. Some of you will disagree substantially with much of what I have to say; others will agree strongly; still others will both disagree and agree. I trust, however, you will all agree that I present this one approach to opening up your classrooms— the learning center approach—without claiming that it is *the* way.

THE EDUCATIONAL SETTING

Sometimes referred to as the informal classroom, the open classroom takes many forms, shapes, and directions. I use the term, "open classroom," simply because of its wide usage in the literature and in educational circles. This usage, however, has its shortcomings in that it is too often emotionally charged—conjuring visions of permissiveness, with the pupil doing his own thing and the role of the teacher in the classroom being drastically diminished. This, however, is not the case in the open classroom.

A casual visitor to a so-called "open classroom" is often struck by the abundance of materials and variety of activities in even the most crowded classroom. Some of the teachers with whom I have been working, in fact, have had as many different activities simultaneously functioning as there were children in their classrooms. On one visit to such a classroom, I noted the following number of pupils and activities at the various learning centers that comprised the classroom, as shown in Figure 1-1.

In this class of twenty-six six- and seven-year old children, some sixteen different activities were carried on at the same time. Every piece of furniture and every nook and cranny was put to use as a learning center. Pupils functioned in corners, at tables, under tables, in the coat alcove, at the sink counter, on book shelves, *in* the book shelves, at the few desks that were in the room, at the blackboard, at bulletin boards, and on the floor. The children had been encouraged to select their own activities. Those who could or would not were guided to activities felt to be appropriate for them by their teacher. Pupils moved freely from learning center to learning center. The single constraint on their movement was the occupation of the desired center.

To ensure successful implementation of movement and activity such as that depicted in Figure 1-1, it is necessary that those of you who plan the

FIGURE 1-1   *Number of Pupils and Activiites Observed in an Open Classroom*

No. of Pupils	Activities
2	Making pottery out of clay
1	Silently reading on the floor
2	Playing an arithmetic checker game
1	Using a spin wheel to study beginning consonants
1	Working on an arithmetic problem
3	Computing arithmetic examples
2	Classifying food according to taste
1	Writing a sentence about something felt, but not seen, in a box
1	Making butter with a churn
1	Identifying airplane ports via an electric quiz board
3	Constructing mosaics out of beads, buttons, seeds, matches, yarn
1	Writing a sentence about a cartoon
1	Constructing sentences by connecting phrases on a worksheet
2	Playing spelling checkers
2	Classifying fruit and vegetables by grouping them
2	Matching words with pictures

implementation of open education practices in your classrooms formulate learning environments in which both you and your pupils explore together, motivate and reinforce each other, and make decisions of *mutual* benefit. In the process you will both need to direct yourselves to such questions as what is to be learned, in which context, for how long, with what materials, and who is responsible for what. These are some of the fundamental questions to which this book addresses itself.

THE OPERATIONAL COMPONENTS

A question I am often asked by students in education and by practicing teachers is: "How will I know when my classroom is functioning in terms of open classroom practices?" This is not an easy question to answer. Because of the various forms, styles, and directions the open classroom takes, an operational definition of it is difficult. However, you can "know" it through identification of the characteristics that make up its dimensions, the ingredients of which I present and discuss throughout the chapters to follow. Figure 1-2 presents these dimensions and characteristics alongside those of the traditional classroom to assist you in distinguishing their differences.

It is not my intention to overstate the contrast between the two classrooms characterized in the figure, for it is highly unlikely that any classroom is completely open or completely traditional. In fact, I have had experiences in classrooms designated as "open" which I found to be more "closed" than some traditional classrooms. For example, during one of my visits to a so-called "open" classroom in a nearby city, I found much to be admired, particularly the diagnostic teaching taking place with the pupils self-pacing, self-managing, and self-evaluating their academic progress. However, despite the results of teacher diagnosis, the pupils' learning experiences were rigidly imposed. A no-nonsense, teacher-directed approach to the tasks to be completed was programmed for the children in the form of contracts. The contracted experiences were teacher-determined, varied little from pupil to pupil, and invited no interaction between them. Pupil input and their preferred choices of activities were nonexistent.

Contrast this with a truly open classroom; there are a number of observable practices that will help you identify it. You will note pupils planning some of their activities, interacting with each other, conferring with their teacher, undergoing differentiated instruction, selecting their learning experiences, moving freely from activity to activity, evaluating their progress, projecting and exploring their interests, working individually, in pairs, or in small groups, testing their ideas, using multilevel texts and materials, inquiring, and experimenting.

Observe Figure 1-2. There is general agreement that the characteristics shown in the figure are representative of those which distinguish open operational procedures from the more traditional practices. Note in particular the persistent attention to the fluidity of pupil movement, the diversity and flexibility of their activities, and the joint responsibility of the teacher and pupils in the open classroom. Note, also, the sharp contrast of these characteristics with those of the so-called "traditional" classroom which are epitomized by narrow, fixed, regulated, routinized, undifferentiated, teacher-dominated objectives and pupil experiences.

Openness, like freedom, has no boundaries. As I have already indicated, the open classroom cannot be defined in precise, absolute terms. Nor need it be. Describing it *operationally* will provide you with a more graphic illustration. To set the stage for the more specific illustrations to follow, permit me to elaborate on the operational functions of six of its major dimensions. These are: (1) the classroom's physical environment, (2) the time allocated for the activities taking place in the environment, (3) the nature of the activities that occur, (4) the materials utilized, (5) the relationships between the teacher and pupils, and (6) the associations of pupils with pupils.

FIGURE 1–2 *Operational Comparisons of the Open and Traditional Classroom on Selected Dimensions of School Practices**

Dimensions	Characteristics	(More open) 5 4 3 2 1 ← | → 1 2 3 4 5 (More traditional)	Characteristics
INSTRUCTIONAL TARGET	The individual pupil	O T	The group or total class
TYPE OF INSTRUCTION	Diagnostic	O T	Textbook Oriented
PUPIL OBJECTIVES	Flexible, variable Personalized Determined by teacher and pupils	O T	Fixed Regulated Determined by teacher
CURRICULUM CONTENT	Varied Wide range Emphasis on multiple texts Determined by teacher and pupils	O T	Constant Limited Range Limited to single text Determined by teacher
FURNITURE ARRANGEMENT AND SPACE DISPOSITION	Moveable Flexible, variable Decided by teacher and pupils	O T	Fixed Routinized Decided by teacher
SUBJECT TIME ALLOCATION	Flexible, variable Unscheduled	O T	Fixed Scheduled Routinized
MATERIAL UTILIZATION	Multi-sensory Multi-level Diversified Wide range	O T	Limited Routinized Undifferentiated Narrow range
PUPIL ACTIVITIES	Flexible, variable Personalized Determined by teacher and pupils	O T	Fixed Regulated Determined by teacher
TEACHER-PUPIL AND PUPIL-PUPIL INTERACTION	Initiated by teacher and pupils	O T	Initiated by teacher
PUPIL MOBILITY	Fluid Unrestricted Wide range	O T	Restricted Routinized Narrow range
PUPIL PROGRESS	Irregular Differentiated Based on diagnosis	O T	Regular Routinized Undifferentiated Based on grade level
PUPIL EVALUATION	Individualized Personalized Self-assessment	O T	Standardized Teacher assessment

O = Open Classroom   T = Traditional Classroom

*Adapted, modified, and expanded from Katz, L. G., "Research on Open Education: Problems and Issues" in D. D. Hearn, J. Burdin, and L. Katz (eds.), *Current Research and Perspectives in Open Education.* American Association of Elementary-Kindergarten-Nursery Educators, Washington, D.C. 1972, p. 6.

The Physical Environment. This dimension of the open classroom is characterized by its fluidity and flexibility, the classroom's form and shape changing as the interests and learning needs of the pupils change. A variety of furniture is employed to decentralize the environment. Assorted tables typically substitute for desks and desks that are in the room are clustered together. Portable screens, bulletin boards, blackboards, bookshelves, and other movable furniture are utilized as partitions. Work benches, science laboratories, art easels, water tables, and homemade learning booths and carrels are mobilized. Rugs, carpeting, mats, pillows, and occasionally a sofa are functional commodities that are sometimes present. In equipping your classroom you may even use such items as rocking chairs and, as I have occasionally witnessed, a bathtub.

Figure 1-3 is presented here to help you visualize the decentralized nature of the open classroom. Please do not construe it as prototypic, however, because at any given moment during the schoolday, its shape and form may change as the needs and interests of the children in the classroom change. Also, I do not intend to convey with this figure that an open classroom must be physically decentralized for you to practice open education. For it is conceivable, although not likely, that open education could be practiced in a classroom where desks are fixed row by row. Note, also, that Figure 1-3 is representative of only one form of the learning center approach to opening up the classroom—that of subject centers.

FIGURE 1-3   *Using Subject Centers to Decentralize the Classroom*

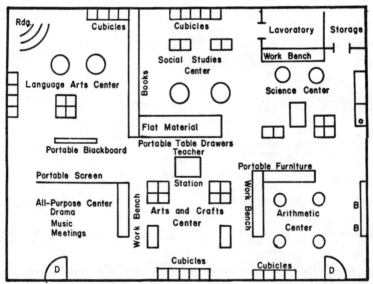

Time Allocation. Characteristically, the time spent by pupils in the learning experiences of the open classroom is unspecified, varying from activity to activity and from pupil to pupil according to the unique needs of each. However, as in the traditional classroom, specified time is allocated for teacher-pupil planning, the sharing of reports, pupil evaluation, general announcements, guest speakers and storytellers, films of general interest, and activities in learning centers which necessitate time limitations. Look at Figure 1-3. Visualize the movement of pupils from subject center to subject center. More often than not, unrestricted by time, pupils at each of the centers shown will fluctuate in number according to the time needed by each pupil to achieve self-initiated or mutually designated goals. To put this component into actual practice, you are going to find it necessary to devote a considerable amount of your time to conferring and planning with your pupils.

Nature of the Activities.   The activities in the open classroom are diverse because they provide for differentiated learning experiences. Pupils do not customarily undergo the same experience at the same time. Based on the various needs, competencies, interests, aspirations, and learning styles of the pupils, the activities are largely oriented to the development of the pupils' curiosity and original thinking, their creativity, and their independence. Progress from learning center to learning center and from activity to activity within a center is typically not fixed, with the content, scope, and direction of each being as varied as the pupils themselves. The activities in each of the learning centers are "gradeless" and open, and the pupils are given much responsibility for choosing the content, materials, and courses of learning suitable to their specific needs.

Utilization of Materials.   Examine Figure 1-3 further. Visualize once again the abundance of multisensory materials you may need to decentralize your classroom should you wish to pattern it along the lines of the one pictured. Ranging from salvage scraps to commercial products, the materials of your classroom need to be sufficiently diverse to encourage pupils to look, hear, smell, and touch. Tapes and records, pictures, films, filmstrips and slides, maps and charts, artifacts and memorabilia, puzzles and games, blocks and rods, clay and paints, science paraphernalia, and other self-instructional materials may be used to develop your pupils to their fullest potential. Books, activity sheets, and associated resources need to be highly differentiated. Gather and utilize materials which are particularly appropriate for activities that your pupils can carry on independently of you, since their independent learning is a necessary component of the open classroom.

Relationships between Teacher and Pupils.   Obviously, Figure 1-3 does not enable you to "see" the relationships between the teacher and the pupils who might function in such a classroom. Given the opportunity to teach in this representative environment, however, you will come to "know" the extent of its openness. You will find your open classroom manifested in one-to-one and in small group interaction between you and your pupils in both formal and informal learning experiences. You will find yourself a friend to your pupils as well as their teacher. Much of your time in the classroom will be spent diagnosing and guiding; your pupils will do the big thinking.

You will know where your pupils are, what they need, and how they are responding to their needs. Consequently, you will find yourself adjusting the rate, quantity, and depth of their learning experiences to fit their levels of motivation, potential abilities, and mental and emotional health. Sounds difficult, doesn't it? Well, whoever said teaching in the open classroom was easy? The ideas presented in this book will help to make feasible for you this difficult but highly rewarding experience.

In the representation of the classroom pictured as Figure 1-3, the teacher displays the courage to be imperfect. If a particular approach to a child fails, the teacher tries another. The teacher gives the pupils the benefit of a doubt and tries not to anticipate a repetition of undesirable behavior. The teacher asks for and receives the help of pupils. In this classroom the teacher serves as a model, and his or her behavior is copied. If the teacher likes the children, they tend to like each other. The teacher reads; they read. The teacher inquires; the pupils inquire. The teacher experiments; they experiment. The teacher debates; the pupils debate. The teacher shows interest in the work of the pupils; they show interest in their own and each other's work.

Associations of Pupils with Pupils.   Divergent behavior cornerstones the interaction between pupils in the open classroom. Turn to Figure 1-3 once again. Picture the variety of ways in which the pupils are involved. Daily, in the all-purpose center, they gather as a group and plan the physical arrangement of the classroom, its activities, and its management. They function according to democratic principles, setting up their own rules for behavior under the guidance of the teacher. In each of the learning centers shown in the figure, they often select their own topics of interest to investigate, write about, and talk about. They select their own music, their own art experiences, and their own literature.

Kids are teaching kids in this environment, invariably motivating, challenging, and supporting each other in the process. They brainstorm, probe, discover, and evaluate together. As a result, they are in frequent communication, flexible and free in movement and direction. Most of their learning takes place in small groups, in partnership, or in individual undertakings. Note, in Figure 1-3, the carrels for those pupils who prefer to work in privacy, the work benches for those who enjoy manipulative experiences and experimentation, and the clustered desks and tables for those pupils who benefit by working together in group experiences.

"How will I know it when I see it?" The succeeding sections will provide you with an increasingly clear picture in response to this question.

CREATING THE CLASSROOM ENVIRONMENT

Almost all teachers I know who practice open education in their classrooms agree that better teacher-pupil and pupil-pupil relationships develop because of the new roles that they and their pupils assume in the learning center approach to the open classroom. They find that they are becoming increasingly receptive to pupil initiative and resourcefulness. Similarly, they find pupils opening up to each other. Teachers and pupils share in the management of the classroom activities—contributing ideas, planning cooperatively, implementing those plans, and sharing in the evaluation of the progress that takes place. In the learning center environment, teachers assist rather than direct the pupils by exposing them to experiences which invite the expression of their natural honesty and their independent action. The teachers move from learning center to learning center questioning, responding, encouraging, and freeing pupils to pursue their selected courses of learning under minimal control of so-called practical consequences.

Important components necessary to the creation of this classroom environment include:

1. A pressure-free setting
2. Independent learning
3. Multisensory experiences
4. Differentiated learning
5. Diversified activities
6. Pupil input
7. Pupil interaction
8. Creative action
9. Self-pacing
10. Self-selection and management
11. Self-evaluation and responsibility

A PRESSURE-FREE SETTING

Aren't the ingredients of the open classroom—love, trust, and respect—also found in more traditional settings? The immediate response is that this indeed is the case. Most teachers assume this; however, there is a wide discrepancy between what some teachers say and what they actually practice. Too often, too many teachers set the example for the behavior of their pupils by identifying the values pupils should have, by limiting their courses of learning, by insisting on prescribed learning experiences for them, by making the class rules, and by ignoring other examples, other arguments, and other values to which the pupils could be exposed. Conditions such as these too often restrict and confuse the pupils. In opening up your classroom, it is important that you build into its structure experiences which help develop your pupils love of, trust in, and respect for each other. Encourage them, then, to express their values, suggest courses of learning, and assist in formulating responsible rules of behavior so that this development may take place.

The open classroom, through the diversification of its activities, tends to free pupils from the pressure imposed by adult standards, fixed curriculum, fragmented knowledge, regulated progress, and restricted movement. It focuses on what children can do for themselves rather than on what should be done *to* them. That is to say, the open classroom places very special emphasis on what pupils think of themselves. It seeks to accomplish this by capitalizing on the pupils' innate honesty, natural inquisitiveness, initiative, resourcefulness, and independence, thereby enhancing and enriching the pupils' self-concepts.

Another major factor which distinguishes the open classroom from the traditional is the mobility it provides for the pupils' personal growth. It reduces pressure on the pupils because it provides the conditions whereby they determine their movement in the classroom—where to go, what to choose, what to do. In fact, the opportunities for preferred choices of the pupils sharply differentiate the open classroom from that of the more formalized classroom. The decentralized setting of the former, as reflected in the learning center approach, makes this possible. Consequently, pupils are apt to turn inward to find direction and discipline. They tend to become increasingly self-reliant because of the many and varied alternatives of learning to which they can respond.

Provision for more elbow room in the open classroom also enables pupils to explore, to stretch, and to expand their learning experiences, thus lessening the pressure of limited areas and restricted movement. As a result of this mobility, spontaneous participation and interaction are more likely to occur. Pupils are not boxed into one learning environment; the diverse learning centers available to them prohibits their becoming a captive audience.

The pressure-free setting of the open classroom has another advantage in that it tends to establish more positive relationships between the teacher and pupils, and between the pupils themselves. It invites the teacher to increase her or his knowledge of the students through the observation and personal contact that the decentralized, learning center environment makes possible. Conversely, because of the extended and more intimate contact between teacher and pupils, it encourages the pupils to view the teacher as a human being with feelings not too dissimilar from their own. Under this arrangement, a teacher recently made this startling statement to me, "God, this is the first time I've seen—really seen—my kids in the five years I've been teaching!" Needless to say, these views of both the teacher and the pupils will determine the direction the open classroom will take.

INDEPENDENT LEARNING

The warm, supportive climate of the pressure-free classroom unquestionably nurtures self-expression by the pupils. This nurturance is epitomized in the diversified activities that present the opportunity for them to work independently of the teacher. You must trust the children, care enough to accept their mistakes, and believe in their capacities to learn from them. In formulating plans for your open classroom, it is necessary that you encourage independent action by your pupils. Unfortunately, "letting go" of pupils is sometimes construed by some teachers as a risk. In my judgment, however, it is essential that you let go of your pupils if you are to institute the learning center approach in opening up your classroom, for you will rarely work with the total class at the same time on the same objective.

The need for children to be independent and responsible for their own actions is well-recognized. The open classroom attempts to promote and extend this need through experiences in the learning centers that constitute the total classroom environment. The fact that pupils are encouraged to find their own directions and make their own decisions conveys to them the feeling that the teacher is genuinely interested in what they choose to do. This respect for their actions, in turn, tends to motivate the pupils to justify such trust. Consequently, it is likely that pupils will try to become worthy of the trust placed in them. The more trusting the learning environment you create, the better your pupils are apt to think of themselves. This, of course, is the foundation on which the open classroom rests. For it is through trust in each other that pupils and teacher will open themselves to one another. As a result, they are apt to reach out and make contact with each other. Therein lies the openness of the classroom.

Question: Are children capable of working independently of the teacher? Far more than most of us give them credit! Consider, for example, what they have already learned independently long before they enter school. They have discovered, solved, and learned to use that most difficult and complicated symbol of communication—language—*without any formal instruction in it.* They have experienced life through close observation, exploration, experimentation and development of their own unique models of behavior. Their personal contact with objects, events, and people has enriched their independence because, in the process of their growth, they have experienced a reasonable degree of freedom to test this contact, observe its consequences, and make appropriate adjustments until, in their own eyes, a refined product suitable to their needs has resulted. Thus, those of you who intend to open up classroom experiences for your pupils would do well to build on what they have already learned before they entered your class.

The open classroom seeks to extend the natural learning attributes of pupils by providing extensive opportunity for work independent of the teacher. The wealth of materials necessary for it to function well ensures this extension of independent thought and action. Materials which are free of judgmental consequences are particularly important. Here, for example, you may wish to include experiences in your classroom which call for painting, constructing, solving puzzles, playing games, and inventing, just to name a few. Pupils working together, helping each other, and judging their own work also increase their independent behavior. The broader the exposure to independent experiences you can provide your pupils, the freer they tend to become. The variety and extent of the learning centers you institute will likely create the conditions for varied experiences, thus increasing the likelihood of your pupils' freedom.

MULTISENSORY EXPERIENCES

The open classroom's emphasis on providing sensory experiences for pupils is a strong component of its structure. See to it that you utilize the total range of sensorial materials. Cuisenaire rods, cubes, prisms, cylinders, abaci, test tubes, magnets, fabrics, sea shells, tuning forks, records, pictures, chemicals, spices, and other materials designed to help your pupils experience their senses will help them to relate their schooling to the outside world. It is clear that children develop their knowledge of the world on the basis of what they see, hear, touch, taste, and smell. Children, like adults, develop their ideas of sharpness from sharp things, of smoothness from smooth things, of sweet fragrances from sweet things, and of bitter taste from bitter things.

I don't mean to imply that all your learning centers must include concrete objects. However, the discriminatory and intellectual skills developed through multisensory experiences in the learning centers you establish are important to your pupils' everyday life. Many of the decisions they will be called on to make will be based on their ability to discriminate. Therefore, in implementing your learning centers, attention should be given to activities through which your pupils may learn the skills of careful observation, exploration, and inquiry. In this respect, sensory-motor aids which invite definite movement and response by pupils toward definite ends are very valuable, particularly when they are designed to build on and extend what your pupils already know.[1] Representative sensory-motor materials especially appropriate for younger children are shown in Figure 1-4. You may find them useful for inclusion in some of the learning centers you plan to establish.

The materials shown in the figure are but a few of the many that you can utilize to develop your pupils' discriminatory and intellectual powers. It should be clearly understood at this point that your use of these sensory aids does not necessarily guarantee learning. It's what happens *after* the initial encounter of the pupils with the materials that constitutes learning. It is important, therefore, that you make provisions for extending the initial attraction and stimulus of your learning centers.

FIGURE 1-4   Sensory-Motor Materials Useful for Inclusion in Learning Centers

Item	Purpose
Movable alphabets	Provide practice in composing words and sentences
Number rods	Develop number relationships
Sandpaper letters	Learn letters, e.g., Kinesthetically trace letters and sound names simultaneously
Sound boxes	Distinguish sounds
Bells	Discriminate pitch, develop scale, learn notes, play tunes
Grammar boxes	Identify parts of speech by touch and sight e.g., pick nouns from slips of paper of same color
Beads	Note relationships with numbers by matching with number card
Color tablets	Master sense of color, e.g., Match identical colors Graduate colors from light to dark
Cylinders	Develop senses of sight and sound, e.g., Via putting pegs into appropriate holes
Bottled odors	Classify various smells
Textures	Develop sense of touch, e.g., Through use of cloth, plastic, sandpaper, etc.
Cards with painted leaf forms	Compare shapes, e.g., match real leaf with its painted counterpart
Geometric objects	Identify shapes, e.g., Place cut-out forms in appropriate socket

DIFFERENTIATED LEARNING

There is general agreement that failure to differentiate instruction for individually different children constitutes a major dilemma in the schools. Which of your pupils need to learn which skills? Derive which ideas? It is an accepted fact that no unique learning sequence exists for all pupils. Thus, in establishing your learning centers, you need to utilize *different* approaches to motivate your pupils, *different* methods of presenting sequences of learning to them, *different* ways of organizing the materials they are to use, and *different* opportunities for your pupils to select sequences of learning and to choose the work within the selected sequences.

I have often been asked if pupils can choose wisely from the different opportunities that may be available to them in various learning centers. Indeed they can! Given the choice of several different levels of learning experiences, or of different emphases in a specific learning level, many, but not all, pupils consistently pick those experiences which best fit their needs. Some need to be guided by you, of course. Daily diagnosis and ongoing evaluation are necessary to provide this guidance. The experiences called for may be determined by formal pretesting by you, may be the result of your observation of your pupils' behaviors, or may result from their expression of their needs. Figure 1–5 illustrates a sequence of diagnosis, prescription, and evaluation you may wish to use to implement individually appropriate experiences in your learning centers.

It is important that you recognize the activities of the open classroom and the learning centers as unique expressions of your pupils. To personalize their experiences it is necessary that you differentiate their activities on the basis of their interests, the concepts they hold, their skills development, their value systems, and their experiential backgrounds. This differentiation may involve vertical (rate) progress, horizontal (depth) progress, or both. The experiences outlined in the learning center component of Figure 1–5 have not been identified because each may constitute any one of a variety of activities. For example, Experience No. 1 might be composed of the lowest level of work in a particular phase of an arithmetic sequence. Experience No. 4, at the other extreme, might consist of the most demanding activity. On the other hand, Experience No. 1 might include activities of a project nature, say in social studies; Experience No. 2 might involve a problem-solving opportunity; Experience No. 3, peer tutoring; and Experience No. 4, programmed instruction. Two approaches to guide you in the appropriate selection of the experience to fit each pupil are: (1) You may direct your pupils to the particular learning experience in the center which best helps them to work toward the objective in question, or (2) You may give your pupils the opportunity to select freely the experience which they feel can best result in the realization of the objective.

You may need to direct your pupils to learning experiences which require vertical differentiation, e.g., the various levels of a nongraded or individualized instruction sequence in reading or arithmetic, or direct them to activities based

FIGURE 1-5   *Relationship of Pupil Diagnosis and Prescription to Experiences in the Learning Center*

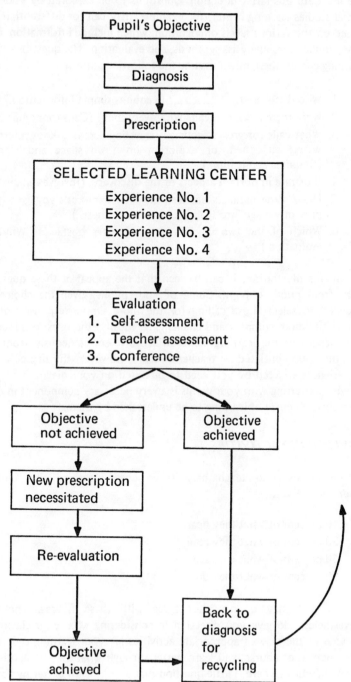

on horizontal differentiation of the experiences to be undertaken by them. Let me illustrate this latter direction. Questions to be explored by your pupils in a social studies learning center, for example, may call for differentiated responses based on the various levels of cognition, which include information, comprehension, application, analysis, synthesis, and evaluation. The questions placed at the learning center, then, might assume the following pattern:

1. Who discovered_____? (Requires simple information.)
2. Were there risks involved? What were they? (Calls for comprehension.)
3. What calls for greater courage—traveling across unknown territory (land, water, air) then, or exploring unknown space and planets today? (Requires application.)
4. Illustrate important aspects of the discovery. (Involves analysis.)
5. Draw some parallels between an early explorer's voyage with that of a present voyage into space. (Demands synthesis.)
6. Which of the two voyages entails greater obstacles? Why? (Requires evaluation.)

From this illustration, it can be seen that the appeal of these questions would vary from pupil to pupil. Some of your pupils, given the choice, would be inclined to select those calling for the more simple responses; others would prefer the more complex and challenging. Ideally, the questions included in the experiences of the learning center will evolve spontaneously from the pupils. Whether pupil-initiated or teacher-directed, however, the degree and kinds of experiences selected by you need to be based on your diagnosis of your pupils' needs. Conferring with your pupils is a very necessary component in deciding the appropriate course of learning to be undertaken by them.

DIVERSIFIED ACTIVITIES

Those of us who teach have often been informed that children learn approximately:

10 percent of what they hear
20 percent of what they read
50 percent of what they see
90 percent of what they do

You and I may or may not agree with these figures. The statements, nevertheless, do give you direction in considering what your classroom should include in the way of appropriate activities for your learning centers. Some of your pupils, of course, will learn better through what they read; others through what they hear. There is little question that all will learn better by actively doing something they *want* to do. The more varied the activities you include in your centers, the more likely will emerge the impressions necessary to motivate pupil expression. Activities should be sufficiently diverse from learning center to learning center to heighten your pupils' responses. Creative experiences, great music and literature, historic moments, good poetry, problem-solving, role-playing, culture contact, and exercises for the development of needed skills are but few of the diverse activities that may be built into the different centers of your classroom.

In planning the learning centers, it is important that you provide the proper balance of activities. Both formal and informal learning experiences are necessary. You will find that certain of your pupils learn better in structured learning centers, preferring more formalized activities rather than informal. Other pupils will prefer an informal setting. Those who function best in step-by-step learning experiences may need to be provided with activities with specific guidelines. On the other hand, pupils who need little or none of your direction to function well in learning centers may benefit from activities in a center which invites them to proceed on a more independent basis. Some pupils may prefer to work alone. Others may be more productive when working in the company of their classmates. Provision for both should be included in the learning centers you establish. In sum, your classroom needs to be planned so that all learning styles and personal preferences of your pupils are taken into account.

The appropriate balance between formal and informal activities in learning centers is difficult to achieve. The important thing is that you avoid an undue emphasis on either. If, for example, each learning center in the classroom is to consist of only formalized activities, each calling for written responses by your pupils, you may be reasonably certain that not all of your pupils will be attracted to them or respond well to them. The opposite kind of environment—that which consists solely of fun-focused learning centers in the form of games, puzzles, "soft" reading, art, and the like—may similarly lack appeal to some of your pupils. What seems to work best is a little of each approach.

You'll need to create a balance between noisy and quiet learning centers as well. Note the differences in work styles of your pupils. Gregarious children may prefer to work at centers which are designed for verbal interaction, while the more reserved children may choose to work in privacy. Creating a learning environment which takes into account the total range of pupil preferences is important. The greater the diversity of the learning centers, the greater the opportunity for pupils to exercise their preferences. In implementing the activities in each of your learning centers, separate, wherever possible, the noisy activities from the quiet. You can use portable screens, book shelves, moveable furniture, alcoves, make-shift booths and other components for this purpose. Language lab compartments can easily be constructed by using sheets of cardboard or pressboard to separate clusters of desks, or desks within a cluster as pictured in the diagram. (See Figure 1-6.) The cardboard or pressboard should extend high enough so that pupils occupying adjoining desks are not in view of each other, thus ensuring privacy for each.

FIGURE 1-6   *Using Sheets of Cardboard to Create Individual Learning Carrels*

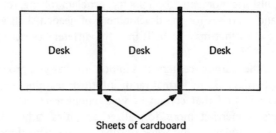

Sheets of cardboard

If certain of your pupils prefer even greater solitude, make-shift learning booths may be constructed out of freezer or refrigerator cartons obtainable from appliance stores (Figure 1-7). Booths such as these are often used as "think tanks" or "dream centers" by children, or put to other imaginative uses. For example, various textures and materials can be pasted to the inside walls for pupils to feel in the dark; constellations of stars may be outlined on the ceiling for pupils to observe and study; or the construction of these learning booths may be left up to your pupils as special projects—to be built and decorated as they wish. The construction of the booth is relatively simple, as shown in Figure 1-7.

FIGURE 1-7   *Utilization of a Refrigerator Carton as a Learning Booth*

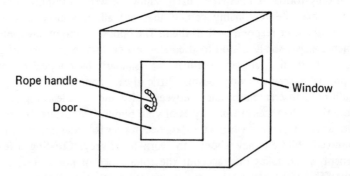

The inside of the carton may be equipped with a desk or small table and a chair or a rug on which to squat. Depending on its intended use, it may include a tape recorder, a record player, reading materials, or possibly a filmstrip projector. The student teachers under my supervision invariably construct interesting variations of the learning booth. One teacher, in the context of a unit of work on Indians, invited the construction of a tepee for use as a powwow center. Another teacher encouraged her class to construct a rather imaginative "spaceship" (of paper and chicken wire) in which a blanket, lamp, and source materials were placed for independent study in the class' unit of work on space.

PUPIL INPUT

Central to the formulation of the open classroom are the contributions made by pupils. It is important that you invite your pupils' input openly and freely. The kind and extent of their input will naturally vary with the circumstances. Ideally, the form and direction of your classroom will be shaped by the input from your pupils, consequently, its structure cannot be other than flexible. Therefore, in planning the format of your classroom you need not, and must not, feel restricted to a particular arrangement of its physical space and activities.

I am familiar with a number of classrooms where pupils have determined their physical arrangements and have formulated many of the learning centers. In one such classroom, during the course of a study of Japan, two girl pupils—one of Japanese extraction—created a learning center which generated much interest in the culture of that country. Through the simple process of clustering four desks together and placing on them a teapot and several small handleless cups, a few small bowls of rice, and chopsticks with Japanese characters, the pupils attracted to the center were motivated to hypothesize about Japanese life. Dressed in kimonos, each of the girls took turns as hostesses, serving tastes of tea and inviting discussion.

Subsequent responses to this experience were as follows:

Jimmy: "They must live where it is warm because they grow a lot of rice and you need sun to grow rice."

Maria: "It takes a lot of water to grow rice."

Elvia: "They must not have very many animals since they did not serve meat."

Ruperto: "Do they have a written language? The marks on the chopsticks look like words."

Alice: "These people may be little because you need little hands to hold these cups without handles."

Andy: "They must not have iron or silver since they use wood to eat with."

Celia: "Maybe they use wooden sticks instead of spoons and forks to eat with because they have a lot of trees."

Albert: "If they don't have many animals, is it because rice takes a lot less room to grow? To have animals you need a lot of pasture for grass."

Patricio: "Yeah, but why rice? Is it cheaper to grow? Healthier?"

Martha: "These people must be happy. The clothing they wear is full of pretty colors."

Whether or not these conclusions drawn by the pupils are accurate is not the central issue here. From an adult's point of view, the responses may indeed reflect the pupils' narrow, distorted, or incomplete insights unsubstantiated by facts. However, when the responses are looked upon as testable conclusions or as points of departure for further inquiry, then their value is evident. This is precisely what occurred in the learning center initiated by the two children. Certain pupils were motivated toward a more extensive, more authentic exploration of life in Japan.

Countless other illustrations of pupils' input into the activities of a classroom may be cited by many teachers, some of which I include in Chapter 6 in the section on teacher-pupil planning. Unfortunately, this input has been sporadic rather than consistent in too many classrooms. In opening up your classroom, it is necessary that you capitalize on the input of your pupils as an authentic, sincere, and natural contribution to the formulation of the classroom's learning centers.

PUPIL INTERACTION

Kids *can* teach kids! Closely allied with pupil input as a necessary ingredient of the open classroom is the idea that pupils are capable of interacting with each other so that each gains. Teachers often speak of the development of the "whole child" as the crux of the educational process. The open classroom seeks to implement this concept. This implementation starts with *activity*. Children question; they talk; they decide; they do. It is through the subsequent interaction, especially when it is self-initiated, that the pupils grow both academically and socially.

Watching a group of children in action is a revelation. Observe your pupils. Which of them is inclined to question, to probe, to test, or to initiate, confront, and argue? Who is apt to get tired, bored, and difficult? Who is attentive and cooperative? Who are the isolates? Who are the active participants? Are there some who get easily discouraged and withdrawn? Who relates well with whom? Which of your pupils tend to lead? Who are the followers? Who does what, when? The interactive experiences you provide your pupils with will help make these behaviors visible to you.

The diversified activities of the open classroom will enable you to study your pupils in action. Consequently, your observations will help you to make appropriate determinations as to subsequent courses of learning by them. Are there experiences in learning centers where a follower can be given opportunities to exercise leadership responsibilities? Can the easily discouraged child have successful experiences? Should the incessant talker be placed at a learning center with other talkers who will not permit his monopoly on conversation?

Earl Kelley in *In Defense of Youth* identifies basic standards of learning as:

the need for other people

the need to communicate with other people

the need for a loving relationship with other people

the need for a workable concept of self

the need for freedom[2]

I couldn't agree more. It appears to me that taking these needs into account justifies pupil interaction as a key component of the open classroom. Peer grouping is very important in personalizing the education of your pupils. You will find, I am certain, that your group activities are often compatible with the diverse interests, directions, and aspirations of each of the pupils making up the groups. The interactive experiences you institute in learning centers will clearly provide opportunities for your pupils to learn from each other. They can turn to one another for help, thus lessening, if not completely diminishing, the anxieties that each may have. It is reasonable to expect, then, that each of your pupils will be less reluctant to postulate an idea, suggest an experiment, or test a conclusion. Furthermore, the fact that the interaction taking place at a learning center often exposes the pupil to different ways of thinking, different ways of feeling, and different ways of behaving cannot but help to develop his self-concept in positive directions. He sees himself through the others. "It is okay to be different," he thinks, "after all, who isn't?" Or, he may realize, "Man, I'm not so different after all!" Once your pupils have positive feelings about themselves, their work is more likely to be that which they wish to achieve.

Formal as well as informal programs attest to the effectiveness of kids teaching kids. Team or partnership learning programs have been successfully implemented for years. Other formal programs, such as the Cross-Age Helping Program available through the University of Michigan's Center for Research on the Utilization of Scientific Knowledge, are designed to help older children teach younger children. Many teachers, of course, are not in a position of having such programs available to them. However, you can do much with what you have in your classroom. Those of us who were fortunate enough to teach in the team-taught schools of Lexington, Massachusetts, placed considerable effort in the direction of pupils teaching pupils. Frank Lyman, a member of my teaching team, was eminently unique and imaginative in this respect. I illustrate a classic example of his work in the form of an eight-year-old pupil teaching another pupil about cause and effect. I use the language of the pupil-teacher himself as he describes his teaching.

1. Ask him if he knows what themes are. If he knows, ask him what cause and effect is.
2. If he doesn't know, tell him that a theme is a subject, like space, sea, etc. A theme needs someone to probe it with his stick of knowledge.
3. Give him an example of cause and effect. If a kid (Joe) punches another kid (Pete) on the nose, the other kid punches him in the stomach. They become rude and mean to each other. A week later they may not still speak. Then ask him, "What do you think made Joe punch Pete in the nose in the first place?" "Why did they keep on fighting each other?"
4. Give him some other examples.
5. Show him some pictures of disasters. Ask him what he thinks caused them?
6. Ask him to tell you a cause and effect story.
7. Ask him if he'd like to make a tree. (A way of diagramming cause and effect). Your trunk is the *cause*, your branches the *effects*.
8. Test him.

What was the cause of the girl's being rich?

What caused this man to say "ouch"?

This illustration is but one of many approaches used by my colleagues to encourage pupil interaction, particularly in the area of the language arts. Numerous teachers have used, and continue to use, pupils to help other pupils. But much of this has been incidental rather than an integral part of their classroom experiences. In opening up your classroom, it is a *necessary* component of the experiences that are to take place.

Should you need a rationale for instituting "kids teaching kids" experiences in the learning centers you plan to implement, consider the help your pupils will receive which you alone cannot possibly give them. Consider also these advantages:

1. Individualization of the instructional process
2. Increase in the motivation of your pupils
3. Enrichment of pupil-teachers and pupil-learners
4. Development of resourcefulness by your pupils
5. Increase in meaningful experiences

6. Development of pupil respect for pupils
7. Development of friendship among pupils

If you need still further reason for implementing pupil interaction, feel certain that in some instances children can teach other children better than adults can. Experiences in our own homes clearly reveal this: e.g., an older sibling teaching a younger one how to make a bow knot, as the latter learns to tie his shoe laces; big brother demonstrating to his kid brother the proper stroke in tennis; sister helping her twin solve an arithmetic problem, the explanation of which she found difficult to understand in school. The fact is, kids talk kids' language. Teachers who encourage this interaction in their classrooms report less tension, greater participation in class activities, more initiative, more positive attitudes toward school and peers, and pride in accomplishment of both the pupil-teacher and pupil-learner.

Is it as simple as it sounds? Are there no problems that arise when the pupils teach pupils? Certainly there are! Most formalized programs, such as the Cross-Age Helping Program, insist on preservice training to lessen the occurrence of negative attitudes, impatience, and frustration that may arise. However, in my own experiences with elementary school children, I found informal discussions with the pupil-teachers and careful consideration of whom they were to teach sufficient to communicate the procedures essential to their working together. In the area of arithmetic, for example, almost no attention was given the need to cooperate, to listen, to speak one at a time, etc. Here, pupils found themselves on an equal plane, each contributing to the progress of each other. The fact that they were called on to work independently of the teacher must have, in their eyes, implied trust. The approach I utilized—team learning—is discussed fully in Chapter 4. My intent is to provide you with practical and feasible suggestions adaptable to your own circumstances.

CREATIVE ACTION

A tin can. A C-clamp. A candle. Some screws. A few rubber bands. A golf ball. *How good an inventor are you?* When placed in an "invention center," the attraction of these objects to pupils is immediate. The impact is one of action as pupils respond to the challenge to invent. Creativity, as you know, calls for new arrangements, new combinations, and new patterns. Similarly, the open classroom requires these ingredients, for creativity is its essence. Pupils are stimulated to produce numerous and varied ideas and approaches, many off the beaten track. Originality, flexibility, elaboration, redefinition, and sensitivity to problems are all vital components of the classroom's creative action. It is important, therefore, that you reward your pupils for the unusual. Ventures into the unknown, oddball questions, ideas, and strange solutions should be looked upon favorably. Make it clear to your pupils that new possibilities are always just over the horizon, to be sought or invented.

The urge to create is at its very height in the young. Note, for example, the unrestricted flow of color and movement in the young child's art, not yet given to the preconceptions and imposed generalizations which dull the senses of too many adults. You will find experiences calling for invention especially attractive to your pupils. In an invention center, the pupils are provided with the opportunity to rise to their creative peaks—their intuition, instinct, and spontaneity finding an outlet for expression. Encouraging your pupils to invent a new contraption out of a tin can, C-clamp, a candle, and a golf ball, invites the inventor to explain his creation, verbally or in writing.

Most experienced teachers are very familiar with the numerous ways of stimulating creative expression in their pupils, including the use of pictures, sentence starters, composition derbys, box cameras, startling statements, catchy titles, and assorted objects. To encourage this expression, it is important that all contributions of the pupils are accepted. By doing this, you are likely to find that each of your pupils will subsequently see himself as having something of importance and value to express.

I feel that the decentralized environment of the open classroom lends itself to creative action by pupils, because they are provided considerable opportunity to respond to their own thoughts and feelings in learning centers of their own choosing. Ideas for such opportunity come from many sources—classroom texts, college courses, workshops, publishers' monographs, professional journals, colleagues, and the pupils themselves. The beginning teacher as well as the experienced teacher would do well to take advantage of the very specialized magazines that deal with art activities, creative writing, and the collector's world. The latter have already used many ideas that are appropriate for inclusion in learning centers. Some teachers, however, lack the experience of gathering, accumulating, and classifying the many ideas that are available. One simple expedient is to develop a personal card file of activities from which appropriate creative experiences for your pupils may be selected as needed.

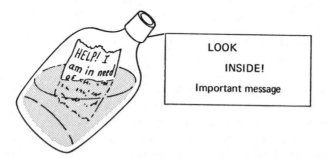

Creative ideas for learning centers need not be contrived in the sense of forced experiences for your pupils. A bottle, such as that illustrated, inviting pupils to explore its contents may lead to challenging questions and regarding bottles as a medium of communication. What does the bottle contain? A message from a sinking ship? A cry for help? It is known that all kinds of bottles are found bobbing up and down in ocean waters, many of which are very old. In the past, even though uncertain, they were sometimes the only means of communication available. Known to old salts as the "mermaid express," bottles, pupils are interested to discover, were very much a part of the history of sea voyages. Columbus himself, for example, similarly used wooden casks to relay messages, a discovery which never ceases to delight those children who express interest in exploration. The "bottle center" can be used in various ways to invite creative action by your pupils, for example, pupils may be directed to hypothesize about the content and meaning of a message in a bottle through creative story-writing, or to pursue their interest in sea-borne bottles through further study. Presently, bottles are used by the United States Fish and Wildlife Service to determine the tidal patterns and flow of ocean currents, as well as being used as markers to tip off fishermen on the location of haddock and codfish. (*Hint:* Eggs of fish float on the ocean's surface.)

Children as well as adults need to create. Creative learning and creative teaching go hand-in-hand. The connection between the two, that of the "creative learning process" is defined by Torrance and Myers as:

> ... one of becoming sensitive to or aware of problems, deficiencies, gaps in knowledge, missing elements, disharmonies, and so on; bringing together available information; defining the difficulty or identifying the missing element; searching for solutions, making guesses, or formulating hypotheses about the deficiencies; testing and retesting these hypotheses, and modifying and retesting them; perfecting them; and finally communicating the results.[3]

Simply stated, this process may be construed as one of problem-solving.

Experiences at a problem-solving center typically invite creative action by pupils. One activity they often find fascinating consists of animal tracks drawn simply on a sheet of paper with the purpose of eliciting pupil hypotheses as to what the tracks reveal. The hypotheses may take the form of a picture to be drawn, a story to be written, or simply a listing, the pupils choosing the response of interest to them. I illustrate one such procedure for you.

A group of seven-year-old children, after hypothesizing the larger footprints were those of a dog and the smaller those of a rabbit, decided:

"The dog fought the rabbit."

"The dog ate the rabbit."

"The rabbit ran away."

"The rabbit hid under a bush."

"The rabbit ran into a hole."

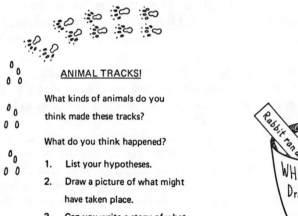

ANIMAL TRACKS!

What kinds of animals do you think made these tracks?

What do you think happened?

1. List your hypotheses.

2. Draw a picture of what might have taken place.

3. Can you write a story of what might happen?

I illustrate the foregoing example, as well as the "bottle center," simply to point out that creative action by your pupils can often be stimulated by your capitalizing on experiences a bit different from the usual activities of the classroom. I do not intend for the procedure I outline to be construed as *the* way to begin. There are many ways. The "track center," for example, may be introduced effectively through the observation of animal tracks after a good snowfall (should your school be located in the appropriate climate), via a story or film about the mystical "Abominable Snowman" of the Himalayas, or through the countless Westerns which revolve around the sheriff's ability to follow the outlaw's trail. Furthermore, "tracks" need not be studied strictly in the narrow sense of "footprints." Interested pupils may see fit to follow the footsteps of man exploring new territories by way of animal trails, or may wish to pursue the theory of evolution through the "tracks" of animals preserved in fossil form. Still other pupils may wish to study the characteristics of the animals to which the footprints belonged, the habitats in which they lived, their relationship to the natural life cycle, and their utility to man.

It is true that creative action by pupils often begins with their personal experiences. But when unaided, your pupils' self-expression may not advance beyond their immediate thoughts and feelings. As long as the pupils' self-determined goals do not become so distorted that they become reflections of your goals, you need not feel that you impose upon them when you go to their aid. In my judgment, providing teacher-facilitated experiences for pupils for the purpose of raising their sights or redirecting their pursuits does not necessarily constitute an imposition upon their personal goals. However, I strongly believe that each pupil has innate aspirations, the expressions of which have been repressed so often that they hesitate to reveal them. If you feel as I do, it is your function, then, to open your pupils to experiences which expand

and enrich their natural self-expression without fear of having their creative products exposed to judgment which may reveal their inadequacies. To encourage their creativity, it is important that you provide a place for your pupils in which they can express themselves. The learning center is one such place. Try not to measure its activities in terms of a certain amount of accomplishment in a certain amount of time, or as something to be turned on and off at your direction. More likely than not, initially at least, you can expect a mass of "low-grade stuff" to be produced by your pupils because of the nonjudgmental setting of the center. However, teaching by you is in order. Differentiating the rich artistry of your pupils' creative products from the replicated and the mediocre is definitely within your responsibilities in the open classroom. To dismiss this responsibility as judgmental is to also dismiss the artistic standard and original invention in the pupils themselves. H. Caldwell Cook spells this out clearly:

> The development of personality demands freedom of expression and every opportunity for the exercise of originality. . . . For such work as this the teacher must sink himself in the needs of his class as a group of individuals; must take care not to thwart natural inclination, and yet at the same time insure that the efforts of his pupils do not run away into fantastical conceits, blind imitation, affected novelty or sheer tomfoolery. He must know a good thing, actual or potential, when he sees it, and must neither let pass unchallenged any work which the author [the pupil] could improve, nor reject as unfit anything which has life in it and a true inspiration, however feebly showing. He [the teacher] must be ready to set aside all convention in method, all blind rigidity or discipline, and pin his faith on no stereotyped formulae. There is a different way every day.[4]

"There is a different way every day." Especially is this true in the open classroom. Recognition of this by you is an important component in helping your pupils grow toward standards of their own adulthood. Children are quick to realize that you are in the classroom to help them learn, and that honest, fair, and constructive criticism of their work serves this purpose.

SELF-PACING

The primary responsibility of a teacher in the open classroom is two-fold: (1) to develop an honest relationship with and between pupils; and (2) to help pupils in their personal growth through the teaching processes. The learning center approach to opening up the classroom lends itself to this primary function by creating the conditions which encourage optional and, therefore, optimal participation by pupils. Open access to materials and activities ensures the likelihood of their participation. This access, in turn, invites self-paced experiences by the pupils.

As discussed in one of the preceding sections of this chapter, each of your pupils is different from every other pupil. Self-paced learning experiences are integral components of this differentiation. Your pupils' abilities to pace their learning is, of course, grounded in their emotional, physical, social, academic, ideational, and experiential make-up. Therefore it is important that you take into account their maturational development in establishing your learning centers so that they may function optimally. I suggest, here, that you provide learning options from which your pupils may choose on the basis of their experiences and levels of personal growth. This optional route is necessary because of the differences in your pupils and because they are constantly confronted with vastly different slices of society.

To encourage self-pacing opportunities and optimal participation in the learning centers you plan to implement, it is pertinent to consider the characteristics of your pupils. Take pupils in the six- to eight-year-old age bracket. What are they like? If you are a primary school teacher who wishes to open up your classroom, you will do well to study the available literature for this age group.[5] It is especially in the late stages of these years that peer grouping offers satisfaction to the emotional needs of pupils. Although some pupils find it difficult to share the attention of their teacher, some are ridden with tensions, and some have fears of not being liked, there is little question that all want to feel they are needed. You can capitalize on this by inviting and encouraging your pupils to contribute to the formulation of the learning centers and their activities, thus acknowledging that their contributions are needed and valued.

Youngsters at this age level tend to learn more effectively through concrete experiences. The knowledge that they are most interested in these, and in specific information, than they are in generalizations may help you to determine the appropriateness of the activities you plan to include in your learning centers. Note, also, that pupils in this age bracket tend to interpret stories in light of their own experiences. They display interest in dramatic play, collect things, enjoy all kinds of games, and put a premium on "correctness." Here, too, you are given direction pertinent to the self-pacing of their experiences. Based on these characteristics, for example, you may wish to create a "dramatic play center," a "collection center," a "game center," or a "story center," thereby capitalizing on the interests ascribed to children in this age category.

Pupils in the nine- to eleven-year-old age span have the same basic emotional needs as the younger pupils. They also want to be loved, to have security, to achieve success, and to work independently. All, of course, look toward new experiences in the intermediate grades. If you teach on this level, learning centers constructed on the basis of new activities and directions are appropriate for these children.

During this period of your pupils' maturational development, their interests vary greatly. Reality rather than the imaginative play of their earlier years comes into clearer focus for them. Seeing how things work, dramatics, the creative arts, and even career opportunities draw their attention. Taking this first characteristic into account, for example, it would seem a natural consequence that you implement a "see how it works" or "junk center," towards which your pupils may contribute. The broken-down typewriter, the malfunctioning clock, the battered radio, the discarded toaster, and a worn-out vacuum cleaner invariably attract most pupils in this age bracket, especially when they are invited to take these apart to see how they work. Some of us, in fact, have had the experience of seeing these become operable because of the ingenuity implemented by pupils at such a learning center.

This is also a period of extensive reading. Some nine- to eleven-year-old pupils are capable of reading adult materials with effectiveness. Others find reading difficult, which leads them to frustration and, on occasion, causes or results in emotional problems. Thus, self-paced activities are necessary to meet these wide differences in their capabilities. Both boys and girls enjoy books about travel, nature, and people's lives, as well as culture contact studies, science, and historical adventures. From this, then, you may see the need to establish a "travel center," a "nature center," a "biography center," a "multi-culture center," a "science center," or a "historical center." By the time these children reach the age of ten, many of them are ready to solve algebraic problems, are capable of instituting plans, modifying them, evaluating the consequences, and taking the appropriate action for each situation.

This age group is noteworthy for still other characteristics. Boys and girls hug! They punch! (Need for a "punching bag center"?) They are attracted to animals, plant life, modes of dress, cars, boats, and planes. Those of you who teach pupils in this age bracket would do well to acknowledge and encourage these characteristics, along with those discussed in the preceding pages, by implementing learning centers which capitalize and build on them. Figure 1-8 summarizes the characteristics and interests of children ages six through eleven.

When deciding *what* should go into each of the learning centers on the basis of who should do what, you should take into account your pupils' capacities to learn, as well as their interests. Self-pacing is especially important here because there is a physiological limit to the amount of learning a pupil can accomplish. Consequently, the specific task to be achieved must vary with the learning capacity of each pupil. The degree of security, energy, intelligence, sensitivity, dependency, stability, attitude, and ambition of each student strongly influences this capacity.

Look at any child's behavior in any home, for example, where self-pacing based on these characteristics is clearly evident. My three-year-old son is no exception. To a large degree, he "manages" his education according to his own pace. One moment he is playing with blocks, perhaps constructing a building or road. If he tires of this, he may browse through a picture book. A playmate may barge in and interrupt this involvement, and off they go to the sandbox in the backyard. Back in the house, out come the pots and pans. He "cooks," or he fits container into container. Thus he sets his own time, place, and pace. The intriguing aspect of this is that the child's self-paced behavior is not aimless. In fact, he has a definite purpose and design for his actions.

So, too, in the open classroom. Given the opportunity, your pupils will also self-pace their activities. As in the preschool world, it is pertinent that you provide both structured and unstructured materials in the various learning centers for this self-pacing to take place. Structured materials (model cars, boats, planes, kitchen utensils) as miniature imitations of the adult world are important in helping pupils to identify with and grow toward adulthood. Unstructured materials (paints, clay, rocks, sticks, sand, blocks, crayons) are also important in inviting pupils to expand their immediate world by creating forms of their own choosing. Thus they shape their personal world.

FIGURE 1–8   *Characteristics and Interests of Pupils, Ages 6 to 11*

Ages 6 to 8	Ages 9 to 11
Interested in . . .	Interested in . . .
Simple construction activities	How things work, tinkering
Checkers, dominoes, monopoly and assorted simple card games	Cars, planes, engines, and mechanical devices
Simple puzzles of all kinds	Planning and evaluating their activities
Comic books	Reading biographical, travel, nature and science stories
Listening to stories, animal stories in particular	History, other cultures
Collecting things, but not organizing them	Organized collections of all kinds (coins, shells, stamps, cards of sports figures, minerals, insects, dolls)
Drawing and labeling pictures	Complex puzzles and games that challenge (chess, checkers)
Arithmetic and science	Experimentation and exploration
Reading and writing	Peer relationships
People and events of the past	Seeking new experiences
The larger world community	Creating and inventing
Specific information, not generalizations	Working independently
	Abstract thought
Concrete, multi-sensory immediate activities	Discussing and sharing ideas
Riddles, jokes (except on themselves)	Facts, real things
Singing games, action songs,	Painting, music, art, dramatics
Information about sex	Career education
Being liked, being wanted	Being liked, being wanted

It is no secret that different children pace themselves differently for a variety of reasons previously discussed. Some respond best when not governed by timetables, step-by-step progressions, or grade-associated tasks. Others feel rewarded when working toward specific targets under tight deadlines. It is necessary, therefore, that you plan the opening up of your classroom with provisions for self-paced activities. A valuable ingredient of these provisions is opportunity for your pupils to self-select and manage their learning experiences.

SELF-SELECTION AND MANAGEMENT

Pupils choosing their learning experiences are given persistent attention in this book. It is perhaps the most important factor in opening up the classroom because it invites and encourages self-directed change in pupil behavior. It is clear that the opportunities for pupils to learn increase under this arrangement to the extent that they are able to behave openly and freely in the classroom. The learning center approach helps to teach pupils self-management through the choices of activities they make, and by their focusing more specifically on what is to be learned. This tends to become a natural occurrence because the pupils' attention is narrowed down to the particular object, problem, or activity in the centers they select for learning.

Not all pupils, of course, are capable of selecting and managing their educational experiences. Some teachers feel, in fact, that certain pupils need to undergo "training" to increase their ability to choose wisely. Let me illustrate. An initial step you may take is to make only two equally beneficial stories available to your pupils, either one of which they may choose to read, or offer two science experiments with the provision that only one may be selected. After a period of time, the options available may be extended to provide your pupils with an increasingly wider range of activities from which to choose, each of equal benefit to them. Subsequently, the decision-making process may be expanded to provide even more extensive opportunities for them to select learning experiences not of equal benefit to them, for instance, difficult stories to read, easily-read stories, and "just-right" stories. In using this approach as training for decision-making by your pupils, you need to provide enough differentiated experiences to give them sufficient opportunities to demonstrate their increasing good judgment by selecting activities appropriate to their objectives.

Mrs. Sandra Abernathy, a second-grade teacher at the University Hills School, Las Cruces, New Mexico, illustrates training for decision-making as follows:

1. Practice in decision-making—no chance of "wrong" decision.
    a. Choice of *time sequence.*
       Pupil does assigned work in any order he wishes.
    b. Choice of *work area.*
       Pupil chooses one of two different work areas of interest to him.
    c. Choice of *task.*
       Pupil selects one task from two or more tasks in the same subject area, each of equal benefit to him.

       d. Choice of *time sequence, work,* and *pacing.*
         Pupil chooses five areas of interest each week.
         Pupil chooses one out of two or more equally beneficial tasks in each
         of the areas selected.
         Pupil may choose one area per day, resulting in free time each day; or
         pupil may choose more than one area per day, resulting in accumula-
         tive free time each week.
    2. Use of judgment in decision-making—some risk involved because not all
       choices would be equally beneficial to the pupil.

Other teachers initiating open-concept programs in their classrooms feel differently. They take the position that in the truly open classroom, pupils are being educated in decision-making processes constantly because they are often placed in positions of deciding what to do, where to do it, and when to do it. I feel that the appropriate way to learn to make decisions is a very personal matter for both the teacher and the pupils. The best method would vary from teacher to teacher and pupil to pupil. It is to the pupils themselves, then, that you must look for the answer.

In my own experience, allowing pupils to freely select their own learning activities produced almost magical results. I can never forget one of my most enthusiastic and dedicated student teachers attempting to motivate a class of nine-year-old youngsters in a reading "lesson" not of their own choosing. She was warm, personable, and pedagogically knowledgeable, but to no avail! The pupils she was "teaching" expressed absolutely no interest in the story selected *for* them in the basal reader required by the school's administration. Obviously, this called for a change in tactics. It was decided that henceforth the pupils were to select their own readings. Two simple procedures were agreed upon. First, the pupils were permitted to select *any* story they wished in the basal reader, and second, they were encouraged to respond to the story selected in *any* manner they wished.

On my very next visit, I was almost stunned by the behavioral changes which had taken place in the pupils. Where formerly I had witnessed extremely passive, disinterested pupils in a rather deadly "homogeneous" classroom setting (after all, how many children are interested in poppy seeds—the subject of the assigned story?), I now observed a lively, interactive group of pupils in a highly responsive environment. The classroom had been decentralized through the simple process of clustering desks, and provision for pupil mobility had been made. Previously, the children were sitting row-by-row at their desks throughout the reading. Six children were now in costume, rehearsing a play they had written from a story selected out of the basal reader. Four boys and girls were taping another story they had chosen. Two pupils were conducting a flash card drill on vocabulary picked out of another story. Two other children were almost out of view under a table, reading to one another passages from a story they had chosen. Seven pupils were planning a "television program" based on a story in the reader which lent itself to a visual presentation. One child was painting her impression of a story she had read. Five boys and girls were reading silently, each absorbed in a different, freely selected story. Two children were engaged at the blackboard undergoing syllabication exercises under the teacher's direction, this being their choice of reading activity.

This occasion when the pupils selected their own stories to read and made decisions on what was to be done with their selections was to set the pattern for their subsequent reading experiences. The decentralized setting of the classroom is shown in Figure 1-9.

FIGURE 1-9   Pupil-Selected Reading Centers

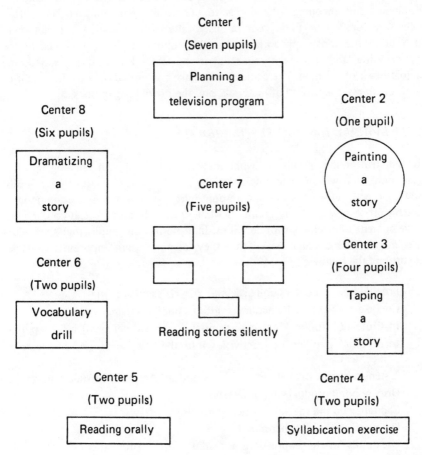

You may use almost any learning experience in the classroom to encourage the self-selection process. Your pupils can pick the arithmetic examples they wish to compute, the words they wish to spell, the science experiments they wish to do, the social studies projects they wish to implement, the art medium they wish to express, etc., even within the prescribed boundaries of curricula dictated by policy-making bodies. Under nonrestrictive curricular guidelines, of course, many more options are available to pupils. Providing each of your pupils with the total list of words to be used in a block of time, or even during the course of a year, so that they may freely select those words they wish to learn to spell, define, or apply is a case in point. A functional list such as the *Dolch Basic Sight Words* or the *Barbe Reading Skills Check List* can be used very effectively for this purpose, as well as to develop your pupils' abilities to recognize, analyze, and use the words selected.

It is conceivable that the selection of words from a list you have provided is not enough for some pupils who may not choose the words appropriate to their needs. Therefore, guidance may be in order. You must ensure the necessary minimum and encourage the pupils to pursue the potential maximum. It is necessary for you to guide your pupils to alternative routes, yet to let them determine the most appropriate route to follow. That is, you clarify the opportunities and encourage your students, but in the final analysis, they do the actual work of learning. The choices they make are limited only to the extent of your openness, the variety of materials, and their own imaginations.

SELF-EVALUATION AND RESPONSIBILITY

It is a truism that pupils are what they think they are. In opening up your classroom, you will need to emphasize the positive development of your pupils' self-concepts. Self-evaluation and responsibility are two necessary components of this process. What really counts is what turns kids on! How can you, in your development of open-concept activities, indicate to your pupils that their ideas are important and valuable and that they, as people, are important? Consider instituting the following:

Provide free and open pupil access to materials and activities.

Create activities which encourage optimal pupil participation.

Institute decision-making opportunities (class and personal) by the pupils.

Incorporate pupil-created activities into the class' programs and learning centers.

Listen to pupils. Invite questions, solicit ideas. Act on their suggestions.

Display pupil products and interests.

Capitalize on the special abilities of pupils.

Use pupils to teach other pupils.

Use pupils' written expressions as reading materials for other pupils.

Have pupils demonstrate their hobbies, skills, and talents to other pupils.

Record pupil stories, reports, and experiences for use in learning centers.

Establish *successful* experiences for pupils.

Carry on frequent, ongoing conferences with pupils.

Invite pupils' parents to show their hobbies, talk about their work, express their talents, and assist in the classroom.

Promote indigenous language and colloquial speech unique to pupils.

Provide for pupil self-selection, self-pacing, and self-evaluation of learning experiences.

Reinforce, reinforce, reinforce!

Once these processes become ritual, rather than sporadic, it is reasonable to expect that your pupils will assume responsibility for their own behavior. You can build toward the opening up of your classroom by instituting still other conditions and processes which will help to develop their sense of responsibility. Begin by planning to supply your pupils with the tools and experiences they need to create, build, and apply the processes necessary for them to interact responsibly. They need to learn what they can and cannot do. Self-evaluation is a necessary component of this responsibility. To help your pupils do this, you can implement procedures which invite them to correct their performances in both academic and nonacademic areas so that they may determine for themselves their capacity to pursue subsequent steps of learning.

In the field of arithmetic, for example, you might provide open access to answers to encourage the self-correction process. You may further encourage your pupils to assess their progress by calling on them to evaluate incorrect responses, for instance, "I came up with the wrong answer because I forgot to carry over one 10 to the tens' column when I added." If a pupil needs guidance in evaluating an incorrect solution of an arithmetic example, a grammatically incorrect sentence, etc., you may simply place one or more question marks by the example or sentence to indicate to the pupil that one or more processes need his further attention, for example, "$5 \times 25 = 105$" (?), the question mark indicating that the pupil missed a necessary process. Or, in writing a sentence, for instance, "the book i red was a good one." (???), the question marks suggest to the pupil that he needs to make three corrections. The importance of this approach is that the pupil is called on to find his own mistakes.

Whatever the subject, the intent should be to help the pupil clarify his operative thinking and see the consequences of his procedures. Once you provide this help, the brunt of the decision-making process falls on the pupil's shoulders. You guide; the pupil evaluates and corrects. In this manner, you will find your pupils progressing beyond operative thinking and operative understanding to operative application.

The self-evaluation process is active rather than passive because it provides pupils with referral points for managing their own learning. The learning centers you plan to implement need to take this active orientation into consideration. Each, therefore, should contain activities towards which the pupils can direct their operative skills of evaluation. Include activities that have meaning for your pupils. They will then have reason to recall, to apply their learnings, and to evaluate their own effectiveness. This evaluation is crucial in determining the kind of self-concept the pupils will develop, for it is through the self-evaluation process that they will recognize their strengths, weaknesses, and resources.

Consequently, through this process they will be given the guidance and direction necessary to the management of their subsequent courses of learning.

POINTS TO REMEMBER

- Trust in and respect for pupils constitute the central tenets of open education.
- The open classroom takes many forms, shapes, and directions.
- The teacher's outlook and role are pivotal in opening up the classroom.
- The input and contributions of pupils are important components of the open classroom.
- Self-selected, self-directed, self-paced, and self-evaluated learning experiences of pupils are fundamental in opening up the classroom.
- Learning centers should include materials and experiences important to pupils.
- Experiences in learning centers should be difficult enough to challenge yet not discourage pupils.
- Free access to materials and preferred choices of pupils for activities are necessary to open up the classroom.

NOTES

1. The teacher contemplating the utilization of multisensory materials in the open classroom can gain much by reading books about the Montessori method of teaching. Among those available, the following are particularly helpful:

    Dr. Montessori's Own Handbook, Introduction by Nancy McCormick Rambusch, illustrated (New York: Schocken Books, 1965), cloth and paperbound.

    The Montessori Method, Introduction by J. McV. Hunt (New York: Schocken Books, 1964), cloth and paperbound.

    Spontaneous Activity in Education, Introduction by John J. McDermott (New York: Schocken Books, 1965), cloth and paperbound.

    The Montessori Revolution in Education, E. M. Standing (New York: Schocken Books, 1969).

2. Earl Kelley, *In Defense of Youth* in Phillip W. Jackson, *The Difference Teachers Make* (Washington, D.C.: U.S. Department of Health, Education, and Welfare, Office of Education, 1971), p. 3.

3. E. Paul Torrance and R. E. Myers, *Creative Teaching and Learning* (New York: Dodd, Mead and Co., 1970), p. 22.

4. Hughes Mearns, *Creative Power: the Education of Youth in the Creative Arts* (New York: Dover Publications, 1958), pp. 39–40.

5. Many books are available on this subject. One that focuses on children in the five- to eleven-year-old range which may be helpful is Dorothy H. Cohen, *The Learning Child* (New York: Pantheon Books, 1972).

One spon a tumm.
a king was haggy
He wnt to bee
haggy and He was
haggy.

Susie, Age 6

two

Defining and Clarifying Learning Centers

Implicit in any institutional model for instruction and learning is the necessity to raise specific questions relating to the school curriculum, the experiences of the children to be involved, and the functions of the school's staff. The open classroom is no exception. Before deciding the form, substance, and direction of your learning-centered classroom, you first need to determine the:

1. Objectives appropriate for each of your pupils
2. Pupils' position with respect to each objective
3. Experiences necessary to achieve the objectives
4. Organization needed to implement the experiences
5. Composition of pupils essential to each objective's attainment
6. Learning styles or approaches to be emphasized
7. Reward system which works best for each of your pupils

Undergirding these components and at the heart of the organization of your classroom for open education is this question: what kinds of learning experi- do your pupils need and who is to determine these needs? These are not easy questions to ask or answer. What objectives do your pupils hold to be appropriate? Why not ask them? I think you will find their responses helpful in providing you with guidelines for shaping the classroom you plan to organize. Plan *with* your pupils. Appropriate objectives may be determined by you, an individual pupil, a group of pupils, or by your class as a whole. The manner and extent of your involvement will vary with the experiences of your pupils and their need to expand their experiences. Should you have some doubts about the extent of pupil involvement, you should keep in mind that children learn *what* and *when* they wish to learn. The learning center approach to the open classroom capitalizes on this fact by making learning a personal matter for each pupil. Thus, in constructing your learning centers, it is important that you facilitate the ability of your pupils to take responsibility for their own learning by taking advantage of their natural bent to initiate and direct their own activities.

PURPOSES AND CHARACTERISTICS OF LEARNING CENTERS

Learning centers occur any place, in and out of the classroom, where pupils direct themselves or are directed by the teacher toward the pursuit of learning. They may exist as permanent locations for specific purposes, for instance, an arithmetic center, or they may be flexible in their structure, such as those depicted in the introductory page. They are designed to encourage pupils to achieve open choice-making, problem-solving, and creating opportunities by providing them with secure, comfortable, and when possible, natural settings.

Too often, learning centers are construed as areas "set aside" for extracurricular experiences, each with a specific set of directions for pupils to follow. This view has led some teachers to construct them so that pupils can experience them *only* when their assigned work has been completed. Consequently, no pupil is given the opportunity to integrate his own interests with classroom activities according to his unique abilities and aspirations. In my opinion, this ignores the very essence of the learning center approach to the open classroom. For the center themselves should be the *starting point* for pupils from which subsequent experiences will evolve. "Setting aside" activities in which pupils may participate *after* completing the required work of the classroom misses the point of the learning center. In fact, it denies the well-documented theory that children inform us when and what they wish to learn.

My three-year-old son illustrates this theory. Browsing through books readily available to him, he, as did his older brothers and sister before him, invariably institutes a learning experience by asking; "What's this?" "What's that?" as he points out the letter "o," for example. I then "teach" him that the symbol which interested him is an "o." This is diametrically opposed to the more conventional form of teaching, for instance, "Paul, today I am going to teach you what an 'o' is." Ideally, then, the activities of learning centers would stem from your pupils' first-hand experiences and needs, and pupil participation in the centers would not be restricted to special times.

Nor should the activities in a learning center *necessarily* be determined by a set of directions devised by you, to be followed rigidly by your pupils. Whether or not this would be appropriate will depend on the particular circumstances and the kinds of activities your pupils wish to undertake in the center. To provide appropriate experiences for your pupils, your learning centers must assume a variety of forms for a variety of purposes. They may be subject-centered, interest-centered, problem-centered, skills-centered, theme-centered, or simply fun-centered, to name but a few.

As indicated earlier, you may institute learning centers in advance with specific assignments for your pupils, or learning centers may be formulated out of the spontaneous input of your pupils with no specific directions attached. A center may consist of a single, fossilized rock in a designated area on the classroom floor designed to attract and stimulate the interest of your pupils, or it may be composed of an expansive set of related activities clustered at a table, focusing on the development of specific skills or concepts. In between these extremes are many variations of the learning center—some teacher-constructed, others pupil-constructed—the form and direction of each dependent on the special needs of your pupils. Whatever their form, learning centers consititute the total learning environment and should not be construed as areas set aside for extracurricular activities. In my view, learning centers constitute the open classroom itself.

What are the advantages of opening up your classroom by using learning centers? The obvious answer is the flexibility that such an arrangement provides. First, it allows for greater movement by the pupils and capitalizes on their individual natural spontaneity. Second, the variety of centers provides diverse settings in which pupils can work autonomously or in small groups in self-selected experiences. Third, the provision for opportunities to make choices encourages pupil commitment to learning experiences which are likely to result in productive follow through and attainment of individual goals. Fourth, the flexibility of the environment imparts the feeling of freedom necessary to open the pupils' minds and emotions to the pursuit of knowledge. Furthermore, the learning center approach to opening up the classroom changes the teacher's role to one in which greater attention is given each child. Thus, most of your time will be oriented toward individual and small group teaching, which will often require you to use new methods in evaluating your pupils' progress.

In setting up your version of the flexible, modified, open space environments, it is necessary that you construct each learning center in terms of: (1) the characteristics of the content and skill to be learned, and (2) the characteristics of the pupils who are to make use of the learning center. It is necessary that you keep in mind the following components in planning for the material to be learned in each of your centers:

Your pupils' *familiarity* with the material
The *complexity* of the material

The *amount* of material
The materials' *value* to your pupils
The *organization* of the material

PUPILS' FAMILIARITY WITH THE MATERIAL

It is well known that the child enters school with his intellect developed much more than his spoken language would indicate. His preschool experiences have caused him to develop many ideas about the world. This became apparent to me during the summer of 1971 when I worked with teachers in the beautiful kingdom of Nepal. My American school experience left me in a dilemma. What does one do in a classroom where virtually no books exist? Where charts, maps, globes, counting frames, alphabet cards, and other instructional aids are not to be found? It was under these conditions that I tried to utilize in a learning situation the familiarity the child has with the materials of his world. In Nepal, the typical child is exposed to environmental circumstances which cause him to think operationally, as do children in the United States. He "reads" the weather, plants, rocks, trees, faces of people, coins, the time of day, building signs, birds, insects, and the topography of the land. He knows, for example, that plants are green, yellow, brown, large, small, prickly, smooth, dead, or alive. Consequently, I attempted to encourage the institution of learning centers based on the Nepalese child's familiarity with his environment.

It was expedient, for example, to take advantage of the children's operational thinking about natural objects. They brought in plants, abandoned birds' nests, rock specimens, leaves, insects, and other things found in nature. Out of these, various centers were begun, such as an "insect center," a "rock center," and a "plant center." The familiarity of these learning centers and others based on the Nepalese pupils' real-life experiences eliminated stress and capitalized on their spontaneous interest simply because they agreed with the pupils' attitudes. The centers provided concrete situations in which the pupils could apply their ideas and extend their operational thinking. What the pupils thought, they could talk about; what they talked about, they could express in various forms. When supplied with paper, paint, and crayons, this expression often took the form of drawing and painting (of themselves, mothers, fathers, water buffalo, homes), classifying (plants, soil, people, buildings), and writing by association. Thus, I tried to enhance what was strongest in the Nepalese children—their inner motivations—a natural consequence of their awareness of, and curiosity about the world around them.

Similarly, in devising a center based on your pupils' familiarity with its materials, it is necessary that you keep two important criteria in focus: (1) the provision of experiences for which they are ready, and (2) the extension of these experiences to help advance them to subsequent stages of personal development. For every new idea to be derived or skill to be developed, the initial experiences of your pupils must be composed of relevant actions that they can perform. Remember, also, that the initial activities of your pupils are but a starting point and, therefore, do not consititute the total criteria to be utilized in constructing a learning center.

COMPLEXITY OF THE MATERIAL

Learning may not take place if your pupils do not encounter obstacles in the learning centers. At all levels, the materials of the centers need to be differentiated so that they are difficult enough to cause each of your pupils to seek solutions, yet not so difficult that they are discouraged. It is important that your learning centers be well-balanced to meet the diverse abilities and interests of your pupils and to prevent their indoctrination into *one* system of ideas. The complexity of the materials you use should challenge and push your pupils toward their goals. Attempt, therefore, to construct your learning centers with materials that engage your pupils in activities which help them to meet their personal needs.

AMOUNT OF THE MATERIAL

The amount of material to be included in your learning centers affects the extent of their attraction to pupils. For example, I am familiar with a teacher who, in the development of a unit of work on Mexico, had constructed a learning center which utilized memorabilia of that country. The teacher had clearly acknowledged her Mexican-American pupils' *familiarity* with the Mexican culture and had sufficiently differentiated the activities of the center to capitalize on the range of pupil interests and academic potentials. The memorabilia, in fact, did attract the pupils' curiosity. But despite the pupils' association with the materials of the center and their initial attraction to them, none of the pupils was inclined to participate in the activities of the center. In my opinion, the reason was clear. In constructing the learning center, the teacher had required that *all* of its activities be completed by the pupils. I feel that this had the effect of turning them away from the center because no options were provided for them.

In my view, the teacher in the foregoing illustration had not considered a necessary point in the construction of the learning center by not making provisions for the pupils to select only those activities of interest to them. Subsequently, by redirecting guidelines for the activities so that her pupils could select any *one* of the five included in the center, she was able to recapture their attention. Where previously none of her pupils had been attracted to the center, almost all now responded. Therefore, when planning for your classroom, it is very important that you give your pupils the opportunity to choose from the activities within the centers they select, as well as the opportunity to choose the centers in which they wish to work.

Should you implement a center which consists of only one activity, preferred choices by the pupils of tasks to be performed within that one activity also need to be provided for maximum effect. For example, if a center is designed to include just one set of mathematics examples, for instance fifteen in number, your pupils might be given the option of *how many* and *which* of the fifteen they would like to do. A transitional step would be to direct them to the number of choices available, such as stipulating that they could do *any* five to ten (or any arbitrary range decided by you) of the mathematics examples. "Do you really mean it, teacher? I can do any five to ten examples? I can do only five if I want to?" Teachers report that this approach has generated much interest in the children and is applicable to all the subject matter fields. They report, in fact, that some pupils find it so exciting that they go beyond the stipulated minimum. They also report that under this arrangement, pupils choose wisely in selecting the tasks which fit their personal needs.

Given progressively difficult and different examples to choose from, teachers state, pupils pick those problems that they can deal with *successfully.* That is, each pupil performs at the level of development which seem to be suited for him. This very important matter of choice constitutes the very core of the open classroom. It is totally unlike the often-used procedure whereby "slow children" are called on to do the first five examples, "average children" the first ten, and the "best mathematicians" all fifteen examples.

What else is there to learn from this approach? One teacher prided himself in giving fifty-item quizzes to his high school chemistry class, often with disastrous results. Without arguing the merit of fifty-item tests of any kind—and I think I can argue against such a weekly procedure—I asked him to consider the approach of permitting his students to select *any* ten to twenty items on which they wished to be tested. Put into practice, the change in their response was dramatic. As is often the case with elementary school pupils, they picked the quiz items they could do successfully. Furthermore, the consequences of this approach gave subsequent direction to the teacher. By noting the items his students did not pick, he was able to reassess and redirect his teaching to their special needs on the assumption that they did not understand the items not selected. The end result was the establishment of "needs centers," where each group was provided with problems tailored to the specific requirements of each pupil. This is one approach you may wish to consider in diagnosing the needs of your pupils.

To sum up, in planning the construction of your learning centers, you need to consider the amount of material to be placed in each center in terms of:

1. The *quantity* of work required of your pupils
2. The opportunity for your pupils to select *what* they wish to do
3. The provision for your pupils to decide *how much* of the work they need to do.

THE MATERIAL'S VALUE TO PUPILS

What pupils feel to be important is closely tied to their *familiarity* with their world, as previously discussed. Clearly, the construction of your learning centers should embrace materials which the pupils in your classroom feel will be of benefit to them. Personal experiences vary from child to child, as do the values each holds. Consequently, it is important that you make available a wide variety of materials to your pupils—not necessarily in each of your learning centers, but in the total range of the centers.

In the preceding pages I have stated that the idea of pupils' choosing their courses of learning necessitates alternatives from which to choose. This opportunity to choose, furthermore, is crucial to the pupils' *valuing* what is chosen. It is not likely, for example, that pupils will feel their choices to be important when put on an "either-or" basis, with neither being their *preferred* choice. In constructing your classroom centers, therefore, it is important that you provide alternative learning experiences which include their preferences. How, then, do you find what your pupils feel to be important? Obviously, time must be taken for planning with your class and for conferencing with individual pupils to find this out. This procedure is discussed in Chapter 6.

Both the preferred choices of your pupils and meaningfulness of the material they choose can be brought into play by you simply and effectively. To illustrate this point, let us turn to mathematics once again. In planning for a mathematics center, rather than your stipulating what work to do, encourage your pupils to construct their own problems. Assume, for the moment, that work in the area of multiplication is necessary, or has been expressed as an interest by a number of your pupils. You might provide directions at the center which invite the pupils to devise ten examples of their *own* choosing. This simple expediency capitalizes on your pupils' preferred choices because they are likely to construct examples which mean something to them. It also constitutes a better mode of teaching than does the strict assignment of examples from a book or those made up by you. Should you, furthermore, deem it necessary that the ten examples include some attention to two-place multipliers or various other number combinations, you can arrange it by requiring that a certain number of the examples to be constructed by your pupils includes some. Your pupils, consequently, will create those examples which they feel are important to them within the parameters set forth by you, yet they will maintain their freedom to choose the examples to be constructed. The result is that the experience becomes a personal one for each of your pupils because each set of mathematics examples will differ from pupil to pupil.

It should be increasingly evident to those of you who are planning open classroom environments that you are responsible for establishing the realm of your pupils' choices and boundaries within which they are to function. I do not feel this subverts the pupils' choosing their courses of learning or in any way coerces their freedom to choose. For tantamount to this freedom is your helping them to see and understand the limitations and consequences of their decisions. To help your pupils develop their personal values through this process in the context of the learning centers to be included in your classroom, it is important that you encourage and help them to:

Consider what they prize and cherish
Make choices, and make them freely
Discover and examine available alternatives
Weigh alternatives thoughtfully and reflect on their consequences
Affirm their choices
Act, behave, and live in accordance with their choices.[1]

The six points paraphrased here are necessary ingredients in the construction of your centers, wherever appropriate, and in the organization of your total classroom as well. Consequently, to the extent that it is necessary and feasible, it is very important that you provide your pupils with experiences in learning centers which invite opportunities for them to choose, to reflect, to decide, and to value.

ORGANIZATION OF THE MATERIAL

The organization of a learning center embodies and integrates the four preceding characteristics of the materials to be included in the center. It should be understood that this integration is not necessarily equally proportionate, or in a particular order. Conceivably, there will be times when your pupils' *familiarity* with the materials in a center will have less bearing on its construction than will the *complexity, amount,* and *value* of the materials. To discover the appropriate emphasis of each of these characteristics as it affects your pupils' learning in a center, considerable time must be spent by you in conference with each pupil. If your learning centers are to be well-planned, therefore, you will need to take into account the individual differences of your pupils. Whether the conference is initiated by a pupil: "I'd like to start a project on _____ ," or by you: "What do you wish to explore today? Read? Learn? Complete?" the basic questions essential to the achievement of the individual pupil's personal targets must form the guidelines of your conferences with your pupils.

1. "What do you already know about what you wish to do, Maria?"
   (You find the extent of the pupil's *familiarity* with the material to be learned.)
2. "Do you think you can handle the work by yourself, or will you need some help?"
   (You determine the *complexity* of the task to be achieved.)
3. "How long do you think it will take you to achieve your objective?"

(You determine the *amount* of work required. Perhaps a contract is formulated and agreed upon at this time.)

4. "How do you intend to use your results?"
   (You discuss the *value* of the experience and its application to further learning.)

5. "How do you plan to get at your objective? What do you need to do to meet your goal, Maria?"
   (You agree on the *organization* needed to expedite the pupil's learning.)

Figure 2-1 shows the integration of the five characteristics and, hypothetically, the degree of their emphases with respect to experiential differences that may be found in a pair of pupils. Each segment in the figure, for instance the familiarity of pupil A with the material of the center as contrasted with the familiarity of pupil B, is shown proportionately different to indicate that the amount of knowledge brought to a learning center differs from pupil to pupil. Therefore, your learning centers need to be planned for the development of each pupil's potential.

FIGURE 2-1   Variances in the Characteristics of the Learning Center

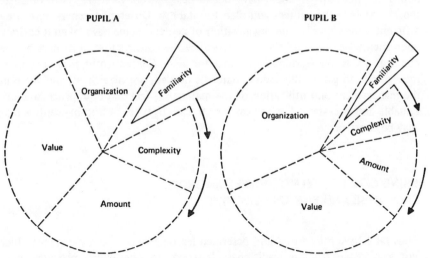

Note that I indicate the flexibility of the characteristics of the learning center (broken lines). I suggest here that the final determination of the centers you plan cannot be made until you assess the experiential backgrounds of your pupils. This assessment may take place in conferences with your pupils, as I have already illustrated, or through your observations of their behavior, by testing, through questions submitted by them, by information revealed in their personal biographies, by anecdotal and cumulative records, and by other diagnostic measures with which you are familiar. Once you have obtained the necessary information, the complexity and amount of the work to be experienced in the center, the selection of work important to the pupil, and the type of organization needed, these factors can be used as criteria to shape your learning centers. For example, Figure 2-1 shows that pupil A has more familiarity than pupil B with the material in the center. Consequently, you may surmise that he should be provided with more complex and extensive experiences than pupil B who, because of his more limited background, may need less difficult experiences in order to respond successfully.

Conversely, just the opposite determination can be made. You may argue that because of pupil A's greater familiarity, he is able to achieve his goals with less effort than is necessary for pupil B. The appropriate action varies with the objectives to be realized by each of the pupils. Whatever the determination, the preferred experiential choices of your pupils need to be built into the center on the basis of what is of value to each. Again, this is not to say that you must include multiple alternatives from which your pupils are to choose in each of your learning centers. Rather, these many and varied alternatives need to be integrated into the total fabric of the learning centers that are to constitute your classroom.

After the first four characteristics of the materials to be learned and the pupils' relationships to them have been assessed, your next step is to organize the materials in the centers you plan to establish. Different teachers have tried different approaches to the organization of centers. Some have taken it entirely upon themselves to build them. Others view the construction of centers by the pupils as a valuable learning experience for them. Consequently, they encourage their pupils to gather the source materials needed, organize them, and share in the management and utilization of the materials. I feel that both procedures are valuable and necessary. Let us now turn to various types of learning centers that may be constructed.

USING CENTERS TO MOTIVATE, DIAGNOSE, PRESCRIBE AND ENRICH LEARNING

Thus far I have introduced and described learning centers as a means by which you can move from a traditional classroom to one which provides open, personalized experiences for your pupils. By now, you are perhaps sufficiently interested to want a more extensive explanation of the term, "learning center." Certainly, what kinds of learning, by whom, and for what purposes are questions which need to be considered in explaining this term. Figure 2-2 illustrates the learning center. As shown in the figure, the term "learning center" is classified under four broad categories, each with a different purpose for pupil activity. In establishing your learning centers, it is important that you have a firm grasp of the purpose of each. What is to be your intent? To arouse the interest of your pupils? To find out what they know or may need to know? To guide their skills development? To broaden their experiences and extend the quality of their lives? Your response to these questions will, in large measure, determine the types of centers you need to establish.

FIGURE 2-2   Categories of Learning Centers

Type	Objectives	Methods and Media
1. Motivational	Determined by teacher	Selected by teacher
2. Diagnostic	Determined by teacher	Selected by teacher
3. Prescriptive	Determined by teacher and pupils	Selected by teacher and pupils
4. Enrichment	Determined by pupils	Selected by pupils

Note in Figure 2-2 the four major types of learning centers—motivational, diagnostic, prescriptive, and enrichment centers. In implementing these centers, the question arises of who is to determine their objectives and the methods and media needed to carry out these objectives. I feel the appropriateness of the answers is tied closely to the types of learning centers to be implemented. Figure 2-2 suggests guidelines for determining the objectives, methods, and media. However, these are simply guidelines and are not intended as hard-and-fast prescriptions for making your decisions. It should be clear, for example, that the objectives, methods, and media for each of the centers need not be determined as indicated in the figure. Both pupils and the teacher may issue input into each of the centers. The type and extent of this input will vary with the purposes and circumstances of the learning centers.

LEARNING CENTERS BROADLY DEFINED

Different methods, of course, may be utilized by you to organize and implement learning centers in your classroom. Clearly, the variety of the centers you implement is limited only by your and your pupils' imaginations. The particular kinds of centers you employ need to revolve around your pupils' interests, learning needs, and personal enrichment. Thus, I feel, some of your centers should be designed to motivate your pupils, others to discover what is necessary to encourage them to act on their motivations, and still others to extend and enrich their learning needs. What, then, is a motivational center? A diagnostic center? A prescriptive center? An enrichment center?

The Motivational Center.   Everyone agrees that all pupils are motivated to learn and, whether this motivation stems from their inner needs or is the result of their environment, that it does affect their performance in the classroom. However, you may find that certain of your pupils have difficulty in using their built-in motivations. As their teacher, one of your functions is to help them seek and find techniques by which they can meet their needs. This is to say, you attempt to "motivate" your pupils by providing the stimuli needed by them to fulfill their needs. The motivational center is a particularly useful vehicle for providing such stimuli for at least four reasons:

1. It appeals to pupils' innate curiosity.
2. It develops the pupils' awareness of their needs.
3. It encourages the pupils' desire for peer approval.
4. It provides a rewarding environment.

Generating the spontaneous interest of your pupils is, of course, the most important objective and should be the central purpose of your motivational center. Without question, the kinds of materials you select and the activities you devise for inclusion in your center will strongly affect the direction and extent of your pupils' interests. Appeal to their curiosity. Dare to be different! Utilize materials and approaches with built-in fascination for your pupils. Place a "bucket of ideas" in your center from which they may select things to explore and do. Set up a bulletin board to attract their attention, for instance, "Chuck needs information on_____. Can someone help him find the sources and materials he needs to get this information?" In conjunction with appropriate materials placed in the center, invite further response by your pupils:

"What can you make with this clay?"

"Which of these materials will float?"

"When will these seeds sprout?"

"Why is this sponge curled up?"

"Who might use these tools?"

Try other approaches. Motivate your pupils with a mystery box, an ant farm, mice in a maze, a display of old objects, of toys, of dolls! Give them something else to be curious about: a bug climbing a wall of a jar, a horned toad in a box, a tape recorder with different sounds to explore. Consider, also, puzzles for your pupils to solve, worms to dissect, blood cells to examine. Use talcum powder, a glass, and Scotch tape to pick up fingerprints. In short, include in your motivational center(s) the unusual and the novel. Spark a freshness through the innovative activities of the center not typically encountered by your pupils in their daily classroom routine. Maintain this excitement by changing the stimuli as needed, for even the most attractive goals may lose their appeal if the experiences you provide in the center become repetitive.

The Diagnostic Center.   Whereas the motivational center is designed to capitalize on the curiosity of pupils and stimulate their interests, the diagnostic center takes this important purpose a step further. It is constructed and implemented with the specific purpose of providing you with the opportunity to analyze your pupils' behavior as they undertake the experiences of the center. It is intended to guide you to the kinds of centers you need to institute to meet the needs and interests of your pupils as revealed to you as a consequence of their activities in the center. Equally, if not more importantly, is what happens within the pupils themselves as they experience the work of the center. Each of your pupils needs to:

> ... understand with some precision what is to be learned and "what it is all about" (i.e., why it is important, how it relates to other subject matter and to himself). To whatever extent he has succeeded, he needs to know about it, for a sense of success contributes energy for the next task; to whatever extent he has not yet achieved mastery, he needs to know what the gaps are, so that he can figure out what to do about them. In some degree he has to be his own diagnostician, because in the final analysis he will be his own diagnostician anyway—he is the person who is in control of his learning energies—and it is better that he do the job well.[2]

Clearly, instructional diagnosis will facilitate the best possible kinds of learning by your pupils. Indeed it lies at the very heart of the learning-centered classroom, for the more you find out about your pupils, and the more they find out about themselves, the greater is the likelihood that you will know how to implement the learning centers needed to move your pupils forward. It is important, therefore, that you institute some of your learning centers with the purpose of finding out who your pupils are, what they can do, and where they might go. To realize this purpose, you should spend considerable time observing each of your pupils in action. Which center does the pupil select to work in? What activities does he select? Who does he prefer to work with? How well does he perform his activities? What obstacles does he encounter? What will he need to do to overcome these obstacles? How can I help him to assess his progress and recognize the next step? Is he able to self-direct and manage the experiences of the center? These are a few of the questions you may find useful in determining your pupils' needs, interests, and aspirations.

Let me now assume that one of your diagnostic centers is to be established for the purpose of discovering the needs and interests of your pupils in the area of reading. Place books, magazines, and assorted reading materials which cover a wide variety of topics and levels in your center. Observe your pupils as they move about the center. Which materials do they select? Do they read the materials selected? Or do they flit from book to book, magazine to magazine? Do they express a variety of interests over a period of time? A narrow range of interests? Do they find it difficult to read the materials they select? Easy? Do they share their reading? With whom? Follow through and confer with them on their reading. Discuss the important points and call for substantiation of these points. Ask them to summarize, predict, and relate similar experiences to those read. Similarly, through the establishment of diagnostic centers in other subjects, such as science, arithmetic, and social studies, you will gain information essential to the appropriate organization of your classroom.

Your diagnosis of your pupils' readiness to work openly in a learning-centered classroom may also be conducted through more formal procedures. Various commercial instruments may be used for the purpose of finding out your pupils' academic interests. Too often, however, they call for excessive tabulation and lead to frustration. Usually, observation of and conferencing with pupils are the best methods for finding out what kids are all about. Along with simple, formal pretesting techniques and anecdotal records that you create, I feel these are sufficient tools for the diagnosis of your pupils' needs and interests. In fact, a very important way to begin is simply to ask your pupils what they are interested in, and what they feel they need to learn and do to express their interests.

Your direct observation of your pupils' behaviors in diagnostic learning centers is very important in determining the kinds of centers that you subsequently implement. Coupled with the conferences you hold and the pretesting techniques you utilize, direct observation will assist you in gathering the information you need to choose rationally among the alternative methods available in implementing your centers. It will also guide you to the specific teaching necessary to meet your pupils' individual needs. You may readily expect, then, that the results of your pupils' experiences in the diagnostic centers will bear directly on the organizational format of your classroom insofar as you take advantage of this feedback. Such feedback will invariably affect the materials you will select and use in your centers, the skills developed by your pupils, the concepts they will derive, and the understanding they will achieve. More than likely, you will need to prescribe certain learning experiences if these are to be realized by your pupils.

The Prescriptive Center.   The experiences you provide in the various prescriptive centers you establish will, of course, be a direct result of your diagnostic findings. Clearly, such centers need to be implemented to provide opportunities for your pupils to develop the skills and acquire the information and understanding necessary for them to maximize their learning. Your prescription for the attainment of these goals would naturally vary from pupil to pupil. In addition to the differentiated curricular experiences your pupils will undergo in the centers you establish, each of your pupils will be called upon to function on his own level of ability at his own rate.

Making the transition from the diagnostic to the prescriptive center should pose no real problem, particularly to those of you who are experienced teachers. Consider, for example, a pupil in a diagnostic writing center. Your observation of his work in this center and subsequent conference with him discloses that he hates to write but loves to read. How, then, is it possible to communicate to him the importance of writing, or possibly to help him develop an interest in writing? An obvious step is first to guide him to various materials and activities in a prescriptive reading center established to help pupils pursue their reading interests. Following this, some natural second steps would be to encourage him to write a simple caption to a picture or cartoon he finds of interest in the center, to paraphrase a scene from a story or book he likes, or to construct a diorama of an event in a book and write a brief explanation of it for other pupils to read. The idea, clearly, is to first encourage the pupil to perform in the areas of his interests a￼ d to subsequently help him make the transition to the areas of his needs.

Consider another pupil. He finds it difficult to solve or is uninterested in written measurement problems found in a diagnostic mathematics center. Prescription? Provide more concrete experiences for him to do in the center. Include various objects that he can measure and provide a simple checklist on which he can record his results. Provide him with tools and materials with which he can build something according to specific measurements. Invite him to leave the center and measure a desk, a shelf, a wall, or the room itself using the metric system. Have him investigate the history of measurement and share his findings with the class. If animals such as white mice are available, have him measure their growth and chart the results. Solicit his ideas on what he might prefer to awaken his interest in and ability to measure.

Many of the materials already in use in your classroom can be used for purposes of prescription. Textbooks, films, filmstrips, recordings, artifacts, charts, graphs, maps, globes, arts and crafts materials, and experimental instruments are all useful. Whatever works best for the pupil under diagnosis is what needs to be prescribed. As explained in the next chapter, learning styles vary from child to child. Some children learn best through materials they ￼ ￼ad, others through what they hear, and still others by using materials they can manipulate and construct with their hands. Finding the right prescription for each of your pupils is a tall order. The next few chapters will assist you with ideas for enriching the learning of each of your pupils.

The Enrichment Center.   Dozens of ideas are presented in this book that are applicable for your use in enrichment centers. I focus on enriching ideas primarily because I find that too little attention is given to school activities which raise the sights, increase the intellect, add to the depth, expand the variety, and improve the learning experiences of pupils in the elementary school classroom. In how many classrooms, for example, are children seen teaching each other, making their own decisions, and doing the heavy work of learning? How many are found writing musical compositions, creating photographic stories, interviewing people, examining case studies, exploring ecological systems, studying blood samples, investigating fingerprints, and undertaking units of work on topics such as poverty, city housing, farm surpluses, refugees, pollution, the economy, energy, medicine, and various religions? In my judgment, enrichment activities need to go beyond having selected pupils read filmstrip captions, lead toy orchestras, list favorite readings, help teachers weigh and measure fellow pupils, act as classroom hosts and hostesses, and run errands. It may be argued that each and every one of these experiences is worthwhile. However, to suggest that customary activities such as these constitute "enrichment experiences" stretches the point.

The pupil thinking critically about information, data, and issues is an important component of the learning-centered classroom. Current events lend themselves to this process, especially with older elementary and academically able school children. News items, articles, and editorials from newspapers and magazines are particularly useful in enriching your pupils' abilities to interpret, summarize, and draw conclusions on important events of the times. When placed in an enrichment center for exploration by your pupils, the results are often enlightening. Listen to one of my former ten-year-old pupils who, when investigating the problem of the admission of refugees into the United States, took this written position:

> I agree with the article's proposal that refugees should be allowed to come over from the other countries to the U.S. I think it would be advantageous to the U.S. in five ways: (1) It would help the U.S. get acquainted more with other countries, and to understand them; (2) The U.S. would have a chance to know safely and truthfully what the people of other countries really thought about Communism; (3) It would, in a way, show the other parts of the world what it is like to help other countries, and how advantageous it is to "get together." (4) It might lead to people becoming citizens of the world; (5) It might help the countries of the world into friendlier relationships. This is only the beginning, but it may result in making the world a better, happier, and friendlier place in which to live.

Try placing controversial readings in one of your enrichment centers. Select your readings so that pupils who use the center are called upon to note likenesses and differences, discover real and false analogies, identify distortions, distinguish shades of meaning, and predict the outcomes of issues. Devise the activities of this center so that your pupils learn to identify such features as current information, interpretation, opinion, argument, and special pleading. Include in this center materials such as advertisements, speeches, notices, conversations, bulletins, and memoranda to help them focus on "masked" words designed to influence readers according to the author's intention. This may naturally lead to your pupils' study of propaganda, a study which academically able children in particular often find fascinating.

To develop your pupils' abilities to read and think critically, create activities for your enrichment center which first invite them to separate facts from opinions, and then encourage them to examine the facts. Questions on an activity sheet might take the following pattern, for example, as each fact is examined.

1. Is the "fact" important or unimportant?
2. Is the "fact" relevant or irrelevant?
3. When was the "fact" stated?
4. Who stated or wrote it?
5. Were personal interests involved?
6. Is there agreement or disagreement on the alleged "fact" by others concerned with it?

Consequently, with repeated experiences in reading critically, you may reasonably expect that your pupils will learn that certain kinds of information affect their daily lives, that well-informed people are respected for their opinions, and that the whole theory of democracy presupposes an informed citizenry.

In my work with academically able children, I found it rewarding to make use of the pupils' direct responses in my evaluation of the effect of their experiences in an enrichment center such as I have briefly described here. The following responses were representative:

"I like the way we have a chance to express our thoughts."

"I like to criticize and to be criticized."

"I look forward to language arts in my school."

"Hooray! No More 'Dick and Jane' books."

"I have learned much more than in any other class."

"We no longer have to go through a book we could read backwards."

"For the first time in school, I enjoy reading."

The question may arise as to whether learning centers should be viewed as strictly motivational, diagnostic, prescriptive, or enrichment centers. Certainly these centers should not be viewed as distinctly separate from each other under all circumstances. It is quite possible that certain pupils will undergo enriching experiences in the activities of a motivational center you have established and/or in those of a prescriptive center. Similarly, others will likely be motivated as they function in centers other than a motivational center. My intent in first categorizing the term, "learning center," into four broad types is to focus your attention on the specific purposes that need to be kept in mind as you construct your learning centers. In other words, it is important that you implement the centers while keeping in mind the purposes of motivating, diagnosing, prescribing, and enriching the learning of your pupils. To accomplish these very important goals, you will need to focus on the implementation of more specific types of learning centers.

SPECIFIC TYPES OF LEARNING CENTERS

One goal of this book is to clarify the term "learning center" through definition, interpretation, and illustration. The literature to date has provided no general agreement on precisely what constitutes a learning center. Using the term synonymously with "interest center," for example, only clouds its interpretation further. Consequently, a wide variety of learning centers are presented here to communicate the idea that a learning center may be defined as any place where learning takes place. As shown in Figure 2-3, learning centers encompass many different types, with various goals—some with broad purposes (motivating, diagnosing, prescribing, and enriching learning), some with less broad purposes (developing word analysis skills), and some with very specific purposes (learning to identify and pronounce word endings).

Observe, in Figure 2-3, that the four major types of learning centers previously discussed have been broken down to centers which are more specific in purpose. A prescriptive center, for example, may be established with inquiry training as its main objective. Thus, the prescriptive center may serve as an inquiry center or a problem-solving center. Similarly, a diagnosis center, set up to find out the academic skills your pupils possess or those they lack that are necessary to their progress, may take the form of a subject center in which information in a specific subject is stressed. Figure 2-4 illustrates the further specificity of learning centers. Note, for example, how a subject center—in this case, that of language arts—may be broken down into centers with more specific objectives such as encouraging pupils to learn to read, spell, write, and so on. Each of these centers may, in turn, be divided still further into various skills centers as shown in the figure.

There are literally hundreds of learning centers that you may implement in your classroom. A sufficient number of these are illustrated throughout the book. Learning centers may be constructed, in fact, on almost any topic. These may range from a center as simple as a "Make a Muscle" center where your pupils observe the contraction and expansion of muscles by crunching newspapers, to a center as sophisticated as a space center in which your pupils are encouraged to build rockets. The possibilities are restricted only by the input of you and your pupils. Included in these possibilities are learning centers which focus on the skills development of your pupils and on the expansion of their personal interests. A few are illustrated here.

FIGURE 2-3   *Specific Types of Learning Centers*

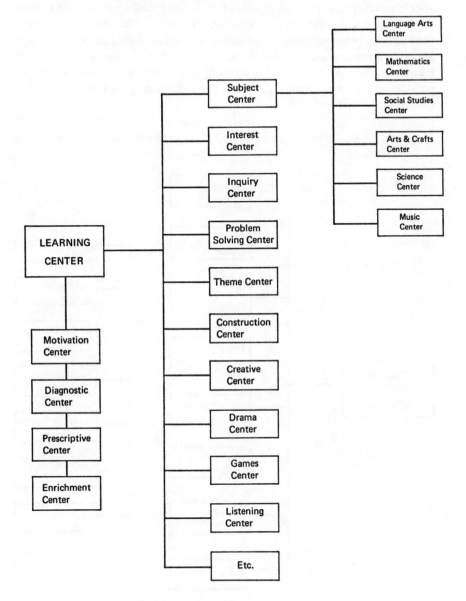

The Subject Center.   As shown in Figure 2-3, the subject center may consist of any one subject traditionally taught in the classroom, for example, a mathematics center, a social studies center, etc. In establishing your learning centers, you may favor this particular approach because of your previous orientation or your current practices. Those of you who teach strictly on the basis of periods of time established for instruction in arithmetic, reading, and other subjects may find it more comfortable to initiate the decentralization of your classroom through subject centers in which the activities are not sharply differentiated from your present practices. You may, in fact, prefer to establish your learning-centered classroom by implementing one subject center at a time. I discuss this process and cite specific examples of subject centers throughout this text, and illustrate their implementation extensively in Chapter 7. Simply pictured, the subject-centered classroom takes the form shown in Figure 1-3 in Chapter 1.

FIGURE 2-4   *Representative Subject Center Subdivided into Specific Topics and Skills Centers*

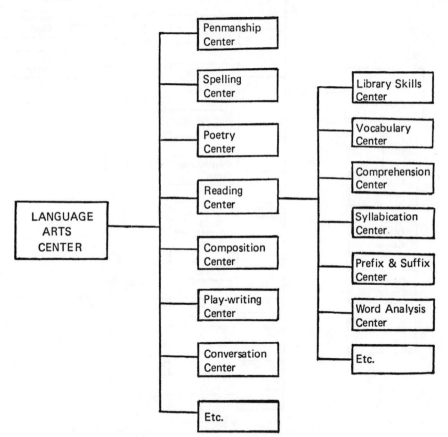

Typically, under the arrangement shown in Figure 1-3, each of the subject centers is self-contained. That is, each exists as a permanent station in which the activities of the center are undertaken. To begin with, the work in each of the centers may consist of only a single activity, involve the use of a single textbook, and follow the work pattern already familiar to your pupils. Eventually, to provide more personalized experiences for them, you will need to differentiate the activities of each of your pupils in the various subject centers as this becomes necessary. You may use either one of two possible approaches here: (1) differentiate the activities within each of the centers you establish; or (2) diversify the activities by dividing appropriate centers to sub-centers, as shown in Figure 2–4. The particular approach you utilize will likely be influenced by the amount of space you have available and by the extent of the diversification that is needed to meet the individual differences of your pupils.

The Interest Center.   Too often the teaching of subjects established by curriculum policy dictates the academic goals of pupils. That is, arithmetic is taught as arithmetic, social studies as social studies, etc., with little thought given to the interests that pupils may have, except as extracurricular activities. In my opinion, many of the skills traditionally ascribed to various subjects can be taught through interests expressed by pupils within the subjects themselves. Consider, for example, the pupils in your class who are interested in sports. Baseball batting and fielding averages, basketball field goal and foul-shooting accuracy, football passing and receiving statistics and yards gained per run, along with won and lost records, time factors, and distances in other sports may be used to teach derivation of averages and percentages, the use of fractions, and the various mathematical processes necessary to compute these.

Capitalize on your pupils' proclivity to collect pictures of athletes by establishing an interest center for this purpose. Fact-finding is a natural attribute of children. Indeed, when allowed to follow their interests, children are avid collectors of facts. Picture cards of sports figures are actually collected by youngsters for the facts they disclose about their favorite athletes. People, places, and events often come alive as a result. Enlarge your collection center to include books about the various sports figures. Include maps and encourage your pupils to find out where their favorite athletes live. Extend the activities of your collection center further. Go beyond athletes to include pictures of composers, artists, spacemen, adventurers, statesmen, and everyday people. Who are they? Where do they live? What do they do? How do they affect our lives? Branch out! Invite other kinds of collections which express your pupils' interests such as stamps, match covers, scrapbooks, insects, records, shells, rocks and minerals, flags, menus, puzzles, and songs. Whatever the interests of your pupils, build on them. Reward them for the individuality of their interests and, at the same time, try to elicit new responses from them.

In my opinion, curriculum developers, administrators, and teachers often underestimate the tremendous potential that exists for capitalizing on pupils' interests. Take, for example, the very widespread interest of the younger generation in folk, country, and rock music. Consider its feasibility for teaching social studies and language arts in an interest center. You will probably find that folk music, as an expression of past and contemporary social problems, is a natural entry point to studying the lives, ideas, and events which helped to shape, and continue to shape, culture. It can be used by your pupils to explore differences in dialects, attitudes, and traditions of various regions. They can be encouraged to interpret the music and lyrics expressive of a region and piece together the history of an era. Woody Guthrie sings of the dust bowl ("Songs of the Dust Bowl"). What was life like then? Joan Baez sings of workingmen defending their rights ("I Dreamed I Saw Joe Hill Last Night"). What is life like in the copper mines today?

In America, epics and other traditional forms of literature common to older cultures are, for the most part, nonexistent. Consequently, folk music is more than ever a valuable primary source of authentic literature concerning American culture. Rooted as it is in the lives of the poor, from whom much of it has sprung, it is a particularly useful medium for sensitizing your pupils to the conditions, problems, hopes, and attitudes of poverty-stricken people. The plight of the migrant, the steel worker, the criminal, and even the drug addict is often reflected in the music of the times. Supplied with appropriate literature placed in a folk music center, your pupils will find delight in exploring the authenticity of lyrics and the settings, people, and events mirrored in them. In the process, you can expect that they will enhance their research skills, extend their vocabulary, recognize, analyze, and interpret components of authenticity, explore prejudices, and examine trends. (Why is it that whereas fifty to thirty years ago, virtually all country blues singers were black, now many country blues singers are young, white, college graduates? Are there similarities? It is a powerful question to consider.)

"If I teach through interest centers, what about the skills development of my pupils? Won't they miss out here?" Indeed, this is a primary concern of a good many teachers. In my opinion, this is a concern that needs to be met head-on. Consider a child's interest in model airplanes, for example. Place the materials appropriate to his pursuit of this interest in a hobby center. Include models of airplanes, balsa wood, glue, paints, pen knives, measurement tools, a saw, directions for constructing models, and literature pertaining to principles of flight, history of aviation, and general information on airplanes.

Certainly, when given the opportunity to read about airplanes and to actually construct a model, the pupil must develop and use a variety of skills. Appropriate materials need to be selected, measured, cut, assembled, and pieced together. The pupil reads directions for constructing the plane, jots down essential notes, sketches models or their components, searches the literature for information on aerodynamics, and summarizes his findings. He learns to select and mix paints, notes their effect, and chooses the appropriate medium for painting his plane. In shaping and assembling his plane, he takes into account essential principles of flight. Mathematics, science, art, and various components of language arts come into play. In the process of pursuing his particular interest, consequently, he goes beyond mere acquisition of skills to their actual application.

Or, consider one of your pupils who is interested in wild animals. Given the opportunity to pursue his interest, will his skills development be neglected? I think not; in fact, they may well be enhanced. Skills of research, map reading, note-taking, classifying, and report writing are some skills that will likely develop. The interested pupil may explore habitats of animals, observe the terrain in which they live, note the food they eat, seek out their water supplies, study their survival skills, examine their place in the natural scheme of things, and discuss their usefulness to man.

Take, for example, the primary school child interested in horses. Your initial lesson plan for his skills development in writing, drawing, and dramatic expression at a "horse center" composed of a variety of pictures, horeshoes, branding irons, and reading materials might assume this pattern.[3]

MARE OR COLT?

1. Choose a picture of a mare (mother) and colt from the pictures on the bulletin board. Can you give each a name? What might the colt be saying to its mother? Draw a picture of them and write what they are saying to each other on the picture you draw.

2. Choose one of these sentences as a story starter and write a story. I will be interested in what you have to say.
   a. If I were a pony, I'd . . .
   b. If I owned a horse, I would . . .
   c. To take care of a horse, I would . . .

3. Choose any one of these to do, or suggest an idea of your own you'd like to do instead.
   a. Draw and color the horse you would like to have. Can you make it run across a field, around a corral, or jump a fence or small brook?
   b. Make your brand from your initials or your name (JRJ, BOB). Read about some famous ranch brands in our books about ranching. Make a chart showing the different brands you find.
   c. Show how a horse is cared for. Draw a picture of a horse in a stall, being rubbed down, eating grass or hay, or lying down in the stall.

4. How good an actor are you? Choose some friends to act out one of the following:
   a. A round-up
   b. How you would train a horse
   c. How you would make friends with a colt

The interest-centered classroom is a natural environment for discovering your pupils' strong points and capitalizing on them. How, then, might this discovery take place? Clearly, the changing times have resulted in changing the interests of children. To find out these interests, you may need to explore current research findings concerning the changes that have taken and are taking place. Surveying the findings described in the various journals of educational research is an important step. Inquiring about the interests of your pupils is another. Go beyond these steps, however, and listen to the questions your pupils ask. You will find, I'm certain, that their interests are often reflected in the questions they pose. Understandably, some of your pupils may not be inclined to question. Establishing inquiry centers can do much to foster this most important component of their learning and extend and refine the learning of those of your pupils who love to inquire.

The Inquiry Center. The "culture" of your classroom will, without question, play a significant role in shaping the interests of your pupils. An invaluable ingredient of this culture is the development of your pupils' attitudes for inquiry. Why are cowboys disappearing? Why are there literacy campaigns today in the river valleys where writing was first invented? Why do Bindibu Tribesmen dress as they do? Why is New York the largest city in the United States? Are camels still used on the desert? Should we dam up all our rivers? Why do Navajo Indians work on modern ranches, yet still hold on to customs and beliefs of long ago? The inquiry center rarely fails to attract the attention of children. Analytical, critical, reflective thinking by them invariably takes place. They apply facts and data, project hypotheses, make inferences, and derive concepts and generalizations.

Start simply. Attract your pupils to an inquiry center with a picture, an exhibit, a bulletin board display, a strange-looking artifact, and a discovery box. There is so much for them to be curious about. The discovery box, for example, can be used in multiple ways to stimulate the thinking of your pupils. They can dig for artifacts buried in a box of sand, feel for various textures of materials through fist-sized openings in a sealed box, explore shapes, sizes, and weights of objects through similar apertures in another box, and assemble and connect bell wire, a dry cell, and a buzzer mechanism in still another sealed box to discover the magic of an electrical flow.

As further illustration, place a raised relief globe in a sealed box. Cut an opening through one side of the box large enough for any one of your pupils to put his hand through to feel the unknown object—in this instance, the globe. Conceal the opening so that the globe cannot be seen. Cut off one end of a sock or a short sleeve and attach it to the aperture for this purpose. Or, paste retractable strips of paper over the opening. Encourage your pupils to hypothesize about the box's concerns. Attracted to one such box in an inquiry center, one group of six-year-old pupils proudly proclaimed:

"It's something round."

"It's something that turns."

"It feels rough and smooth."

"There's nothing around it."

Is there a better way to introduce and develop further these four important generalizations about the earth with primary school children?

To carry this further, uncover and place the globe in the inquiry center in a prominent place. Invite your pupils to find out all the additional information they can about the globe. Assuredly, certain pupils will find that there is more "blue" (water) than "brown, green or yellow" (land) represented, that portions of the "blue" (lakes) are encircled by the "brown, green, or yellow," and that parts of the "brown, green or yellow" (islands) are surrounded by the "blue." Other pupils will discover that still other portions of the "brown, green or yellow" (peninsulas, capes) jut out into the "blue," that "black lines" and "blue lines" (rivers) cut across the globe in a variety of directions, some from blue to blue portions or from line to line, and that some of the "black lines" are long, some short, some thick, and some thin.

All of your pupils will likely note that some of the colored portions of the globe are higher or lower than other portions. Some will wonder about the significance of the "browns," "greens," and "yellows." Such findings, and more, are likely to take place without your instruction. Through this self-seeking discovery process, you may reasonably expect that even your most unsophisticated pupils will be able to visualize land terrain, islands, lakes, oceans, rivers, peninsulas, capes, deltas, etc., when the appropriate terminology is associated with their findings. Subsequently, as you introduce additional landmarks on more sophisticated globes and maps to your pupils, you can expect more sophisticated learning to take place about geography, the factors causing day, night, and seasons of the year, and about the people who inhabit the regions of the earth.

Place a number of rolled-up paper towels in a sealed shoe box. Puncture a hole the size of a pin head in the box. Put this box, a paper clip, and a magnet in an inquiry center. What will your pupils discover? I continue to be amazed at the processes of inquiry most children develop when they are challenged. More than likely they will move the magnet along the sides of the box to see if the content of the box is attracted. Noting the punctured hole, they will invariably elongate the paper clip to poke into and probe the interior of the box. They are likely to weigh the box in their hands, shake it vigorously, and gently tilt it from side to side to discover its contents. In this illustration, they may generalize that the contents of the box are round, light, rough, and soft. "Knowing this, boys and girls, what might the content be?" It's been my experience that some of your pupils will, with time, discover the exact contents.

What is it? Place an unfinished sketch in your inquiry center. Invite your pupils to complete it, perhaps color or paint it, and write a caption for it. Some may wish to write a story about their finished product. Use a picture of a gnarled, misshapened stump to provoke the imaginations of your pupils. What do you see? What is it doing? Place a way-out drawing of a hypothetical being from a distant undiscovered planet in the center. Draw the figure with three eyes, two noses, four arms, several mouths, extremely long legs, and completely covered with hair. Encourage your pupils to hypothesize about the planet. Why does the figure have three eyes? Is it because the planet is perpetually cloudy, dark, dusty, or stormy? Is one eye for the purpose of looking straight ahead, one to the left, and the other to the right? Why does it have long legs? Is the terrain of the planet rough or smooth? Are giant steps needed to cover the walking distances? Perhaps your pupils will develop new theories, new places, new events.

Do you remember the now defunct "Hot Dog" television program? Questions of interest to young children constituted its appeal. You might place similar questions in your inquiry center to attract interested pupils. How do you get lead in a lead pencil? What makes popcorn pop? How do cartoons move? Why are the beach and desert sandy? How do you get the fortune in fortune cookies? Who invented hot dogs? Questions, when interestingly presented in inquiry centers are invaluable in attracting the natural curiosity of your pupils and enriching their learning. How do you feel about inquiry? Can you translate this odd-looking sentence? Place strange-looking symbols in a center to challenge your pupils. Invite them to create a language of their own to challenge each other.

Challenge your pupils further. Can you "prove" that there is air in a brick? Make a "Cartesian diver"? Measure your lungs' air capacity? Push a paper boat completely under water and get only the bottom of the boat wet? Use "Did you Know" questions to stimulate their interest further in experimentation. For example, "Did you know you can . . .

Float a pin on water?

Stick a paper drinking straw through a potato without bending it?

Shape an arrowhead from stone with a piece of soft, green wood?

Tell whether an egg is raw or hardboiled without cracking it open?

Extract heat from a rock?"

Or, to extend your pupils' interest in directions other than experimentation, you may include questions in your inquiry center which lead to their reading for explanations, such as "Did you know . . .

Egyptian women who lived 5,000 years ago used as much make-up as do Hollywood movie stars today?

Whales have an underwater language?

An African tribe scratched a multiplication table on an antelope bone more than 7,000 years ago?

There's no blue in a bluejay?

Spear points similar to those used by some Eskimos today have been found in California and Florida?

The earth is a rock?

Ancient elephants' fossil teeth have been found on the bottom of the ocean off the eastern coast of the United States?

Certain frogs survive without water for many months?

Birds do not sing just to make music?"

The questions asked by children themselves are particularly useful for inclusion in the inquiry center. Because they typically reflect a wide range of interests, they are especially useful in personalizing the learning experiences of your pupils. Why doesn't the moon fall down? Why do trees lose their leaves? Why is it cold when the sun is shining? How does hair grow? Why do people speak different languages? Where do the clouds go? What happens when you cross the equator? I am sure that you can agree that questions such as these are likely to open up a multitude of activities for exploration in the centers you establish.

Simple "what" questions may also be used to initiate learning by your pupils. Listen carefully as they inquire as to the what of things. What is gravity? What is a verb? What are freckles? What is "few"? What is love? What are the insects that live in the ground? For example, a startling amount of insect life almost beyond human imagination can be found in soil. Experimenting scientists of the United States Department of Agriculture found the following in a piece of earth only ten inches deep and a yard wide: 3 spiders, 5 centipedes, 10 millipedes, 40 pill bugs, 50 snails and slugs, 3,340 worms of all kinds, 150 grubs, 160 fly eggs, 480 ants, 2,000 springtails, 20,000 mites, hundreds of rotifers and nematodes, and 5,000,000 protozoans. Additionally, one mole and two mice were found in the same patch of earth.[4] Similarly, you may wish to include in your inquiry center various containers of soil for your pupils to inquire about the life that exists in each. Construct a screen so that they may sift the soil to note, count, and observe the insects. The top of a candy or shoe box to which a screen is stapled and into which the soil can be poured is useful for this purpose.

Clearly, the most important thing you can do in fostering inquiry by your pupils is to establish your classroom environment so that they are free to examine their own ideas and to test them against available data. Central to this climate is teaching your pupils to accept and, at the same time, challenge each other's ideas openly and freely. Encouraging your pupils to explore so that they are not afraid of being wrong and doing more than is expected of them is a major step in opening up your classroom. Closely allied to this exploration is the process of problem-solving. Establishing learning centers for this purpose invites valuable learning experiences for your pupils because it goes beyond the very important process of inquiry to their hypothesizing about possible solutions.

The Problem-Solving Center.   There are three necessary ingredients you will need to consider in constructing a problem-solving center. Your pupils should view each problem to be explored as: (1) a *task*, (2) *problematic*, and (3) *personal*. Conceivably, for example, the scarcity of food in India, the slums in our cities, and the unproductive dry, barren lands of the world may all have personal meaning to the pupils. The problem-solving activities you establish in your center may range from simple, conventional tasks involving rudimentary computational skills to complex tasks such as those involved in exploring more serious problems such as the above-mentioned.

Both boys and girls are interested in the problems that exist today. Consider the problem of land erosion, for example. Can we prevent the occurrence of "dust bowls" in the future? Picture fertile farmland surrounded by ponds, alongside a stream winding down from snow-capped mountains. What would make it a desert? Pose this question to your pupils. Place such a picture(s) in a problem-solving center, along with various desert scenes and readings on the ecology of deserts. Invite your pupils to invent a recipe for a desert. Primary school children, in particular, often find this approach intriguing. Given the opportunity to compare pictures, read, and discuss their findings, perhaps your pupils would come up with some of the ingredients that make up the following recipe:

Many, many days of sunshine
No rain (except for flash floods)
Persistent hot winds
Excessive grazing by farm animals
Disappearing mountain snows

Mixing these ingredients together, you can readily expect that your pupils will guess the end products—the subsequent withering of plant life dependent on water, the depletion of top soil necessary to the growth of plants, and the erosion of land by wind and flood.

Consequently, your pupils are likely to match the ingredients of their recipe for a desert with the conditions of deserts that exist throughout the world. Place atlases, maps, and globes in the center to expedite their exploration. More than likely, they will discover similar conditions of abundant sunshine, lack of water, and excessive winds exist in the various desert regions. Along with this, they are likely to discover the dissimilarities among deserts. That, in spite of abundant sunshine, not all deserts are hot or are similar in terrain. Some students may be amazed to find that many deserts are very mountainous, and that certain types of plants and animals adapt themselves well to life in the desert.

A natural second step to this experience is to invite your pupils to explore the problem of land erosion. Expand the materials of your problem-solving center so that this process may take place. In due course of time, you can expect that your pupils will become increasingly knowledgeable about vast irrigation projects underway throughout the world, the huge dams being built, the planting of trees, shrubs, and grass, the use of fertilizer, contour farming, and other processes used to convert dry, barren, and eroded lands to fertile, productive soil. Divergent, convergent, and evaluative thinking by them result from their investigation.

The importance of economics and the nature of economic understanding may be explored through interesting problem-solving experiences. Concepts of supply and demand, savings, scarcity, and factors of production may be derived. Take the latter, for example. Place materials in your problem-solving center which invite your pupils to compare and contrast the problem of productive resources of different regions, of different cultures, or of different eras. To investigate this problem, the materials of the center must be sufficiently diverse to enable your pupils to study the availability of natural resources, labor, transportation, markets, tools, and other factors of production. This can be initiated on a very basic level. Those of you who teach primary school children may begin with the structure of the family. Gather as many pictures as you can depicting family life. Saturate your center with magazines. Who are the producers of the family? Who are the consumers? Invite your pupils to cut out those pictures in the magazines which point these out. Does producing goods and producing services vary from culture to culture, region to region? Are some people non-producers? (the very old, the very sick, the very young, etc.). What are the goods being produced in the family? (Mother and father cooking and building shelves for the kitchen). What are the services being produced? (Brother and sister cutting the grass and cleaning the bedrooms.) The idea is to use the materials and activities of the problem-solving center so that they stimulate questions and raise problems.

Problem! How can the efficiency and welfare of all the members of a family be increased? Supposing that each member were to cook, wash the dishes, feed the cat, cut the grass, etc., would this be the most efficient way to conduct the affairs of the family? In response to this problem, your pupils more than likely will see the need for a division of labor. Create other problem-solving experiences. Who determines the kinds of goods and services produced by people? To raise questions and problems concerning the various factors of production, arrange the activities of the center so that the similarities and differences of technological progress in various cultures and regions are apparent to your pupils. Carefully selected pictures, films, and filmstrips may be used for this purpose. Different tools can be compared, skills in using the tools can be contrasted, and different standards of living can be investigated. For example, pupils in the upper grades can compare the economic system of early settlers in America with that of the native Indians; that of the early 1900s with the present-day economy; that of the rural family with the urban family; and the economy of developing nations with the more industrialized countries.

Introduce the concept of choice simply. Set up a variety of realistic problems for your pupils to explore, such as:

You've cut your finger and wish to stop the flow of blood. What are you likely to need most? A piece of chewing gum? A book to take your mind away from the cut? A Band-Aid?

You're camping out on a beach infested by mosquitos. What are you apt to choose for your comfort? An electric fan, a toy truck, mosquito lotion?

Build the activities of the center up to the point where your pupils generalize that the choices they make determine the kinds of goods and services produced by people.

Similarly, other facets of the economy may be presented in the center in the form of problem-solving experiences. Problems pertaining to the use of income, the conflict between unlimited wants and limited resources, scarcity, specialization, interdependency, and competition may be explored. Depending on the experiences and interests of your pupils, you may move from simple to very complex problems. Is the earth producing enough food for its inhabitants? Some of the factors involved in studying this problem are how climate, soil, and culture affect food consumption and production. Consequently, your pupils will be called upon to study weather, growing seasons, rainfall, erosion, glacial deposits, conservation methods, and diets based on cultural beliefs. Alternatives may be explored. These include substitute foods, importing, reallocation of peoples, etc. Extensive ideas for economic activities applicable for inclusion in the problem-solving center are readily available from numerous sources. The Joint Council on Economic Education (1212 Avenue of the Americas, New York, New York 10036) is one such source. Its monographs are replete with the experiences of practicing teachers in the area of economic education.

Legend or fact? Literature, as such, is another important source you can draw from to place your pupils in problem-solving situations.

> Out from Ur of the Chaldees went Abraham. Out from Ur, the city of his birth, went the man who recognized that "God is one." But where was this mysterious city of his birth? No modern map marked its location. No modern scholar knew of its existence. Was there such a city?

> Old Indian legends whispered of some mysterious fortress—a city high in the Andes Mountains of Peru. They called it Tamputocco, meaning "place of many windows." Was this just a myth invented to explain the coming of the first Inca?

> The Minotaur, half-man and half-bull, was said to have existed on the island of Crete in a building called the Labyrinth designed for him by the royal architect of Crete's great King Minos. Did such a creature really exist?

> The "Curse of the Pharaohs" suggested that death would come to those who disturbed the tombs of Pharaohs in Egypt. Was this superstition or fact?

Fascinating accounts of myths, legends, and historical events more than likely will intrigue most of your pupils. Begin now to look for and gather such accounts. Newspapers and magazines, as well as books, are replete with literature you will find useful for instituting problem-solving experiences in your centers. Personalizing the activities of your pupils around common themes of human experience is yet another approach to the implementation of learning centers.

The Theme Center.   Children watch two television dramas. One is a documentary account of unrest in the Middle East, the other is the proverbial *Wizard of Oz*. Prejudice, friendship, freedom, justice, motivation, honor, insult, revenge, rebirth, and change are recurring themes. How can you increase your pupils' awareness of and extend their natural sensitivity to the many themes of human experience? Consider implementing theme centers for this purpose. A theme center may be composed of almost any topic of study. Kite-flying in various parts of the world, exploration of space, settlement, revolutions, ecology, and the characteristics of life itself are among the many themes that your pupils can explore. Let us turn once again to the use of literature as a vehicle for participating in the themes of human experience.

Themes, ideas, concepts—flypaper for knowledge![5] Begin, first, by exposing your pupils to the themes of "appearance and reality," and "cause and effect." Place a few books in your theme center, such as *The Emperor's New Clothes*,

Tower by the Sea, and *Charlotte's Web*. Invite interested pupils to respond to synopses or examples taken from these books. More than likely you will need to set the stage for their responses by first discussing examples of appearance and reality: what something appears to be and what it really is. Explore the difference with them and then encourage them to develop their own theories. The following examples are particularly useful to those pupils who are academically able and show a strong interest in reading.

In *The Emperor's New Clothes* it is rumored that anyone who cannot see the Emperor's new clothes is stupid and does not deserve his job. The Emperor parades his gorgeous clothes proudly to the admiration of everyone, especially himself. He "appears" to everyone—except to one small child—to be wearing fine stitches when in "reality" he is stitchless as a jay bird. Read or see this play and you'll be in stitches!

In *Tower by the Sea* a cat has one blue and one green eye. The cat and a magpie move through the streets of Katverloren, a fear-ridden, medieval town in Holland. A frail young woman searches in a graveyard for a dead baby she never had. A kind old woman comforts her. Old crones, rumor hags, take notice and pass the word around. An epidemic breaks out. Babies are feverish. The mayor's baby is stolen. A crone shrieks, "It's the witch!" The kind old woman is placed at the stake.

In *Charlotte's Web*, Wilbur is a doomed ham. His path is thorny. Pigs are pigs and are to be eaten—that is the "reality." Charlotte, a bloodthirsty friend, doesn't see Wilbur as any old pig. She creates a new "reality." Wilbur is "terrific"; Wilbur is "radiant." The future "ham" becomes a blue-ribbon pig!

To help develop your pupils' theories of "cause and effect," it may be necessary for you to guide them first through questions based on their readings. You may, moreover, need to work directly with some of your pupils. The most talented of your readers, on the other hand, may be entirely capable of responding to the questions independently of your direct guidance. Representative questions may take the following pattern:

What *causes* the "blindness" of the Emperor's subjects and the people of Katverloren?

What *causes* the farm people to change their minds and see Wilbur as a "terrific" pig?

Is Wilbur, in reality, a "terrific" pig?

What *causes* of this "appearance and reality" gap are common to all of the examples taken from the books?

What *causes* show up in one example and not in the others?

Can you now create a theory of "cause and effect" that will explain the appearance and reality gap in other books you have read?

Will your theory apply to:

The Great Oz?

Alphonse, The Bearded One?

Prejudice?

The Salem Witch Trials?

Advertising?

Cheating?

Will your theory apply to what you think you are and to what your classmates think you are?

In similar fashion, you may develop this process further by using other selected themes of human experience. Consider, for example, the themes of honor, result, and revenge. Encourage your pupils to read for examples of these themes. Augmented with personal experiences, the following are representative of examples taken from literature.

Greek *honor* was defended at the walls of Troy. *Revenge* was taken on the Trojans.

I'm on my *honor* to do my own work on a test.

Mary Poppins' outlandish behavior was an *insult* to the *honor* of Mr. Banks.

His *Honor*, the Mayor.

In "Call it Courage," Mafatu went to the cannibal island to recover his lost *honor*.

With these examples as referral points, invite your pupils to extend their thinking about cause and effect. Nations, great men, kings, warriors, and people of certain cultures take pride in "honor." Are "pride" and "honor" the same? Why do people seek "revenge"? Do you ever take "revenge"? Does an "insult" or "teasing" bother you or your friends? How do people who do something "dishonorable" feel?

Literature may be used in a number of other ways to explore the themes of human experience. Invite your pupils, for example, to search for proverbs with the idea of developing theories of cause and effect. Called upon to interpret the proverb, "He who would catch fish must venture his bait," one eight-year-old youngster developed the following theory:

This proverb is like cause and effect. It means you have to lose something to gain something. It occurs in everyone's life. If I want to keep a pet (I have a cat), I have to call and feed him every day. I "earn" a cat by calling him. He earns a meal by coming. I get to pat a clean cat by brushing him. He earns a birthday party by being a good cat. I get money by earning it or finding it. I earn it by doing one of millions of jobs around the house. I kind of "steal the money" by sitting and reading a book while my brother (I'm baby-sitting) tears up the room.

Certain pupils may find a center built around themes of human experiences in literature not to their liking. Perhaps other subjects may appeal to them.

Consider the built-in appeal of social studies. Try, for example, building a center on the theme of exploration. Invite your pupils to sail with the Vikings, Columbus, or with Thor Heyerdahl on the Kon Tiki. Have them fly into space with John Glenn, Neil Armstrong, and other astronauts, or, if they prefer, travel overland with Marco Polo, Daniel Boone, Lewis and Clark, the conquistadores, and Juan de Oñate. Let the choice be theirs.

If possible, capitalize on the exploration that took place in your location. For children who live in New Mexico, what is more natural than the theme of northward exploration by Oñate? To develop this particular theme, place in the center a variety of utensils, tools, trinkets, potsherds, a metate and mano, a handplow, some corn, arrowheads, stone scrapers, ornaments, maps, grass, soil and sand, and rocks and shells indigenous to the Southwest. Include guidelines for pupil activities where and when appropriate. These may take the form of activity cards[6] or activity sheets designed to invite pupil response.

You may, if you wish, place all the materials in the exploration center. Should space pose a problem, an alternative approach would be to reduce the number of activities to take place at the center. This will, consequently, necessitate fewer materials and require less space. Additionally, the interest of your pupils will probably be sustained as you add and substitute new materials and new experiences to the center. To suggest how the theme of Oñate's exploration may be carried out sequentially, a few activities are listed below that are particularly appropriate for upper grade children. In an exploration center they can be presented as follows:

> How good an explorer are you? Can you make important decisions? Note the objects in this center (utensils, tools, weapons, trinkets, etc.). If you were exploring with Juan de Oñate north of Mexico, which of these objects would you take with you? Think thoroughly. List those you would take on the activity sheet provided for this purpose. Compare your list with the equipment actually taken by Oñate. Read to find out.

> On their trip northward, Oñate's men found pieces of pottery such as those you see here in the center. What do these pieces represent? Can you put them together? Sketch your representation. Who were the people who might have used what you've sketched? For what purposes? Where did they come from? Where did they go? List some ideas you have about them.

> Look at the metate, mano, handplow (rock), corn kernels, and pottery. These were also left by some people unknown to Oñate's men. How were they used? Can you put the mano, metate, and corn to work? Can you tell how the pottery was made and colored? See me if you need help.

> Near Santa Fe, some of Oñate's men found arrowheads, scrapers, and ornaments just like these at an abandoned settlement. Who were the people who used them? How were each of these items used? Read to see how well you have hypothesized.

At times on their trip north, some exploreers would leave their expedition to establish permanent settlements. One such location is represented by the outline map you see here in the center. Note the river, its tributaries, the ponds, and the forest land represented. Establish your settlement. Use the map to mark the location of homes, the sawmill, trading post, blacksmith shop, and church. Where will you graze your cows? Plant your crops? Think hard. Your plan and ideas will be shared with others and then matched with actual settlements established by explorers.

This box contains long grass, short grass, dark soil, sand, wood bark, and rocks. With these as reference points, can you make some good hypotheses about the kind of terrain (land features) early Mexican pioneers crossed to reach their destinations? How might the pioneers have used the terrain to their advantage? What were some of the obstacles the terrain presented to the pioneers? Be prepared to present your views when we meet to discuss these questions.

Observe the shells, sand, and rounded stones you find in this center. Hypothesize about the following:

Where were Mexican pioneers traveling northward likely to find these? (Alongside rivers, lakes, and ponds.)

Why are the stones rounded?

What is the sand made from?

What do the shells represent?

Can you now trace the pioneers' route to the north? Show me the results.

The theme of exploration can, of course, be carried on in multiple ways and settings in learning centers. Your pupils may study the effects of myths on exploration (Atlantis, Cibola, El Dorado), contrast the motives of various individuals and countries for exploration, research the evolution of ships and navigation instruments, and write historical fiction, to cite just a few possibilities. Additionally, you may wish to consider still other themes unique to the social studies. Themes of special interest to primary school children might include those which focus on celebrations, shelters, mining, agriculture, water control, and the oceans. Those appropriate for older pupils might revolve around power and technology, food and population, cities and transportation, migrations, revolutions, law and government, archaeology, architecture, education, and writing systems. All of these, I might add, were used successfully in the Lexington, Massachusetts schools during my tenure there.

Science also will provide you with multiple opportunities for developing theme centers. By way of illustration, picture the many activities that can be built around the theme of plant life, with a special emphasis on seeds. The following are particularly pertinent to those of you who plan to teach, or are presently teaching, primary school children.[7]

How do these seeds travel?   Enclose various seeds in individual cellophane wrappings. Invite your pupils to place each in containers that designate their individual mode of travel, e.g., those that fly, hitchhike, or swim. Label each container clearly so that your pupils understand that they are to place seeds that fly in the "fly" container, those that swim in the "swim" container, etc.

What part do we eat?   Place a series of cards in the center, each picturing a fruit or vegetable and their names. Invite your pupils to record the names of the fruit or vegetable on an activity sheet under the appropriate headings designated on the sheet (leaves, fruit, stems, seeds, roots). In response to the question, for example, the word *cabbage* would be listed under the heading of *leaves,* the word *pear* under the heading of *fruit.*

Measure these!   Place various plant life, such as carrots and leaves, in the center for pupils to measure. Provide an activity sheet on which they may record their results. I think you will agree that pupils love to measure all kinds of things.

What will these seeds grow up to be?   Place various seeds in the center for your pupils to examine and hypothesize the answer to the question. Use pictures of the "grown-up" seeds for comparison purposes. Better still, if feasible, use fruit that is cut so that the pupils can actually see the seeds inside.

Describe a flower!   Place a flower(s) in a cup or box of soil. Invite your pupils to list words appropriate to it, e.g., pretty, yellow, etc. Watch their vocabulary grow! Have them design their own flowers as an added treat.

Guess! How many seeds in each?   Cut an apple, orange, avocado, or squash. Encourage your pupils to estimate the number and then count the seeds in each. How many plants can they grow?

Make a seed collage!   Place construction paper, glue, and multiple containers of various seeds in the center. Who knows? This experience may show the beginning of a great artist!

Play science checkers!   Place a checkerboard and flash cards composed of words such as root, stem, leaf, etc., in the center. To play the game, each pupil takes a turn showing a flash card to the other. If the word is identified correctly, the pupil may move a checker forward. The object of the game is to get across the board first. The more words known, the more likely this is to take place. Consequently, you'll find your pupils working hard to develop their science vocabulary.

How green is your thumb?   Place containers of seeds and various kinds of soil in the center. How well can your pupils plant? Invite them to select the seeds and soil of their choice. Have them keep a record of the growth that takes place or doesn't take place.

There are, of course, literally hundreds of activites that you can use or perhaps are already using that may be added to this partial list. Note, moreover, that the skills development of your pupils is not being ignored as they undertake experiences such as those illustrated here. Vocabulary, reading, spelling, arithmetic, writing, and art skills, as well as scientific learning, all come into play. However, there will be times when you may need to direct more specific attention to the development of your pupils' academic skills. You may, consequently, prefer to establish skills centers for this very important purpose.

The Skills Center.   Education involves, certainly, more than the transmission of knowledge and the development of academic skills. In my opinion, too much emphasis is placed on academic skills and not enough on the personal experiences of the pupils and their relationships with others. However, there need not be any conflict between the development of your pupils' academic skills and their personal objectives. In implementing the skills center, it is important to design its activities so that your pupils see the connection between the skills to be developed and their goals. Thus, it is necessary that you confer with them on a continuing basis.

Also important to the establishment of your skills center is the degree of creativity you bring to it. Even the most boring of subjects—from your pupils' point of view—can be taught with imagination. The study of verbs is a case in point. One approach could be to attract your pupils to this study by the use of nonsense-type sentences, the idea being to encourage them to identify each verb in a sentence by whatever method possible. Generally, they will be able to identify the verb by its form, position, and action.

Can you find the verbs?
1. The glorpans gleeped at mone.
2. Slon has pliting furbs.
3. Bopey hickled.
4. The zop is miting.
5. Kaffy lobed laf nan.
6. Twa corbies were traking amon.
7. Nom ganed dan slathered kinerth the simbly.
8. Yancey gerbered.
9. Are the blunkies fering?
10. Is Wanie kining?[8]

Activities such as this are not only useful in developing the skill in question, but will probably be considered fun by your pupils.

Think of other imaginative approaches to develop your pupils' academic skills beyond identifying the parts of speech. Prerequisites to your pupils' being able to write and express themselves well are the skills of observation and description. Use your skill centers to sharpen their acuity. Perhaps the following activities will stimulate your thinking and help you spin off to more imaginative approaches. To develop your pupils' powers to observe and describe concisely:

Place any object in the skills center. Invite your pupils to touch, smell, rub, hit, squeeze, move, and study it from all angles. Encourage them to list words which describe their responses to the object such as its shape, weight, feel, color, and smell. Or, ask for a direct comparison. For example, a ball of clay may bring to mind an apple or orange, the moon or sun, a planet, a baseball, or a man's bald head. Have them develop similes and metaphors with the words they think of.

Put your pupils inside a wave, up a tree, or flat on a haystack by using pictures in the center. Have them describe the way they feel in each of these situations to a classmate, record them on a tape, or list them. Encourage them to use words that say exactly what they mean.

Place a mirror in the center. Invite your pupils to make faces and list what they see. A variation would be to place assorted pictures in the center and have your pupils note and list the different emotions they see expressed in the faces of the people.

Place a recording of various sounds in the skills center. Ask your pupils to describe exactly what they hear. Perhaps they will create a new language by making up their own words.[9]

As well as using creative experiences to develop the academic skills of your pupils, it is very important that you capitalize on their maturational characteristics to further develop their skills. For example, those of you who are preparing to teach or who are presently teaching in the primary grades would do well to consider your pupils' interest in checkers, monopoly, dominoes, and simple card games. Put this interest to work in your skills center. More than fun is involved, for a good number of arithmetic, spelling, and language arts skills can be taught effectively through this game approach. Similarly, older children's interest in these games and in hobbies such as cars, planes, various kinds of collections, and experimentation can be utilized to teach skills in the upper grades. Build on this interest whenever and wherever it is feasible.

The activities of the skills center will naturally vary with the needs of your pupils. As is true in any classroom, they may range from the very simplest to the most complex. The idea in the learning-centered classroom, however, is to add activities to the skills center only as they are needed and not on the basis of a set of predetermined skills you want your pupils to learn. Keep in mind, also, that although the skills center is established for the specific development of academic skills needed by your pupils, these skills are obtained in all types of learning centers.

The Invention Center.   What can you invent, create, or construct? If invited with these questions, your pupils are likely to generate more interest and enthusiasm in an invention learning center than in any other type you could implement in your classroom. Can you imagine your pupils inventing a "flying picture," an "electric perkball," or a "Jensenda"? Simply designating a center as an invention center is usually enough to excite their imagination.

Start on a very simple basis. An assortment of scrap wood and a bottle of glue is sufficient. Encourage your pupils to invent anything they can with the wood. Watch their ability to express themselves grow! They will typically name their invention, talk about it, and sometimes write about it. Extend the variety of materials you place in the center. Try a strange mixture such as a penny, piece of wire, string, paper plate, comb, Scotch tape, and brass fasteners. You can't possibly imagine all that your pupils are apt to invent!

The Construction Center.   In my opinion, all elementary school classrooms need to have an area where children can saw, hammer, and build things. However, a complete workshop for this purpose is not possible for most of you. Turn, then, to the establishment of a construction center in which your pupils can be provided with simple cardboard carpentry experiences. Put cigar, candy, and shoe boxes to work. Utilize milk cartons. Watch your pupils develop their mathematical skills as they measure, cut, saw, match, and assemble portions of cardboard to build dioramas, insect cages, and electric boards. Note their increasing knowledge as they use milk cartons to build wind vanes, anenometers, hygrometers, and other instruments to study weather. Miniature houses and municipal buildings and even entire villages wired for electric lights may be built through experiences with cardboard carpentry.

Go beyond the use of cardboard. Provide your pupils with opportunities to build models of all kinds which require other materials. Your older pupils most likely will enjoy the construction of model bridges, locomotives, and airplanes; younger pupils will play with blocks, Lincoln logs, and erector sets. Some of your older children may find that "film-making" appeals to them. Before beginning, have a film cleared by a processor so that it becomes transparent and ready for use. Invite your pupils to create a story on the film. They will need to use a pen and India ink, or a Kohi-noor pencil to draw their ideas on the film. Constructing musical instruments usually appeals to both boys and girls of any age level. Ask your pupils to contribute empty bottles, blocks of wood, sections of rubber tubes, elastic bands, coffee cans, cigar boxes, wire, gourds, string, large nails, and other items with this purpose in mind. With a bit of imagination and some know-how, your pupils will create a rather amazing variety of musical instruments for their enjoyment.

Ideas for construction-type activities are numerous. Those of you who are experienced teachers, I'm certain, already have a great number of ideas. Additionally, when given the opportunity to do so, your pupils themselves will suggest many activities for inclusion in the construction center you establish. Activities which encourage children to build are extremely important to the formulation of open learning experiences in your classroom because they will invite the social interaction necessary to complete a project. Equally important, in addition to their natural appeal to your pupils, building activities will serve to invite and encourage *constructive* behavior by your pupils.

Other Learning Centers.   This discussion of various learning centers should have made you increasingly aware of the almost limitless possibilities for constructing and implementing other types of centers in your classroom. Indeed, just about any activity you are currently using in your traditional classroom may be presented in a learning center. These may be broken down as specifically as is necessary, for example, as a sculpturing center, puppet center, tangram center, tall stories center, measuring center, geoboard center, autoharp center, bone center, word shop center, fishbowl center, dinosaur center, etc. The next few chapters will acquaint you still further with various types of learning centers and with the techniques for their implementation.

POINTS TO REMEMBER

- Appropriate learning objectives may be determined by the teacher or the pupils.
- Pupils learn what and when they wish to learn.
- Preferred choices of activities by pupils are necessary to open learning experiences.
- Learning centers should be constructed on the basis of pupils' interests, academic needs, and personal enrichment.
- Instructional diagnosis facilitates learning experiences essential to pupils.
- The interest-centered classroom is a natural environment for open learning.

NOTES

1. L. E. Raths, M. Harmin, and S. B. Simon, *Values and Teaching* (Columbus, Ohio: Charles E. Merrill Publishing Co., 1966), pp. 38–39.

2. Fred T. Wilhelms, "Evaluation as Feedback," *Evaluation as Feedback and Guide* prepared by the ASCD 1967 Yearbook Committee, Fred T. Wilhelms, Chairman and Editor (Washington, D.C.: Association for Supervision and Curriculum Development, NEA, 1967), p. 4–5.

3. Adopted and modified from a plan submitted by Doris Burress, Mesa Verde Elementary School, Farmington, New Mexico, in my workshop course on learning centers and the open classroom, San Juan College, New Mexico State University, July 8-26, 1974.

4. Richard F. Dempewolff, *Nature Craft* (New York: Golden Press, 1965), p. 10

5. In this section on literature, I draw heavily on the ideas of Frank Lyman, previously cited in the first chapter.

6. Discarded, used computer cards are useful in this respect.

7. Adapted from the experiences of Mary Sumner and Jo Ann Zembiec, White Sands Elementary School, White Sands Missile Range, New Mexico.

8. Adapted from an activity sheet devised by Mrs. Betty Dirk, Central School, Las Cruces, New Mexico.

9. Drawn from activities suggested by Frank Lyman, Estabrook School, Lexington, Massachusetts.

Dear Dr. Thomas,

The Ice w l ml t. I DiD it at hom. I Lick to xsprmt.

Love
James (Age 7)

three

Attracting Pupils
to Learning Centers

"Our kids actually get so involved and enthused, we literally have to push them out the door at recess and at school dismissal time!"   —Phyllis Gleyre, 3rd Grade Teacher, University Hills School, Las Cruces, New Mexico.

I have often been similarly greeted by teachers who have taken steps to open up their classrooms. Pupils, they state, discover themselves in the decentralized environment of the learning-centered classroom. Among other characteristics, they note more responsiveness and less "tiredness" and "inattentiveness" in their pupils. Why is this? According to groups of eleven- and twelve-year-old children with whom I've talked, school in this setting is "for real." One such group had this to say about their learning-centered classroom:

"It's neat!"

"I like it. You're not always doing the same things."

"You're moving."

"There's more chance to talk about stuff."

"You can choose."

"We're doing, finding out things."

"I don't have to read aloud."

"We're not being told all the time."

The teacher goes *to* the pupil in this classroom environment. Consequently, teachers increasingly find themselves reaching for their ultimate teaching goals—the development of responsive, life-long attitudes in their pupils and freeing their emotions, senses, and intellects. Building on what the pupils know, rather than on what they do not know, the teacher pursuing open-concept directions invariably encourages the pupils to go beyond the frozen boundaries of a particular book or a particular method of learning. Is it little wonder, then, that the decentralized setting of the open classroom appeals to elementary school children?

PUTTING IDEAS TO WORK
IN SINGLE-OBJECT CENTERS

In the preceding chapter, I stated that the organization of learning centers in the classroom takes a variety of forms. The materials in the centers may be chosen to capitalize on pupil interests, may focus on the investigation of problems, may be oriented toward the study of subjects and topics, or may be designed to develop skills or further understanding. Whatever the intent and emphasis of a particular center, its attraction and subsequent interest to pupils must be considered of primary importance.

Attracting pupils to a learning center is not a happy accident. Considerable thought and planning must go into the organization of each of your centers so that: (1) its activities appeal to your pupils, and (2) its direction, scope and sequence are sufficiently understood by your pupils so that they are able to function independently of you. Consider, for example, the learning center containing a single object. The range of possibilities for implementing such a center and attracting pupils to it is almost without limit. Among the many items I have found useful for inclusion in the single-object center are:

petrified worm	sponge
spinning wheel	tape-recorder
animal skull	potsherds
candle mold(s)	telephone insulator(s)
typewriter	necklace (from India)
hand plow	microscope
tachistoscope	sarangee (Nepalese fiddle)
mortar and pestle	insect collection
oil lamp	film loop and strip
discovery box	railroad spike & portion of track
slide, overhead, movie projector	wagon wheel spoke (from a stagecoach)
record player	Tibetan rug
barbed wire	arrowheads
molino (Mexican coffee grinder)	commercial learning kits

The variety of single objects that might be used by you to attract your pupils to a learning center goes far beyond this list. Use your imagination, ingenuity, and courage. Try the unexpected! Place a mastodon knee bone in a learning center. Hang a skeleton for your pupils to touch and examine. To ensure room for the in-depth exploration by your pupils, yet provide protection for the skeleton, use an upright, elongated school clothes locker from which to suspend it. If neither of these is available, try a boa constrictor! (Sometimes obtainable from a pet shop at no cost). Far-fetched? Unusual? Not in the least! Junior and senior high schools, as well as univeristy science departments and certain industrial plants, are excellent sources for borrowing skeletal remains, preserved reptiles, stuffed animals and birds, insect collections, rock and mineral specimens, fauna and flora, microscopes and bioscopes, scales, geometric figures and geoboards, fabrics, and other assorted items and equipment of interest to children. In Lexington, during the course of studying one-celled animals, for example, our primary school teachers were able to borrow as many as *one hundred* microscopes from a manufacturer of science instruments. What incredible excitement! Imagine *each* six-year-old pupil absorbed in the fluctuation of an amoeba as it changed its form and shape in response to stimuli.

The most important source for unusual and different materials is your own classroom. You will find that your pupils are generally willing and even eager to contribute materially to the classroom environment. An intriguing approach you may wish to consider is that often recommended by advocates of the language experience approach. Those of you who teach in preschool or primary grades may invite contributions by pupils who are entering school for the first time and, at the same time, pretest what they already know. You may initiate this process by encouraging them to bring to class various items such as:

1. A scrap of cloth seven inches long.
2. Something yellow, red, or green.
3. A small, flat, thin stone.
4. A twig with three leaves on it.
5. Five kernels of corn.
6. A dab of red or gray clay.
7. A black or green insect.
8. Something to put together.
9. A flower with four petals on it.
10. Beads, buttons, and bottle caps.

Such a procedure is invaluable in discovering which of your children can discriminate color, are able to count and measure, have some knowledge of textures, can identify certain plants and insects, and are capable of noting shapes and sizes. Based on this information, and especially if the contributory items have been carefully selected for diagnostic purposes, you may then proceed to plan appropriately for the various needs of your pupils. The greater the variety of pupil contributions, the greater are the directions open to you for implementing activities in learning centers on the basis of the knowledge gained about your pupils. This venture need not be commercial, expensive, or restricted to the home for salvage materials of all kinds are readily available in the neighborhood, which will be discussed further in Chapter 5.

HATS, ROCKS, COINS, ARTIFACTS, AND SHELLS

A strange-looking symbol. A moving object. An unusual arrangement. A statement. A change of environment. Something bright. Something to be manipulated or constructed. A question. A foreign substance. A catchy book title. A collection of hats. Even a rock! In short, you can use anything that catches the eye to attract your pupils to a learning center initially. Primary school children, for example, may be intrigued by a "hat center," with broad brim, polka dot, Texas style, roll brim, pony tails, high roll, and black hats—all unique to the Southwest. Place representative hats of *your* region in a learning center and include a mirror or two. Invite your pupils to role-play before the mirrors. "Who am I?" "Where do I live?" "What do I do?" Broaden the experience and incorporate hats worn by a policeman, sailor, pilot, baseball player, construction worker, chef, farmer, or perhaps a witch. Then add hats worn by the Brazilian, the Russian, the Japanese, and the Arab. Encourage the writing of "hat stories," the reading of Dr. Seuss's *The Cat in the Hat*, the sketching and creating of new hat styles, the study of hat manufacturing, the use of hats, and the exploration of the different cultures that contain the hats. This center may be expanded to include clothing and costumes, thereby opening up the possibilities for a dramatic portrayal of occupations, roles, recreation, and customs. Your pupils may subsequently be called upon to design materials and construct props, write scripts, and interact with each other. It is likely that your pupils' attraction to the "hat center" will instigate a comprehensive study of different careers.

In my classroom experiences, almost without exception, pupils were attracted to a learning center which consisted of a single rock with an imbedded footprint about seven inches long and three to four inches across the toes. To entice the children to the footprint, I simply lettered the mark "?" on a piece of oak tag and placed it by the rock on a table. The fossilized imprint never failed to stimulate the pupils' curiosity regarding the origin of the footprint. Was it the print of a bear, or that of an apelike figure who, in fleeing the wrath of a volcano, had stepped into molten lava? Was it, or could it conceivably be, the footprint of a man possibly predating the man identified in Dr. Leakey's historic discovery in East Africa? The questions poured forth. Soon the pupils were inundating libraries, bringing in books from home, digging into scout and tracking manuals, and bombarding teachers, parents, and each other with hypotheses. Subsequently, as a consequence of the initial attraction—a single unique rock—an extended center was created of the many and varied rocks and fossil imprints gathered by the pupils in the pursuit of related questions they had formulated.

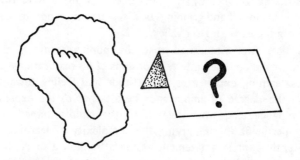

The sequence of events is shown in Figure 3-1.

FIGURE 3-1   Development of a Single-Object Center

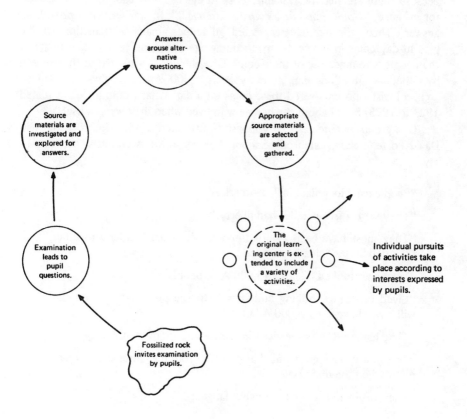

Student and cooperating teachers who have since borrowed my prized possession for use in their classrooms report similar results with the youngsters they teach. In much the same manner, their pupils have created learning centers consisting of fossils gathered from mountain sides, pottery shards and arrowheads found on nearby ranches, open ranges, and construction sites, metates and manos (hand-grinding bowls) dug up from mesas, and shells scratched from the earth of river valleys.

It has been well-established that the pupil's readiness to learn is a consequence of the complex interrelationships of his maturational development, his previous learning experiences, his attitude and feeling toward the subject matter, and the degree of importance he attaches to the experience. Single-object learning centers, when related to the child's immediate world, are particularly pertinent in simplifying the complexity of learning. Teachers, in fact, persistently express amazement at the attraction a single, familiar object often holds for pupils, especially when they are taught to approach the object as a *new experience*. Consider the coin, for example. What can your pupils learn from the examination of a coin if it is uniquely approached? Try establishing a learning center consisting solely of coins minted in the United States, simply because these are readily available. Post an eye-catching caption at the center, for instance, *"Would you cut a coin for change?"*[1] In smaller print, provide an answer. Then, through clearly stated guidelines, make a transition to the present-day coins in the center by encouraging your pupils to hypothesize about the people who made use of these coins. Give the pupils attracted to the center a hypothetical situation, e.g., "The year is 5,000 A.D. Imagine you are an archaeologist who uncovered these coins on a dig! What would the coins (dated 1923 to 1973) reveal about the people who lived when they were in use?"

One group of nine-year-old youngsters, attracted to this kind of activity in David Porter's class, Estabrook School, Lexington, Massachusetts, had this to say:

"People lived in a place called America."

"They were a free people—had liberty."

"They must have been a united people who lived in a land together." ("United States" clearly stamped.)

"Must have looked like us." (5,000 A.D. people)

"Lived in strange-looking buildings." (In the pupils' minds, buildings will have changed by 5,000 A.D.)

"They had a system of leadership—many important men."

"Trees must have grown at that time." (From the laurel and oak leaves pictured on the dime.)

"They wrote and spoke the English language."

"They used a number system."

"They worshipped one God." (In God We Trust)

"They lived over 3,000 years ago."

You may well argue the accuracy of some of the pupils' interpretations as recorded. Indeed, they were questioned by the pupils themselves, with the ultimate result being a search for authenticity through careful observation. Interest in this simple, but "different" learning experience was such that the examination of other cultures took place through the foreign coins the children subsequently brought to the center. The questions that arose took this pattern:

"Why do some coins have holes in their centers?"

"Why are some not round?"

"What is this coin made of?"

"Why does this coin (Nepalese) have mountains on it?"

"What does the lion stamped on this coin (Indian) mean?"

"Do all cultures use coins the way we do?"

It is apparent that questions such as these may serve as springboards to an exploration in greater depth of cultures. Possibilities for further investigation might include the study of metals used to mint the coins, their sources, processing and manufacturing based on these resources, topographical features of countries, the language depicted on the coins, the number systems suggested, architecture of various lands, and the need for a coinage system.

Prior to 1965, dimes and quarters contained 90 percent silver and 10 percent copper. Since that time, silver has been completely eliminated from the composition of these coins. A learning center composed of coins in which these distinctive changes are evident may be utilized to invite your pupils to explore the reasons for these changes. Is silver in shorter supply? Is it more difficult to obtain than copper? Is it more difficult to process? Is its use more essential to other aspects of the economy? What is the metal that has been substituted for silver? Why? Conceivably, such questioning could lead certain of your pupils to want to find out how coins are minted and how paper money is printed. Others may wish to trace the historical development of money. Still others may see fit to explore other forms of money used throughout the world today, for example, the primitive stone "coins" of Yap islanders, each weighing hundreds of pounds. It is even conceivable that some of your pupils might wish to study aspects of banking and the economy.

Similarly, bottles, keys, nails, buttons, medals, toys, stamps, jugs, pottery, post cards, woodprints, dolls, automobile plates, calendars, fruit jars, and countless other memorabilia, artifacts, and household items may be used to explore and study changing tastes, standards, costs, and technological progress in various cultures.[2] Dig up grandma's relics. Peruse antique shops. Explore Goodwill Industries. Scrounge in junk shops and flea markets. Take in garage sales. Excavate a dump! One such expedition resulted in finding a tin can on which Mrs. Flick proclaimed the quality of her cookies at bargain prices. Placed in a learning center, such a container serves as a catalyst for contrasting the cost of cookies early in the century with present-day prices. Changes in the packaging of cookies and other consumable products might also prove attractive to certain pupils as targets of study, for example, why are apples, orange, onions, potatoes, etc., packaged today? Why are certain foods frozen, others dried, and still others powdered? As your pupils investigate source materials and gather essential information, the new experiences will require that they develop new skills. Once such skills are refined and practiced, you can assume that the performances and aspirations of your pupils will reach sufficiently high levels to ensure their readiness for learning experiences which demand a higher degree of performance and stronger motivations.

Effective learning is built on direct experiences. Objects presented here invite direct contact and experiences beyond the initial attraction, as already illustrated. Direct experiences take still other patterns. Take an early vintage bread bowl, a butter churn, or even a labeled wooden slat from a packing case to act as catalysts at a learning center. Post questions in the center to which your pupils can respond concerning any one of these. The utility of the bread bowl, for example, might encourage them to take on the task of making a similar bowl. Pioneers heading west, it is known, made bread bowls by cutting a six-inch-thick block of wood from the trunk of a tree—usually ash—then pouring hot coals into the center of the block, scraping again, and repeating the process until the desired depth was reached. The bowls were indispensable as containers in which the ingredients of bread were mixed, kneaded, and shaped. How are such bowls made today?

Similarly, a single slat from a packing case, such as that used by the Arbuckle Company to ship coffee to the prairie country in the 1880s, may be used as a learning center in your classroom. One group of children, attracted to such a center by the faded lettering on the slat and a brief statement identifying it as a portion of a packing case, discovered through their subsequent investigations that wood slats were used by homesteaders to build shelves, bins, cradle boards (for Indian women), feed boxes for animals, doors, furniture, and well casings.

Learning depends on cues, particularly when pupils attach meaning to the cues. Sensory stimuli, of course, are cues designed to invite responses from the pupils. Another example of the effective use of cues in the single-object learning center is that of a "shell center." The questions which follow are the consequence of pupil contact with shells in a center designed to stimulate their curiosity about sea life. I heard a group of eight- and nine-year-old pupils in conversation at the center ask:

"How do they (the shellfish) eat?"

"How do they move?"

"What do they eat?"

"How are they made?"

"What kind of animals are they?"

"How big do they get?"

"How long do they live?"

"How do they get their food?"

"How do they reproduce?"

"What is their classification?"

"Who puts them in their classification?"

"What enemies do they have?"

"How do they protect themselves?"

"How do they digest food?"

"How are they related to us?"

"What makes the 'sound of the ocean'?"

It is important that pupil-formulated questions constitute the core of subsequent exploration since they reflect their interests. This exploration may take the form of questions posed by individual pupils, or it may assume the pattern of interest groups, each composed of pupils wishing to explore related questions. The appropriate course of action would depend on the particular changes in behavior that you and your pupils want, and on the amount and variety of source materials necessary to bring about the changes. The basic question is whether your pupils stand to gain most in their personal growth by working as members of a group, or through their own individual efforts.

To illustrate how the above-cited questions posed by the children lend themselves to natural clusters of interest, the following diagram (Figure 3-2) is presented for purposes of clarity. The assumption is that all the pupils in the classroom have first had the opportunity to express their interest in the study of sea life. It is understood, furthermore, that the number of questions and number of children per group would vary from classroom to classroom according to the unique interests of each pupil.

FIGURE 3-2   Formulation of Interest Groups

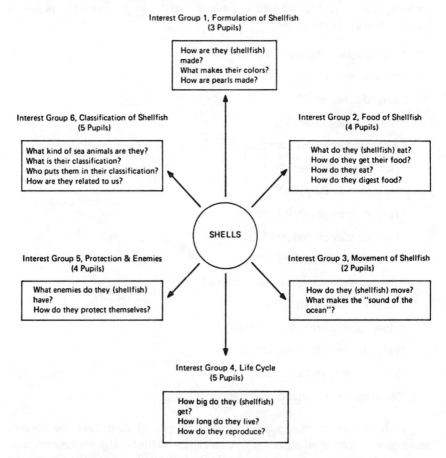

Interest Group 1, Formulation of Shellfish
(3 Pupils)

How are they (shellfish) made?
What makes their colors?
How are pearls made?

Interest Group 6, Classification of Shellfish
(5 Pupils)

What kind of sea animals are they?
What is their classification?
Who puts them in their classification?
How are they related to us?

Interest Group 2, Food of Shellfish
(4 Pupils)

What do they (shellfish) eat?
How do they get their food?
How do they eat?
How do they digest food?

SHELLS

Interest Group 5, Protection & Enemies
(4 Pupils)

What enemies do they (shellfish) have?
How do they protect themselves?

Interest Group 3, Movement of Shellfish
(2 Pupils)

How do they (shellfish) move?
What makes the "sound of the ocean"?

Interest Group 4, Life Cycle
(5 Pupils)

How big do they (shellfish) get?
How long do they live?
How do they reproduce?

USING ORIGINAL SOURCE MATERIALS IN CENTERS

Learning psychologists hold that the individual does not learn unless he can see the results of his input. Typically, the pupil will aspire to achieve in the "range of challenge," where success is possible but not certain.[3] The challenge to those of you who plan to institute learning centers, then, is to construct them so that this range is provided each of your pupils in one or more of your centers. A technique for accomplishing this is to employ a wide variety of sensory stimuli. The wider the variety, the more likely the individually different children in your classroom will function in the "range of challenge" and achieve some measure of success. However, what must be kept in mind is that not all pupils respond best to sensory stimuli. Different kids respond to different cues. Some respond best to situational cues, others to internal memories and associations, and still others to various combinations of the three learning cues. Therefore, it is important that you take into account the diverse learning styles of your pupils as you construct your learning centers.

For those children who respond best to situational cues, learning centers may be constructed to contain "situations" in which either single or multiple objects are used. Examples of the former may include a picture, a map, a historic document, an unsigned letter, a film loop, a case study, or a problem. The list of possibilities, as is true of sensory stimuli, is endless. Consider the unsigned letter[4] on the next page, for example. Who wrote it? The letter rarely escapes notice, and able readers in particular are interested by it. Who is Mr. Dummer? Dr. Spragen? Where was Beardstown? Does it still exist? Pupils note the writer's interest in politics, his need of money, and his "funny" writing style, such as "Henry E. Dummer, Esq.," "Yours as ever," the double hyphen, the unusual "A."

The first steps to learning, I feel, consist of asking questions. Stimulated by the challenge of finding out who wrote the letter, the pupils ask countless questions. Where is Beardstown? Pupils scan encyclopedias, pull down wall maps, and scour through atlases. Was the writer a politician who lived in the 1850s in need of money? Out come the history, geography, and social studies books. A state by state examination of the atlas reveals a Beardstown located in Illinois. A politician from Illinois in the 1850s brings to mind the name of Abraham Lincoln who is agreed upon as a possibility. A natural consequence of this is the investigation of documents written by Mr. Lincoln. A particularly observant youngster subsequently associates the "A" in the letter with that in President Lincoln's signature in the Emancipation Proclamation.

In this illustration of pupil response to situational cues, the important result is not that the pupils actually identify the writer, but rather that they seek out the clues essential to their finding out. That is, it is important that they experience the *process* of educating themselves. Additionally, the skills attendant to finding and using source materials, locating places on maps, interpreting linguistic and content clues, making inferences, and drawing conclusions come into play when they rise to the challenge of the situation.

You can obtain historical documents from a number of sources. Explore historical societies (local, state, and national), town and city museums, and state and national parks. Many of these provide, at a minimal cost, fascinating reprints of original source materials which include maps, posters, letters, diaries, paintings, telegrams, and cartoons. Newspapers such as the *New York Times* periodically issue reprints of newspapers of past eras. Sample copies of still other newspapers are sometimes available at no cost. Write Epitaph, Tombstone, Arizona, 85638 for a free copy of the *Tombstone Epitaph*, for example. Try the back page advertisements of magazines such as the *Saturday Review* and *Boys' Life* for addresses of commercial enterprises which specialize in the retail of historical documents and artifacts. You may wish to consider purchasing "Jackdaws,"[5] —packets of original materials consisting of a wide range of sources such as a letter written by Louis Pasteur to his first patient, a page from one of Shakespeare's school books, Russian Civil War posters, and various eyewitness accounts of historical events. Such packets are attractive, durable, and even washable. Social studies textbooks are also valuable sources. The newer editions include more primary source materials that you can easily duplicate.

July 20, 1858

Henry E. Dummer, Esq

My dear Sir:

When I was in Beards=town last Spring, Dr. Sprager said if I would leave a bill, he would pay it before long. I do not now remember that I spoke to you about it — I am now in need of money — Suppose we say the amount shall be $50.? If the Dr. is satisfied with that, please get the money and send it to me — And while you have pen in hand tell me what you may know about politics down your way —

Yours as ever

Not all children respond well to original documents and memorabilia, especially those which require meticulous and intensive reading. Thus, it is important to take into account the wide variances in the reading abilities of your pupils when constructing source material centers. Include easily readable posters, advertisements, maps, and pictures to attract and provide alternative routes for your less capable readers. Advertisements of the 1800s proclaiming land at three dollars an acre; recruiting posters of the American Revolution; early Sears, Roebuck and Company catalogues; posters of Civil War slaves for sale, etc., are often sufficiently realistic to stir, if not capture, the interest of the so-called non-readers. Who can forget, for example, the advertisements of slaves in bondage? Here, pupils begin to see that *people* were being sold. "Was that the world of the blacks?" they ask. This usually instigates a discussion of what life in America is like now for blacks.

Source materials, such as those mentioned, may lead to more direct studies of causes and effects of societal changes. The possibilities are many and varied. Your pupils may weigh causes and effects, examine personal prejudices, and explore likes and dislikes. They may reason, judge, and make conclusions. Face-to-face contact with historical and original source materials will likely compel them to evaluate evidence and determine the credibility of the sources, thus moving them out of the range of books to life itself. What people did, where they lived, what they thought become foci for further investigation by your pupils.

Learning centers, of course, vary in purpose. Some may require that your pupils complete their activities at particular stations; others invite the pupils to branch out from the centers. A learning center which is constructed of original source materials, for example, may invite the study of local history in the form of direct contact with the community. Your pupils might be interested in the house that once hid runaway slaves, the veteran who fought with General Eisenhower, the old man who knew Pancho Villa, the chest in the attic that sailed with John Paul Jones, or the metate once used by one of Geronimo's squaws.

When was the abandoned schoolhouse first built? Who sat at its desks? What was the composition of the neighborhood? What were the times like then? Your pupils can discover their own historical materials for further exploration in learning centers. They can dig into village, county, and church records. They can explore documents and memorabilia of ethnic clubs, fraternities, societies, businesses, libraries, museums, town and city offices, and chambers of commerce. Often, these reveal much about the social and economic life of communities and their changing patterns. Early replicas (1898, 1902, etc.) of Sears, Roebuck and Company catalogues can be obtained from that company's stores. These can be used very effectively to explore changing tastes, demands, and life styles. Here, your pupils may be called upon to study the clothing, home appliances, agricultural tools, sports equipment, automotive parts, fabrics, office supplies, musical instruments, toys, vehicles, construction materials, tools, and lighting fixtures of particular periods. They may note similarities and dissimilarities with items displayed in present-day catalogues.

Pupils of all levels are usually fascinated with the items presented in such a "catalogue center." Some of your pupils, interested by particular items, may independently study the historical period depicted. What does the clothing pictured in catalogues reveal about the people who wore it? What does the absence of television indicate? What did the people do for entertainment and recreation? Pupils see fit to study the development of tools and weapons and sporting goods from past to present. They express interest in noting the changes in style and composition of furniture—from wood to steel and aluminum, and the cost of home furnishings. They compare prices then with costs now. They explore the similarities and differences of supply and demand of various other items with those today. Process skills are developed as your pupils learn to use indices, compute costs of freight, compare values, fill out order forms, and write letters.

Children may continue to study and record history through still other approaches. What happened to the Wells Fargo Express or to the saloon frequented by Billy the Kid, the old railroad station, or to the broken-down cattle pens? What stories do buildings, monuments, roads, and canals tell? Why are Civil War monuments made of granite, World War I monuments of iron, and World War II monuments of wood? Such objects rarely fail to excite the imagination of youngsters, particularly when they can see and study them. If these objects are not readily available, you can encourage the interested children in your class to tape-record the personal recollections of old-timers or interview them directly. What happened to the harness shop that grandpa talked about? Where were the community's first roads and houses? Who once lived in the homes which once rested on the abandoned stone foundations? Where did they go?

Commercial recordings of historical events, such as those depicted in the "You Were There" series, and folk music can also be used to capture the spirit and times of both the past and present. When placed in a learning center for their use, children find folk music especially appealing. Note the feelings of restlessness, protest, and change conveyed in the music of Bob Dylan, the Beatles, and their contemporaries, for example. Does the music reflect the life of the era in which they sing? What will your pupils think of the sixties as they listen to the music of that period? Was there uneasiness, a movement of some kind, a revolution or perhaps a war? What of ballads of earlier years, when soldiers in battle expressed their loneliness and weariness? How did they feel as they marched off to war? Who did they leave behind? What had they seen in their travels? Whom did they meet? What had they experienced? And what of musical epics of still earlier times, when wandering minstrels sang of what they saw. What was life like then? A learning center in which musical recordings are placed is often attractive to pupils and, for some, stimulates a further interest in the study of a place and its history.

Questions may serve as springboards to still other activities. The following list enumerates some ideas for extending a learning center composed of original source materials. The ideas are simply suggestions. The appropriateness of the specific activities would, of course, vary from class to class to the extent that the questions posed by pupils vary. Two important attributes that should be provided by the extended learning center are: (1) opportunity for your pupils to advance their particular interests, and (2) opportunity for you to ascertain what your pupils have learned through their experiences in the center. The following activities may be included in such a center for pupil selection and action:

Describe a day in the life of a person living during the period you have studied. Choose any person you wish. "Talk" your description into our tape recorder. Perhaps others would enjoy your talk if you make the tape available at the listening center.

Write an "eyewitness account" of an important event that took place in the past as described to you by an old-timer. I'll be interested in seeing your account.

Design and illustrate an advertisement that might have been published in the *Tombstone Epitaph* or in any other newspaper of your choice during a historical period in which you are interested. Compare your advertisement with one of the period you select.

Design a set for a play which might have taken place during times in the past. Make certain that the stage properties are authentic for the historical period you have chosen.

Describe a character in a historical era of your choice. What did he or she wear, eat, and do?

Draw a sequence of pictures which illustrate changing fashions in clothing during the past fifty to one hundred years.

Tape-record selections from original source materials which you feel might have special appeal to members of the class. Place your recording in the listening center so that others may listen to it.

Illustrate a flintrock rifle. Have you researched it accurately? Write a description of your illustration.

Construct a model of any early method of transportation. Be prepared to talk about it in the "meet the expert" center.

Select one item that particularly interests you from one of our "old" Sears' catalogues. Compare it with the most recent edition. Has it changed?

Study the pictures we have of deteriorated adobe forts, abandoned stone chimneys and house foundations, broken-down corrals. Reconstruct a fort, house, or corral by drawing a picture of what any or all might have looked like during the times when they were in use.

Visit the cemetery. Look at a few old tombstones. Select a date and describe the setting in the period of the deceased person's life. What were the buildings, roads, and means of transportation like? Describe an event or custom of the period and record your description.

Choose a book which interests you about a historical period in which you would have liked to have lived. Describe a street scene in the book. What would you be doing on the street if you had lived in that period? Write a description of your activities.

What happened to the town baseball team? Why did it disappear? Any ideas? List a few?

The New Mexican adobe—the New England saltbox—the Navajo hogan. Why is the architecture of each different? Drop me a note about what you have found out.

Write a seven-day diary as it might have been written by a boy or girl of your age in a historical setting of your choice. What language will you use? What will your school day be like? In what kind of house will you live?

Dramatize an event that might have occurred in the past. Several of you may wish to present your dramatization. List the day and time of your presentation on the sign-up sheet at the drama center. Perhaps you can attract the entire class to your performance by posting an attractive cover which announces the event. Good luck! I'm looking forward to your production.

CREATING INTEREST THROUGH PICTURES, PAINTINGS AND CARTOONS

A picture, or a series of pictures as a center of learning opens up many useful learning experiences for children.

FIGURE 3-3   Construction of a Three-Station Learning Center with a Bi-Folded Flannel or Poster Board

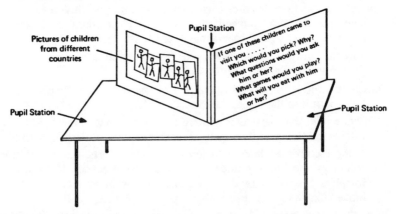

Pictures may be used to develop your pupils' observation, their analytical and interpretative skills, and their proficiency in language. They are also useful in extending the arithmetical experiences of your pupils, amplifying their art-associated skills, and fostering their attitudes of inquiry. The possibilities for using pictures in imaginative and creative fashion are almost limitless. A partial list of activities for your pupils might include:

1. Writing a title caption, or description of a picture
2. Placing pictures in story sequence
3. Discussing the action expressed in a picture
4. Categorizing similarities and dissimilarities in pictures
5. Cutting pictures to construct puzzles and imaginative mosaics
6. Noting visual cues and counting objects
7. Writing dialogue appropriate to a picture
8. Listing visible colors and shapes
9. Listing parts of speech implied in a picture
10. Recording a story based on a picture
11. Dramatizing an event in a picture
12. Discussing feelings evoked by a picture
13. Creating bulletin board and display centers
14. Matching descriptions to pictures
15. Testing recall

Open-ended questions directed toward pictures which invite your pupils to observe and speculate are especially useful in the development of their attitudes of inquiry. Depending on the particular picture, your pupils, through their observations, may hypothesize about the geographical location of the setting pictured, the season of the year, the general climate and specific weather condition, the time of day, the function of the buildings, the kind of population, the different uses of clothing (if people are shown), the life style and productivity of a region, and the extent of the setting's economic development.

FIGURE 3-4   Construction of an Eye-Catching Caption for Use in a Learning Center

Just as anthropologists examine ancient frescoes and historians examine old paintings to find out about people who lived long ago, your pupils can be encouraged to look at readily available reprints of paintings and pictures to find out about the culture of a people.

John White's composite painting of life in an Algonkian (Algonquin) Indian village, Secota (Secoton), in sixteenth-century Virginia, is representative of many that might be used. Set in a forest clearing, the painting's scene of wigwams shaped like Quonset huts, cornfields with plants in different stages of growth, a squatting Indian on a sheltered platform overlooking the fields, outdoor fireplaces, and scantily-dressed Algonkians dancing can be used as a single-object center to challenge the curiosity of your pupils.

"What is the Indian on the platform doing?"

"What does the corn (of sharply differentiated heights) tell us?"

"Why are the Algonquins dancing?"

"Can you guess the main diet of the Algonquins?"

"For what purposes were the fireplaces used?"

"Of what materials and how were the wigwams constructed?"

"Why did the Indians dress as they did?"

Children who surmise that the Indian was on the platform to act as a scarecrow to keep birds away from the ripened corn are delighted to hear that they are correct. Paintings, sketches, and pictures of other cultures in past and present times may be used similarly by your pupils to discover how people lived and live. Thus, it is never too early for student and beginning teachers to start accumulating pictures of all kinds for use in communicating with visually oriented pupils in the form of appropriate learning experiences.

Place various pictures in a learning center. Invite your pupils to look at a human hair magnified 1,800 times, the smallest plant of the food chain, a living diatom enlarged 1,540 times, a forty-million-year-old fossil pollen grain blown up to 4,000 times its size, the eye of a Drosophila fly increased 3,000 times. Magnified objects such as these often stimulate your pupils to further exploration. Place pictures of a boom town, a ghost town, a slum neighborhood, a residential area, a high-rise building, and a sprawling ranch home in a learning center. Invite your pupils to explore the reasons for their existence. Pictures of contrasting cultures may also be placed in a learning center to spur your pupils on to still further exploration. Place pictures of life in the Kalahari Desert of Africa; on the streets of Calcutta, India; in the barrios of San Antonio, Texas; in Appalachia; and in the migrant fields of California. Pictures have so much to tell!

Language development and arithmetic skills are prime targets of the classroom teacher. A "picture center" is invaluable in these respects. In the field of arithmetic, you can invite your pupils to identify and enumerate the number of people, buildings, animals, colors, and assorted items; to identify geometric shapes; and to compute mileage from city to city as indicated on road signs pictured. They can count the number of items beginning with a particular consonant, thereby developing sound association. Your pupils' vocabulary and language may be extended by having them respond to the number of different words (synonyms) associated with a particular object, color, or scene that is shown in a picture.

Picture a farmhouse and barn, a tree, a distant mountain, a hovering cloud formation, a body of water, and a small skiff tied to a post. Is the water a lake, a river, a pond, or part of an ocean? How is the boat propelled? Why is it tied up? How many words can you use to describe the farmhouse? What's the building behind the house? What is it used for? If *you* lived in the house pictured, what would *you* be doing? Building vocabulary and description as they respond, pupils can use this scene to gain in both oral and written language experience. Equally important, the approach utilized permits time for inquiry and reflective thinking by those pupils who may be attracted to such a learning center. Each pupil can proceed in his own time and at his own pace. Ranging from the simple to the complex, the uses of pictures are myriad. If a washing machine could talk, what would it say? (See Figure 3-5.) A dog chases a cat. Why? Did something take place before the pictured event? What do you think will happen? Display a picture of an elephant kneeling, an automobile moving, a child eating popcorn.

FIGURE 3-5   A Single-Desk, Single-Topic Center

What noises do you "hear"? Find two pictures of things that sound alike, for example, *boat* and *coat*. Use a picture to elicit descriptions of settings by pupils. Collect pictures of animals characterized by the unusual use of their tails and use them as stimuli for the discovery of new information and the development of attitudes of inquiry. One group of intermediate grade pupils, stimulated by such "tail pictures," learned the following:

1. Monkeys hang by their tails.
2. Porcupines slap their enemies with their tails.
3. Cows and horses use their tails to brush off insects.
4. Flying squirrels use their tails as rudders.
5. Opossum babies hang by their tails from their mothers' tails.

91732

6. Swimming beavers slap the water with their tails to warn of danger.
7. Anteaters cover their bodies with their tails when they sleep.
8. Sea horses anchor themselves to seaweed by their tails.
9. Woodpeckers prop themselves up with their tails.
10. Some lizards use their tails as weapons when fighting.
11. Alligators swim by moving their tails from side to side.

FIGURE 3-6   A Single-Topic, Multiple-Choice Center

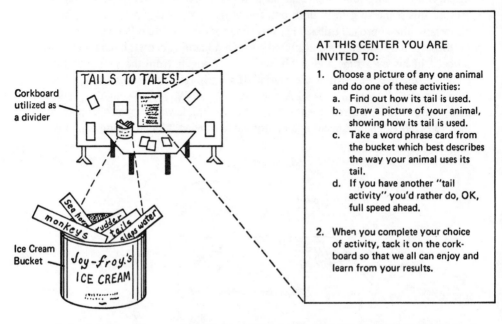

Animals with tails: are there more with tales to tell? Often, children go beyond the picture stimulus to find out more complete information and interesting facts about the habitats and behavior characteristics of the animals of particular interest to them. Others write "tail stories." Some prefer to draw pictures of both real and imaginary animals with unusual tails. Commensurate with their interests, needs, and skill, still other pupils are content to simply associate words with animal pictures.

Art-associated skills can also be developed in a center composed of a single picture. Has the picture been painted or photographed? If painted, what is the technique employed? Was it brushed? Was a palette knife used? What medium was used? Oil? Water color? Crayon? Is the painting's texture dry, coarse, or slippery? Why is the foreground of the picture clearly defined and its background fuzzy? From which direction is the sun shining? What thought(s) is the painter of the picture trying to express? Pictures may be used to extend your pupils' intuition about artistic expression, increase their sensibility, and develop their ability to express themselves visually and creatively.

FIGURE 3-7   Art Center for Clay, Paint and Construction Activities (Two Pupils)

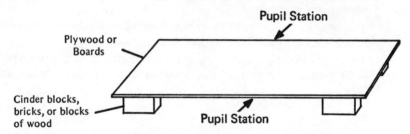

FIGURE 3-8   Extended Art Center Built on Risers (Four Pupils)

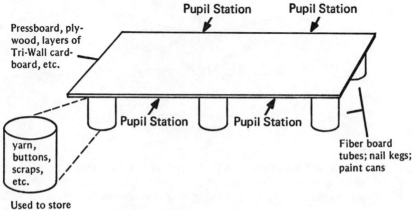

A natural outgrowth of a picture center is the development of an art center in which a variety of media is used to capture, promote, and sustain the pupils' interest in art. Activities that may be included in this extended center are, of course, known to experienced teachers. For those beginning teachers who are less familiar with the wide variety of artistic media and forms that may be utilized, the following materials, used singularly or in various combinations in an art center, may serve as a starting point.

String, sticks, tongue depressors, and cardboard for constructing heddles and looms to be used for weaving materials

Natural items, such as egg shells, orange peels, grass, weeds, and flowers to create picture compositions

Realia (real materials), such as adobe, plants, and branches of trees to construct dioramas

Salvage materials (yarn, buttons, cloth, feathers, seeds, bark, paper scraps, etc.) to create two- and three-dimensional imaginary animals, designs, pictures, mosaics, and mobiles

Chalk for pupils to rub, smudge, and mix with water to discover its different effects

Cardboard, paper plates, sticks, paper bags, and socks for the creation of puppets and marionettes

Sponges, brushes, cotton balls, squeeze bottles, sticks, cardboard, and cloth to provide pupil experience in manipulating paint

Clay for pupils to design, construct, and decorate coil bowls and pinch pots to develop an awareness of clay products such as pottery, bricks, and files

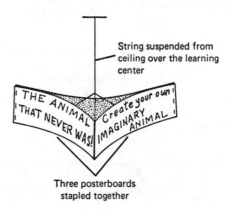

String suspended from ceiling over the learning center

THE ANIMAL THAT NEVER WAS! Create your own IMAGINARY ANIMAL

Three posterboards
stapled together

Recordings of noises that animals and people make for pupils to listen to in order to discover ways that animals and people express their feelings, as prerequisites to pupils expressing their emotions in art

Paper, papier-maché, soap, wax, and wood for expression of pupil ideas in three-dimensional sculpture forms

Yarn and paste to form designs and shapes

Yarn and needle to learn how to make running stitches

Natural and man-made objects to look at, identify, and label as different textures

Crayons and water colors for pupil experimentation with designs to see if oil and water mix

Vegetables, stencils, linoleum blocks, and printing clay to provide pupils with experiences of transferring designs

Finger paints, tempera/wheat paste, and spray enamel for experimentation with different textures of paint and with collage effects

In establishing the art center, it is wise to consider the following points:

1. Sufficient materials and activities to allow for free experimentation by interested pupils so that each finds an enjoyable media and activity

2. Inclusion of "environmental art materials," such as wood, rock, vegetables, fruits, gourds, leaves, and weeds, as well as the more traditional media of crayons, paints, and paper

3. Inclusion of opportunities for spatial, sculptural, and tactile exploration by pupils in the form of "manufactured leftovers," such as scrap lumber, wire, scrap metals, beads, buttons, plastics, tiles, and linoleum

4. Materials keyed to the maturational growth of the pupils, for example, crayons large enough for easy manipulation by children in primary grades and scissors with blunt ends

5. Adequate physical space and cleanup facilities

It is also wise to consider your pupils' various stages of development in art when constructing the art center. This is particularly important because much of the pupils' artistic exploration and expression may be done independently of you. The first stage, the so-called scribbling and manipulative stage, typically occurs between the ages of two and five and is pertinent to those of you who teach preschool children. The second, or symbolic stage, which usually occurs between the ages of five and eight, is noteworthy because it is during these years that children develop their unique abilities to express themselves symbolically. Because children at this stage draw in terms of what they feel rather than what they see, it is important that those of you who teach pupils in this age span understand that their visual representations are indications of their maturational and psychological growth. The media and activities of the art center, therefore, should provide for optimal conditions which encourage your pupils to express themselves in the uninhibited fashion and simple manner which characterizes this age group.

The third stage of the child's artistic growth, occurring between ages nine to twelve, is summarized as follows:

1. A greater awareness of pictorial reality is evidenced.

2. Newer and more relevant symbolic characterizations emerge.

3. Space, distance, and relative size is developed pictorially.

4. Experimentation with values, shades, tints, modeling, and texturing take place.

5. Emphasis on detail increases, at times disproportionately.

6. Subject matter preference is associated with the pupil's sex.[6]

It is helpful to those of you who teach in the upper grades to note these characteristics so that materials and projects appropriate to this age group are integrated into your art centers. You can do much to foster your pupils' creative potentials and personal identities through art centers which provide maximum opportunities for unsupervised activity in a conceptually balanced art program. Art activities, although unsupervised, should not be instituted without direction. For despite the amazing inventiveness of children in this age group, little is gained by inviting their globs, smudges, and hit-or-miss fanciful strokes of brush, pencil, and crayon as artistic expression.

"Kids never get to express the abundant language they have because they're confined to the book." So states Dr. Henry Ray whose work in Warminster,

Pennsylvania's Environmental Center makes great use of photographs and paintings in developing the social perceptions of youngsters who experience difficulty in school. Art, he finds, is one of the best mediums to build their self-images, a crucial prerequisite to learning to read. Teaching your kids to observe accurately and to perceive relationships—what it really means to see—as springboard experiences to reading, writing, and talking may be accomplished through instituting a learning center composed of assorted slides and a simple hand projector. As Dr. Ray advocates, capture the environment through pictures. A man holds balloons. Why? Shoes in a store window—which would fit the larger person? How many chimneys do you see in a downtown scene? Clothes hang from a clothesline. How big is the family? What season is indicated by the clothes? Show a toad in a bush, a squirrel scampering up a tree or city streets. Your pupils look for colors, for something soft or rough. They look *up* above the streets at signs, church steeples, and clouds. They look *down* on the street and see cracked pavement and fireplugs. What do you see when you look at fire plugs? Do you see spacemen or pregnant women? Slides and pictures depicting familiar and relevant scenes such as these will tend to invite your pupils to express themselves.

If a picture center composed of slides and projector poses a problem, try using picture postcards as a medium for developing the imagination of your pupils. Team Kappa of the Estabrook School in Lexington, Massachusetts utilized this approach in teaching children who found it difficult to express themselves in written form, many of whom could not write simple sentences. First, by dramatizing the actions reflected in the pictures and then by describing the pictures in modest phrases, ten- and eleven-year-old children, who heretofore were incapable of writing a complete thought, soon found themselves writing clearly stated, imaginative sentences. In just three weeks, the following unedited sentences were typical of the results.

"A man cocks his hat, steps and swings."   —G.S.

"She felt a ping of fear spring into her."   —S.B.

"The sun sends a farewell message of light as it dies."   —R.D.

"Wary of man, a nimble timber wolf stalks his prey in the darkness of winter."   —S.H.

"One-celled animals with bubbling holes slurp up their food."   —S.T.

"A small alley with rough-ridged walls is squeezing for more room." —M.N.

"It was a beautiful wordless view."   —A.P.

"The last red ribbon of the sunset disappeared."   —C.H.

"This building stands alone in an enormous green stretch of unbroken nature, its purpose forgotten."   —L.W.

"Poor little fish—it just wasn't his lucky day, all caught up in the hands of the lucky boy."   —J.P.

"A teenager squats doing the monkey."   —L.F.

"Fire drill! The buzzer chatters from the well-fed transformer."   —A.S.

"A man is digging by the sunset, digging for a fortune, digging for a future."   —B.B.

What do you think is happening here?
Who are these people?
Where do they live?
How do they live?

Institute a "cartoon center." Cartoons, serious or funny, may attract those pupils who aren't particularly turned on by photographs or paintings. At such a center, your pupils may gain experience in making inferences, interpreting, evaluating, and drawing conclusions about life through political and social cartoons. Through this process, they may develop their powers of investigation and knowledge of current events. Pupils who prefer more humorous cartoons may develop parallel skills through the observation and response to the expression of people's faces and actions depicted by the cartoonist. Other skills may be developed by inviting your pupils to cut and rearrange the characters of a cartoon, ascribing new roles to them, and changing the dialogue to fit the roles. Pupils who have difficulty in expressing themselves may coin simple captions for cartoons from which the original captions have been removed. Subject to your imagination and that of your pupils, the cartoon center, in almost any form, is a useful tool for providing valuable learning experiences because of its built-in appeal to children.

INVITING LEARNING THROUGH MAP CENTERS

It is no mystery! The study of maps appeals to a good many youngsters. This is particularly so when unique approaches are utilized in studying them. Academically able children are especially challenged through the exploration of strange and ancient maps. Start with a single map at a "map center," or include it as one optional activity in a more comprehensive social studies center. One such map that rarely fails to draw the attention of pupils is that drawn in 1459 by Frau Mauro, the Venetian cartographer, the highlights of which are shown here.[7]

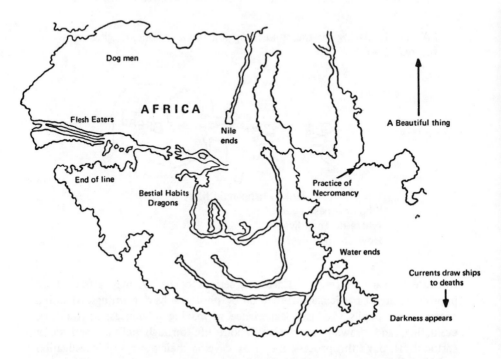

Myth or fact? Why was Africa 500 years ago pictured this way? Reflecting the world of Prince Henry the Navigator's time, Frau Mauro's map stirs the imagination, invites debate, and calls for investigation. As vehicles for developing the importance of distance, direction, and landmarks in charting lands and seas, as well as in examining the significance of knowledge, hearsay, and superstition, early maps such as this have considerable usefulness. Placed alongside a map of modern-day Africa, its shape and notations and their meanings will typically spark the more able children in your classroom to further exploration and study.

Why are the rivers drawn so large? Were they centers of flourishing settlements, used for trading purposes, means of penetrating into the interior, or merely landmarks? Why does darkness appear at the point shown? Was this notation based on superstition, or did the map-maker have knowledge of the relationship between the movements of the sun and earth? Does the shape of the continent show only that portion of Africa known to Frau Mauro or does it reflect inaccurate surveys? How much of the map-maker's work was based on actual exploration and how much on hearsay? Does the Nile River really "end" at the position indicated? What is the meaning of necromancy? Did dragons and

FIGURE 3-9   A Ready-Made Table That Can Be Sanded, Painted, and Decorated by Pupils for Use as a Learning Center

flesh-eaters exist in the Africa of 1459? Do they now? Boiling waters and currents that drew ships to their destruction: are they myth or fact?

Your pupils will search for the truth. They will learn the importance of navigation, the use of charts, compasses, astrolabes, and sextants, and, perhaps, how to read astronomical tables. They learn not about seas "boiling," but about seas racing over coastal shoals at ebb tides. They learn the consequences of sailing with the trade winds and tacking against wind and current as the Portuguese did in the 1400s, which proved essential to their subsequent exploration down and around the coast of Africa. In the process of their study, your pupils may learn to identify peninsulas, isthmuses, bays, gulfs, river sources and mouths, deltas, and other geographic features which add to their quest for knowledge. The children's curiosity is clearly evidenced in the following questions posed by Estabrook School (Lexington, Massachusetts) eight- and nine-year-old pupils, as a direct consequence of their contact with Frau Mauro's map of Africa.[8]

"Why didn't more people explore?"

"If people knew the general shape of Africa, why did the map-maker make up things like 'darkness appears'?"

"How did they know the Nile ended?"

"Why didn't the map-maker make the shape of Africa the right way?"

"Why did he put down a 'Beautiful Thing'?"

"Why were the people so superstitious?"

"Why were all crazy things put down, and not more sensible things?"

"Why did the people believe such silly things when there were wise men around?"

"Where did the superstitions come from?"

"Why didn't they go all the way up the Nile?"

"Did the people have much money?"

"Why did he make some places so big and others so small when they really weren't that size?"

"How did the map-maker make the map if he hadn't been to Africa?"

"Why did he draw Africa curved instead of pointed?"

"What was important to these people?"

Treasure Island! The student or beginning teacher may not be familiar with the usefulness of a "treasure map" to develop pupil skill in problem-solving. A hypothetical map of an unknown island or isolated land area in the midst of a hidden jungle may be created for this purpose and placed in a learning center. Given the "fact" that the treasure is located in the only settlement on the island, for example, the problem is to first locate the settlement. Geographic factors are considered. What are the topographical features of the island? What kind of vegetation does it have? What is the island's climate like? Where is its fresh water located? It is necessary, therefore, to construct the map showing its terrain, types of vegetation, location of water, and climatic conditions as clues for your pupils' intelligent hypothesizing about the settlement's location. Each of these clues may be presented singularly or simultaneously. Pupils accumulate geographic knowledge in the process of solving the problem; they review hypotheses as additional clues are taken into consideration, and they refine original projections. They may subsequently explore life on the island, its economic factors, and culture contact.

It is but a short step to pursue this initial impetus by including regions of the earth that presently exist in the map center, thereby giving your pupils the opportunity to solve problems actually faced by early settlers. Consider the topographical map of what subsequently became the town of Plymouth before its settlement took place, as depicted here. Encourage your pupils to plan its settlement, and then match their final product with that of its early settlers. Two approaches are possible here. Your pupils may simply plan without your direction on the basis of the terrain, vegetation, and bodies of water pictured, and then be encouraged to defend their rationale. Or you may wish to pose questions to serve as cues for planning the settlement. The following sequence of questions may prove helpful. Keep in mind, however, that they present but *one* way that the land might be used.[9] Potential responses are placed in parentheses.

1. In what direction does the river flow? (The pupils may note slope of land, tributaries, marshland.)
2. What kinds of jobs might people do with the available natural resources? (lumbering, trapping, hunting, fishing, tanning, farming, trading.)

3. How might the forest be used? (Cover for wildlife, firewood, lumbering, recreation.)
4. How would you provide for food other than through hunting and fishing? (Clear sections of forest for farming.)
5. Can the flood meadows be utilized? (For cattle grazing.)
6. How might you use the river? (drinking water, transportation, power, fire protection, fishing, ice, movement of lumber.)

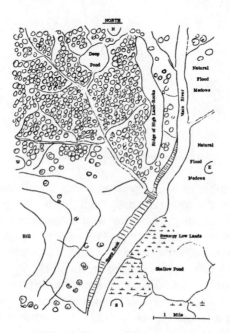

7. Where would you situate your mills, such as flour and saw mills? (Alongside narrow streams, near waterfall.)
8. Where would you build your homes, place of worship, crafts shops? (On the hill and its slopes for protection.)
9. If called for, where would you build a tannery? (By shallow pond to soak hides.)
10. Is there a use for the deep pond? (Fishing, ice in winter.)
11. Where would you construct the blacksmith shop? (Needs water, fairly central.)
12. Where should the trading post be situated? (At south end of settlement where bank is not steep, on the bay.)

Place a series of maps in a learning center, each map showing just one geographic feature of a state or a country. Introduce one map at a time. Note this map of Egypt composed of nothing more than its shape and the Nile River. Present some problems to the pupils using this center: for example, "What kinds of homes would you expect to find in Egypt? Would they be the same as, or different from, those found in our community? Where do you think most Egyptian homes are located? Locate these on the map."

Introduce another map of Egypt on which the amount of rainfall in the various portions of the country is designated. Invite your pupils to hypothesize further and compare their responses with those made on the basis of the information presented in the first map. Probe further. "*Now* what do you think Egyptian homes are like? Is the amount of rainfall a factor in the types of homes built? Would you locate them as you did previously?"

Introduce a third map. This time show the vegetation found in Egypt. Repeat the questioning to see if your pupils relocate the homes because of the added factor. Then, consecutively introduce still newer maps with a different component added each time, such as the minerals located in Egypt, food products, animals raised, types of agriculture, climate, water power, terrain, languages spoken, and religions practiced.

Each time a new component is introduced, continue to probe the previous responses to note whether your pupils modify and refine their thinking as more factors are taken into consideration. Once this process has been completed and final decisions have been made by the pupils as to where they would locate villages, towns, and cities, encourage them to examine maps of Egypt which show these population centers as they presently exist. Compare the differences. Don't be too surprised if certain pupils locate settlements in the middle of the Egyptian desert away from the coastline, the Nile River, the areas of vegetation, and natural resources. Invariably, some children come up with good reasons for doing so, such as the location of oases, too small to be pictured on the map.

Teams Omega and Kappa in Lexington schools found this center of activity, as well as those previously described, effective not only for purposes of problem-solving and as an introduction to the wide spectrum of maps, but also as a springboard from which to derive a multitude of concepts about the relationships between people and the geography of the land in which they lived. Questions which arose as a result of the map activities took the following pattern.

1. How does climate affect food consumption and production?
2. How does soil affect food production?
3. What are man's alternatives to food production based on climate and soil?
4. What is the effect of culture on food productivity?
5. What is the effect of technology on food productivity and consumption?
6. Can man affect climate and weather?

If you plan to institute a single-object center, such as that presented here, you need to recognize that its value as a learning experience goes far beyond the original stimulus. Figure 3-10 illustrates this point further. Note that the concepts to be explored by pupils, although intended to be representative, are in

FIGURE 3-10   Concept Development through a Map Center

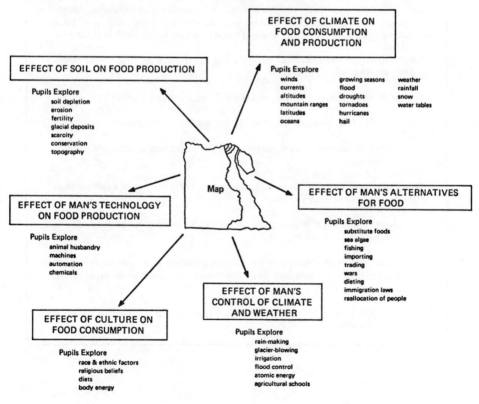

actuality the results of personal experience. Thus, you must not construe them as hypothetical or conclusive.

Moving from a single-object center to a multi-level, multi-experience learning center is a natural transition. The remaining pages of this chapter will acquaint you with a wealth of ideas for making this transition. Dare, design, and do but plan carefully for the construction of such centers. Figure 3-11 is shown here to help you with your planning.

FIGURE 3-11   Guidelines for Constructing Learning Centers

Use eye-catching captions, illustrations, brain-teasers, thought-provoking questions, objects, experiments, etc., which invite pupils to participate.

State objectives and working procedures for pupils clearly. (Note that non-directive instruction may invite more favorable response to certain activities.)

Provide activities which fall within the "range of challenge," inviting a growth experience for each pupil.

Include diverse multi-level materials (verbal, visual, auditory, manipulative, interactive, independent) which capitalize on variances in learning styles and progress of pupils, providing opportunity for each to select those materials which work best for him.

Insure immediate accessibility of materials and information essential to the pupils' growth experiences.

Provide choice opportunities for pupil selection of appropriate activities.

Plan for pupil differences in rate of work. (Flexible time allotment).

Utilize physical facilities (tables, shelves, desks, rugs, partitions, etc.) best suited to the activities.

Create space sufficient for fluidity of pupil movement within each activity area and from activity to activity center.

Post charts or checklists at each center of activity to account for participants and the work initiated and accomplished.

Provide self-correction materials in the form of answer keys, answer booklets, checklists, and verification devices such as electric boards, matching items, experiments, and manipulative objects.

Establish opportunities for pupils to modify, expand and create learning centers of their own choosing.

MULTI-LEVEL, MULTI-EXPERIENCE LEARNING CENTERS

In planning for the implementation of a multi-level, multi-experience learning center, you will need to keep a number of very pertinent factors in focus. First, you need to consider the number of activities to be included in the center you plan to institute. Too few activities may not offer the variety of choices necessary to attract pupils to it, or provide the multi-level experiences essential to meeting the disparities in their needs. Conversely, too many activities may lead them to shy away from the intended purpose(s) of the center, especially when the same activities are included in the learning center for an extended period of time. Rather than have a dozen or more experiments for children to select from at a science center, for example, a lesser number—five or six—from which to choose usually provides a more effective learning environment. Keeping the number of activities within more manageable proportions is less demanding and will enable you to provide a fresh stimulus by more frequently changing those activities which no longer appeal to your pupils. The same experiments in the same learning center, even though initially attractive to pupils, may become stale in your pupils' eyes and thereby lose their effectiveness. On the other hand, too many skills presented within a learning center may sometimes result in pupil disinterest.

As is the case with the learning center composed of a single object, the intended purpose of the multi-experience learning center should be understood and internalized by your pupils. Whatever its purpose, you should plan its construction so that it first wins, then holds, and ultimately assists the pupils who use it to develop and expand their ideas. Insofar as it is possible, it should encompass the personal plans of your pupils and sustain their interests beyond their initial attraction so that each may branch out to individual pursuits.

FIGURE 3-12   A Spill-Proof, Fire-Proof Science Center Constructed of Metal File Cabinets Placed Back-to-Back

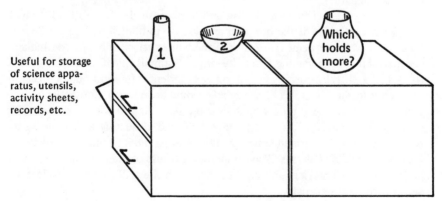

Useful for storage of science apparatus, utensils, activity sheets, records, etc.

Another important facet that must be considered in organizing your multi-experience center is the number and level of demands placed on those pupils who express an interest in the center's activities. Important also to the development of the center is the matter of your pupils' preferred choices of activities, as explained in the preceding chapter. Keeping these aspects in mind in planning for the construction of the center, you may find the guidelines suggested on page 112 of this chapter useful.

BOWS AND ARROWS, RIFLES, AND SOCIAL STUDIES

Because what is important to one pupil is not necessarily important to another, the multi-experience learning center has advantages for attracting and holding pupils' interests that are not always found in single-object centers. Consider, for example, the attraction of a center composed of a bow and arrows, a hunting knife, a powder horn, and, possibly, an old flintlock rifle. Pose the question of the purposes of these artifacts. Although any one of these might ostensibly appeal to individual pupils, it is more likely that, placed in conjunction with each other, the interest of the pupils will be sustained beyond their initial attraction to searching for authentic answers to questions generated by the artifacts. In the process, some of your relatively unsophisticated children who are subject to countless hours of exposure to Indian warfare on television, may well discover that the bow, arrows, and rifle were used primarily for obtaining food and secondarily for protection, rather than for purposes of war. This knowledge may then, conceivably, lead your pupils to a study of the various forms of hunting; the devices, weapons, and methods necessary; the preparation, care, and use of meat; the application of animal skins; the various modes of dress; the raising of domestic animals; the exploitation of wild animals; and the study of other foods essential to man. Learning is more likely to occur because of the number, variety, and level of experiences open to the pupils for their active participation.

How does it feel to be an Indian and to be pushed off one's land? Why, if the primary purpose of the bow and arrows was to hunt food, did the Indians attack the white settlements? Why did the whites attack those of the Indians? Related activities stemming from the original stimuli might take the form of role-playing, thereby opening up still other experiences for your pupils. Accurate research into the life styles of the people would be involved. Consequently, it is conceivable that the pupils would develop skills in gathering and organizing information, analyzing and interpreting data, and evaluating and applying the results. Equally important, through this process your pupils' sensitivity to Indians and white settlers is likely to increase because of their identification with both. Study, role-playing, and vivid contact with the artifacts in such a learning center invite this sensitivity.

The social studies, in almost any form, are rich with source materials for providing multi-level experiences in learning centers. In the area of anthropology, for example, case study readings, plaster casts, pictures, chart and map sites, fossils and documents may be used along with artifacts and resource books and journals. Through contacts with materials such as these, your pupils may be encouraged to trace the evolvement of tools, farming, writing, and architecture. They may explore man's ability to use his environment, the size and organization of populations, the ways groups are socially organized, and the ideas and symbols involved. It is likely that your pupils will develop a clinical attitude. The questions what? when? where? how? why? become guideposts for their exploration. Furthermore, their findings will likely become valuable because materials included in the center are not utilized in isolation, as in studying dates, but are used together. Given essential materials to work with at the center, pupils are invited to reconstruct patterns of settlement and explore the values of various cultures.

The Study of Early Man, adapted from the Anthropology Curriculum Study Project[10] is a case in point. Construct a learning center with the materials provided in this study. Included here, for example, are a map, a chart of an abandoned Kalahari Bushman campsite (Africa) with illustrations of the artifacts found there, a site report, and slides for use in conjunction with this reading. Symbols drawn to scale on the map chart include representations of post molds, hearths, ashes, nutshells, tree trunks, tramped areas, charred bones, and flat and round stones. With these materials as referral points, questions posed at the center may take the following form:

1. How big is the site?
2. What do the "post holds" represent?
3. How many "hearths" are there?
4. How many people lived there?

It is important that the questions be sufficiently clear and that the use of the essential materials be understood so that your pupils are able to function without relying heavily on you. This is not to say, of course, that they should not call on you for approval, encouragement, and direction when necessary.

To encourage your pupils to hypothesize further, questions concerning the climate, plants and animals, availability of water, and location and age of the campsite must be considered to gather the essential information. Thus, those who function in the center are invited to respond to the following questions.

1. How old is the site?
2. Is there anything on the map chart that would give us a clue?
   (Undecayed leather, wood, bones of various artifacts.)
3. Where are we likely to find undecayed artifacts?
   (Dry regions, such as deserts.)

Given the chart of the Kalahari Desert and other maps, your pupils may subsequently locate the site, note its rainfall, vegetation, and animal life. Turning to the site report and slides found at the center, after reading and studying the picture representations, they are then prepared to hypothesize about:

1. How many people lived there? Men? Women?
2. Why did they choose this site?
3. How did they live?
4. How long ago was the site occupied? Permanently?
5. What did they do with their leisure?
6. How did they raise their children?
7. What was their religion like?
8. How were they organized? Chief?

Consequently, pupils who are exposed to the materials of this center are apt to increase their abilities to know what questions to ask, when to ask them, and may go beyond acquiring information, albeit important, to deriving generalizations about archaeology as a technique used by anthropologists to learn about past cultures. Approached properly, like a good mystery which requires meticulous detective work, I think you will find that the experiences in archaeology you provide your pupils will often prove appealing to a good many of them. Indeed, the activities in this area typically generate enthusiasm rarely surpassed by activities in other learning centers. Machu Picchu, Rosetta Stone, Dead Sea Scrolls, Tutankhamon, Stonehenge, Dr. Leakey, Chichén Itzá! These names first draw the attention of, then intrigue the typical elementary school child!

Not all of you, of course, are in the position to have and make use of commercially prepared social studies kits. Home constructed, multimedia kits are good substitutes. In many instances, they are better suited for providing authentic multi-learning experiences for pupils. A social studies kit gathered by McKinley County, New Mexico teachers for use in their fourth grade classes, for example, is readily adaptable for inclusion in a learning center. Included in this kit are samples of copper and uranium ores, finished uranium, cotton, turquoise, wool, maps of the county and state, a historical atlas of New Mexico, an instructor's guide, a folder on indigenous architecture, pictures from the state museum, artifacts of the region, *National Geographic* articles dealing with the area, recordings of Zuni Indian, Spanish, and Anglo-American folklore, assorted readings, and project ideas. Similarly, those of you planning the implementation of learning centers in your classrooms may do well to gather and accumulate materials unique to your regions for inclusion in social studies centers.

Additionally, many social studies activities experienced in traditional classroom settings are appropriate and adaptable for inclusion in learning centers. Consider the following in the field of archaeology alone from which your pupils may select those that appeal to them. Directions for the activities[11] are written here as they might be found in an "archaeology center" at different periods. The center should be equipped with materials such as resource books, atlases, wall maps, journals, diaries and newspaper accounts of archaeological "digs," pictures, artifacts, charts, a tape recorder, filmstrips, and the record sheets essential to carrying out the activities.

Locate the Tigris and Euphrates Rivers in southwestern Asia. Note the land (Iraq) through which the rivers run. This is the area where archaeologists have discovered obsidian objects made by people who lived there a long time ago. Strange, obsidian, a mineral, doesn't even exist in this part of the world! What is the significance of this discovery? Drop your hypothesis in the "hypothesis box."

In 1926 spear points from 9,000 to 11,000 years old were found in Folsom, New Mexico. The site was a "kill site." Indians did not live there. Why, do you think, archaeologists make this claim? Discuss this with a friend. If you cannot agree on an answer, see what you can find in one of our books on archaeology that may help you decide. *Hint:* Look in the index of each book until you find a clue.

⊙represents "sun" or "day." ∿∿∿ represents "foreign countries."

Study the Egyptian picture signs in this center. Can you construct a sentence with these signs? Write your name? Do you prefer our writing system, or that of the earlier Egyptians? Record your ideas into the tape recorder. We'll discuss these later.

Picture restful gardens, imposing villas, bronze statues, wall paintings, and theatrical masks. What sort of town was Pompeii (Italy) before it was buried? Turn on the slide projector for a second look. List a few of your hypotheses. Dig into the readings to see how close your ideas match those you've read. Tell me the results.

Study one of the artifacts you find here. Handle it delicately, the way an archaeologist would. What is its origin? Is it a personal item? For what was it used? How was it made? Record your responses in the appropriate space on the chart.

Examine the animal bones before you. Do you think you can place them together so that the skeleton of the animal is reconstructed? If you wish, ask a friend to help you. Identify the animal if you can. Show me your proof.

Choose an archaeologist you'd like to know more about. Dig into the books we have. Find out all you can about him. Be prepared to give a brief report about him during our "explore and expound" class meeting time.

Ship ahoy! Remains of ships have been found in the Mediterranean Sea. Timbers, lead plates, heavy anchors of ships, and thousands of wine jars, some with the wax seal of the individual shippers, have been uncovered. You're an archaeologist! Where were the ships coming from? Where were they going? What happened to them? Build a "picture" of the events that took place. Compare your interpretation with that found in *Modern Discoveries in Archaeology* by Robert Suggs.

Look in the folder of newspaper accounts which describe archaeological discoveries. Note the one which tells about spear points being found in Clovis, New Mexico. The *same* kind of spear points have been found in Massachusetts, a long way from the sources of materials from which the spear points were made (flint, obsidian, slate). Explain this mystery. Does this tell us something about the life of the people who used these spear points? Talk your ideas about this into the tape recorder. Perhaps we can get a good argument going in the "conversation pit." Be prepared to substantiate your remarks.

Take your pick! Hypothesize about any of the following:
1. The excavation of former Indian settlements revealed hickory nut and butternut seeds larger than those found in their natural state today. What does this finding suggest?
2. In Wisconsin, Indian tools made of copper have been excavated by archaeologists. No copper ornaments have been found. What might this imply about the Indians who used these tools?
3. Archaeologists have considerable evidence that American Indians are related to the Mongols of Asia. They are certain that Mongols did not cross from Asia to Alaska by hopping from island to island. Why, do you suppose, they are certain that this is the case?

Put your hypothesis for either number one, two, or three in the hypothesis box. We'll explore your ideas later.

At the bottom of a deep pool in Chichen Itza, Yucatan lived the Mayan rain god, Yum-Chac. The Mayans kept him happy by throwing valuable gifts into the deep pool. Sometimes they'd fling the most beautiful girl in the land into the pool so that he would send rain to make the Mayans' corn grow. If no rain fell, they knew he was angry. Is this story true? As an archaeologist, how might you find out? Write a brief paragraph which explains your approach. Compare your approach with that of the archaeologists who investigated the story. (See Chapter 2, *Digging into Yesterday.*)

On a map of the world, try to locate the following archaeological discoveries:
1. Rosetta Stone
2. Russell Cave
3. King Rameses Tomb
4. Stonehenge
5. Dead Sea Scrolls
6. Machu Picchu
7. Herculaneum
8. Troy
9. Mesa Verde
10. Abu Simbel

You may need to refer to our resource books and materials for accuracy. When complete, place your map in your personal folder. I'll look at it as soon as I can. Good "digging"!

Look at this sketch of a sunken ship. Note the cargo it has picked up from various countries for delivery to its home port. Can you figure out its trade route system? Where did it pick up its first load of products? Trace its journey from country to country on a map. Where might the ship have been going? You may wish to draw a similar ship identifying some of the products it obtained from each country and stored for delivery.

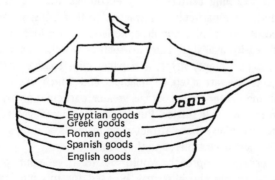

What is a day on an archaeological site like? How does an archaeologist know where to dig? What does he look for in digging? How does he trace the history of the things he excavates? Place your answers in the answer box. I'll arrange a conference with you to discuss your responses.

The aforementioned activities are just examples representative of many others that you may use in social studies learning centers, especially in the upper levels of elementary schooling. Whether the approach is discipline-centered, subject-centered, or concept-centered, it is important that the experiences in the centers focus on high-level thinking which invites extending your pupils' ideas *beyond* the items and exercises that compose the activities of the centers. Thus, it is essential that traditional-type activities be modified so that interpretative skills constitute a major focus, as this is more likely to result in meaningful learning by, and to the satisfaction of, your pupils. The multi-level, multi-experience learning center often provokes associated ideas and information, therefore, it is very valuable in developing your pupils' interpretative skills. Included are the skills of:

Selecting pertinent facts
Differentiating fact from fiction
Weighing facts, evidence, and events
Drawing conclusions from facts
Making inferences
Reasoning from cause to effect
Projecting personal illustrations
Making critical judgments
Applying facts to personal experiences

PRIMARY SCHOOL SCIENTISTS IN ACTION

Primary school children obviously enjoy experiences that invoke sensory impressions. Learning centers which encourage the use of manipulative and tactile materials are particularly attractive to them. Discovery-type activities are cases in point. Start with simple experiences. Consider establishing a science center with easily available materials such as wood, nails, rubber bands, bottle tops, keys, paper scraps, string, and paper clips so that children can discover which objects are attracted to magnets and which are not. Include several magnets at the center to encourage greater participation by your pupils. In a pinch, one magnet will suffice. Pupils may be encouraged to simply group the objects into two piles—those attracted by magnets, and those not attracted. The children discover successfully, and they feel good!

An alternative approach would be to have your pupils record their discoveries. A simple checklist may be used for this purpose, as illustrated in Figure 3-13. There are several important attributes to this approach. Clearly, it

FIGURE 3-13   Checklist Useful in Determining What Pupils Have Learned About Magnets

Name_____   Date_____

WHAT DOES THE MAGNET ATTRACT?

Place a check mark (✔) on the same line of the object that the magnet did or did not pick up. Be sure you check the right column.

OBJECT	YES	NO
Wood		
Bottle top		
Key		
Nail		
Paper clip		
Rubber band		
String		
Paper scrap		
Etc.		

reinforces your pupils' learning, sharpens their observations, and holds them responsible for accurately recording their findings, much as scientists do for verification, consistency, and referral points essential to subsequent investigations. Furthermore, through the process of associating words with the objects utilized, your pupils' vocabulary can be developed and extended. Use a compartmentalized tray in which to tag and place the various items. If commercial trays are not obtainable, a store cardboard carton will do. (See Figure 3-14.)

FIGURE 3-14   Cardboard Carton Easily Attainable and Useful for Storage

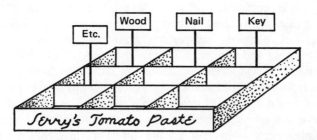

Still other simple activities may be used to construct a multi-object science center for use by primary school pupils. The traditional study of seasons is an example. One approach is to create a center composed of items associated with the seasons. The materials utilized may be pictures, toys, utensils, models and natural objects. Gather four containers such as shoe boxes or ice-cream buckets. Place materials representative of spring in one container, those relating to the summer season in another, etc. Do not label or identify the containers. Given the task of finding out which cluster of objects suggest which season, such multi-media materials frequently instigate further inquiry into the nature of each of the seasons and may extend your pupils' knowledge and vocabulary and integrate their thinking processes. Your pupils are likely to ask for substantiation, generalize, and note exceptions; for example, gloves are worn in seasons other than winter for washing dishes, working in the yard, digging ditches, riding horses; umbrellas and rain don't necessarily reflect spring, etc.

Traditional problem-oriented stories which utilize multiple objects are also adaptable for inclusion in learning centers at a primary level. Household articles are useful in this respect. Create a "lost kit" composed of articles such as a mirror, pencil, book, matches, beads, sugar, soap, safety pin, bottle, shoe strings, bandages, money, candles, nails, and other miscellaneous items. Formulate directions at the center so that your pupils are placed in a hypothetical situation which calls for decision-making on the use of these articles in a survival atmosphere; for instance, if they were given the articles and were lost in the wilderness, which would they keep for purposes of survival? One group of youngsters at such a learning center responded as follows:

Items We'd Keep	Why?
mirror	To signal
matches	To keep warm and cook
safety pin	To catch fish (make a hook)
sugar	For food and energy
bottle	To hold water
shoe strings	To trap animals and for fishing
candle	For light at night
candy	For food
bandages	To stop bleeding

Science experiments, without question, are invaluable in attracting pupils to a learning center, particularly when they lead to discovery by the pupils. Testing for acid or base classification of food constitutes a simple procedure that even the youngest of your pupils can perform. Place in a center items such as orange juice, baking soda and cornstarch (dissolved in water), cola drink, lemon and tomato juice, milk, and water in containers (such as baby food jars), along with red and blue litmus paper. Label the food substance dissolved in each container. Provide a simple check sheet for your pupils to record their findings. Other than for the reasons previously expressed, this is important in reducing the possibilities of aimless exploration "just for the fun of it" that does not extend the learning experience. Figure 3-15 is a representative laboratory record.

FIGURE 3-15   *Laboratory Record Applicable for Use in a Learning Center to Ascertain Pupil Progress*

Name_____   Date _____

Super-Scientist Lab Record

Scientists use interesting ways to find out things. The blue and red strips of paper at this center are tools they use to find out which foods are acid, base, or neutral in their qualities. Dip a red paper strip in each of the food containers. Do the same with the blue strip. What happened? Record what you saw with a check (✓) opposite the food you tested. If the blue paper turns red, the food is acid. If the red paper turns blue, it is a base. Sometimes the strips of paper do not change color. What do you suppose this tells us? Remember to check your results in the right column. When you see me free, tell me what you have discovered.

SOLUBLE FOOD	Blue turns red	Red turns blue	No change	Acid, base, or neutral?
Orange juice				
Baking soda				
Coke				
Water				
Tomato juice				
Cornstarch				
Milk				
Lemon juice				
Etc.				

As with experiences in other centers, it is essential to construe this experience as an ongoing activity. Why is it important that a scientist finds out which foods are acid, base, or neutral? Do the results affect the daily lives of people in any way? Do they affect the pupils? Thus, the learning center must be equipped with materials needed to expand your pupils' interest once it is aroused by the original stimulus. Opportunity for further experimentation and study should be provided and built into the center for those pupils who wish to do so.

A straw, a balloon, and assorted books! "How many books can the balloon lift?" Confronted with these materials and asked this question at a "balloon center," one six-year-old pupil recorded, "It can lift 31 books." An intriguing aspect of the learning center approach to teaching is the reading that takes place. Youngsters not turned on by conventional reading activities, like those taking place with basal readers, often read directions posted in explanation of materials and procedures to be utilized at a center to which they are attracted.

FIGURE 3-16   The Book Case as a Learning Center

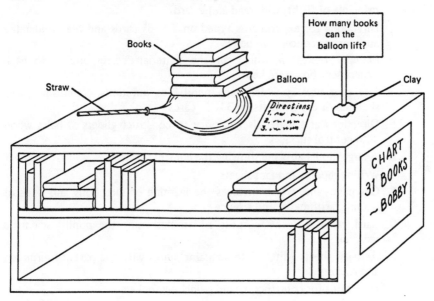

To carry out the balloon experiment, for example, interested pupils in a first-grade classroom I observed were called upon to read the following directions independently of the teacher.

1. Pick up a straw and stick one end of it into a balloon.
2. Rest the straw and balloon flat on the table.
3. Squat down so that your mouth is at the level of the straw and balloon.
4. Place a book on the balloon.

5. Use your fingers to hold the balloon to the straw.
6. Blow up the balloon.
7. Keep adding books.
8. If the balloon flattens out, blow more air into it.
9. Record the number of books the balloon can lift (before it bursts) on the chart.
10. Remember to sign your name by the number you record.

An increasing number of teachers are recognizing the advantages of including both formal and informal activities in multi-level, multiple-experience learning centers to get at the individual interests, needs, and learning rates of pupils in their classrooms. In exploration of the principles of flight, for example, Mrs. Sharon Meier and pupils in her open classroom at New Mexico State University created a science and space center, "Up, Up, and Away!" which included the following activities and materials:

1. A teacher-constructed tape (and recorder) which introduced each principle of flight, with read-along cards
2. Directions for experiments typed on 4 X 6" cards and filed under the appropriate concepts in boxes
3. Material boxes in which all the materials corresponding to each experiment box were kept
4. File card box in which each pupil filed questions, conclusions, and sketches of experiments on 3 X 5" cards
5. Directions and materials necessary to construct gliders of balsa wood with control surfaces
6. A large model airplane showing the control surfaces
7. Writing reports and fact sheets
8. Compass game which involves the learning of directions and skills of reading, arithmetic, and science
9. Card game, for the purpose of strengthening the pupils' scientific reasoning
10. Activity sheets (dittoes) to acquaint pupils with the parts of airplanes and rockets
11. Directions for constructing and launching rockets
12. Assorted books, pictures, diagrams, and magazines on the subject of flight
13. Topics for reports with provision for pupil suggestions of topics
14. Recordings of stories about early sky pioneers, famous pilots, and current astronauts
15. Electric board, used for learning and reinforcing brief facts about flight

It can be seen from this illustration that the activities vary in appeal and levels of difficulty. Inasmuch as there is a considerable range of optional activities from which the pupils may select, it is likely that they will select those activities of interest to them and to which they can respond, even though their success may not be guaranteed. That is, the pupils are given the opportunity to function within the range of challenge open to them.

REQUIRED OR OPTIONAL?
THE LANGUAGE ARTS CENTER ILLUSTRATED

"Bring-brought-do-does!" "What if skunks run loose?" Mrs. Betty Dirk, a teacher in the Las Cruces, New Mexico schools, implements multi-level, multi-experience learning centers on a long-range basis, changing the activities of which they are composed when each has fulfilled its purpose. Figure 3–17 illustrates and includes the materials needed to implement language arts activities for a span of one week at such a center. The physical arrangement, in this illustration, consists of one table and chairs and is not divided into sub-centers as previously described.

In the tradition of things that "must be done" by pupils, some teachers, although they encourage the pupils' free selection of learning centers, require

FIGURE 3–17   Directions for Pupil Activity in a Language Arts Center*

Come-came! Weird Shape! What if skunks run loose? Here are the seven activities we planned for this center, two of which we agreed we all had to do. Choose one assignment to do each day of the week.

1. Required.   Bring-brought-do-does! Follow the written instructions on the ditto sheet. (See Workbook Page number 17).

2. Required.   Come-came! Follow the written instructions on the ditto sheets. (See Workbook page number 23).

3. Optional.   What do they have in common? Be sure to write complete sentences with capital letters and punctuation. Think hard! (See Activity Sheet number 1).

4. Optional.   Weird Shape! Draw something out of this shape. Color it. Write at least eight sentences about it. Remember to use capitals and punctuation! (See Drawing Sheet number 1).

5. Optional.   Creative Writing. (See Activity Sheet number 2). Note the options.

6. Optional.   What If Skunks Run Loose? Color the picture. On the back write a story about it. Use capitals and correct punctuations. (See Drawing Sheet number 2).

7. Optional.   Tell A Story using the Charlie Brown cartoons and captions. Look in the folder for these.

*Adapted from the intermediate grades classroom of Betty Dirk, Central School, Las Cruces, New Mexico.

that they accomplish all of the activities in a center while others require that only certain activities in a center be done. Figure 3-17 illustrates this latter approach. This is a good beginning step in making the transition from a traditional environment to an open classroom. Note in Figure 3-17 that language arts options are provided for the pupils. First, they are not required to do all of the stipulated week's activities; second, they may complete activities in the order they wish as long as the two required activities are completed by the end of the week; and third, they are given the opportunity to select any three of the five options available to them.

A second important step in making the transition is to eliminate the terms, "required" and "optional" ascribed to each of the activities. Simply list the activities and let the kids make the decision on the basis of what they feel needs to be done. Given this option, children are as likely to select the formal, workbook-type activities as they are the more informal experiences. To eliminate the possibility that pupils will do none of the activities when the center is run completely on an optional basis, it may be desirable to state that a certain number of the activities, as shown in Figure 3-17, be done, for instance, any three to five of the seven listed. Should you prefer this approach, it may be of interest to you to note how many of your pupils under this condition complete three, four, or five, or even ask if all seven of the activities can be done. Your input and that of your pupils is essential here. Include the experiences you feel are needed and, at the same time, integrate those of interest to your pupils.

Another important step is to differentiate the activities included in the center so that the needs of the pupils are recognized. Teacher-pupil planning, diagnosis, and observation of your pupils in action are necessary ingredients of this step. Build into the center the experiences you feel are needed and, at the same time, integrate those of interest to and suggested by your pupils.

Those of you who are experienced teachers can, of course, call on literally hundreds of activities that are applicable for inclusion in a language arts center. The student or beginning teacher, however, may yet lack the experience necessary in creating activities which attract and sustain the interest of pupils. I list a few such activities to be adopted, modified, or discarded, as you see fit. The activities are intended to cut across grade lines; thus, they are general enough for implementation at almost any grade level in which children are able to read and follow directions.

> Imaginative thinking! How would you feel if you were a fire about to go out? A puddle of water slowly disappearing? A soap bubble about to pop? A piece of candy disappearing from a dish? Pick one of these to write about.
>
> Magic! If your ruler were a magic wand, what would you do with it? Write a few of your ideas. I'm interested in what you have to say. Show me your ideas.

Water is draining out of your bathtub. Where will it go? What will become of it? Tell me what you think.

If—you were a rainbow fading out of sight, a drip from a waterbucket, a balloon caught up by the wind, how would you feel? What story would you have to tell? Write about any one of these.

If—you were an eagle, or older than you are, or one inch tall, what would your life be like? Drop me a note.

How many of these sentence beginnings can you complete?
I wish I could . . .
I feel good when . . .
If only my . . .
My hair stood on end when . . .
I'll never forget . . .
Share your completed sentences with a friend. Ask him to show you his.

What makes you happy? sad? angry? afraid? Choose one of these to write about. If you wish, write about some other feeling you have instead. Show me what you have written.

Can you draw happiness? fun? a kumquat? Post your drawing on the bulletin board behind the language arts center.

Would you rather have a quirt or a sachet? Why? Be a spelunker or a philathelist? Why? Write a sentence explaining why. (*Hint:* try using the big dictionary.) Draw a picture of your choice.

"Don'ts and do's." If you could list the don'ts and do's of your life, what would they be? List some of those you feel strongly about. Show me your list.

What do you wonder about? Make a list of questions you want answered. Turn in your list to me so I might look at it.

If you could talk for one hour with anyone in the world, who would that be? What would you talk about? Tell me about your conversation.

How to get an idea for story writing! Your character knows something no one else does. Your character has no friends. Your character is always trying to be something he isn't. Your character has a severe handicap. Choose a character. Where does he live? What will he do? What will happen to him? How does he end up? What are your ideas? Can you put them into a plot? Talk your story to a friend. You may wish to write it instead. Show it to me when you are through.

You are a sports announcer broadcasting an exciting moment in a game. Select the sport. What will you say? Describe the moment into the tape recorder. Listen to what you have said. Do you like what you hear? Invite me to listen to it if you wish.

Ideas for implementing activities in your language arts center are myriad. There is no dearth of sources from which they may be obtained. Textbooks, curriculum guides, libraries, colleagues, and your own pupils can offer you all you need, and more. The few representative activities I list here are merely intended to make you aware that many of the activities you already utilize in your classrooms are appropriate for use in the center.

Learning is a personal matter for pupils. The decentralized classroom composed of learning centers is an invitation to a kind of learning admirably suited to the energy level of kids. Serving as referral points for pupils and as stimuli for developing their natural interests, the learning centers you establish more than likely will invite your children's involvement in the experiences of your classroom.

POINTS TO REMEMBER

- Well thought-out plans are essential to the construction of learning centers.
- Children are more responsive to new materials, unique approaches, and direct learning experiences.
- Pupils' questions tend to establish new learning centers.
- Different kids respond to different cues of learning.
- Pupils within a class vary widely in academic aspirations, potential, and achievement.
- Children are capable of directing their own learning experiences.
- Kids can teach kids.

NOTES

1. The Spanish dollar was a common coin of the early colonists. It was cut into pieces to make change.
2. Interested teachers will find *Collector's World* and *Bottles and Relics*, John H. Latham Publications, P.O. Box 654, Conroe, Texas 77301, invaluable for tracking down source materials such as those listed here.
3. Charles O. Neidt and Robert E. Stake, *Taxonomy of Psychological Concepts*, 1962 (condensed paper), p. 2.
4. See: Roy P. Basler, ed., *The Collected Works of Abraham Lincoln*, vol. 2 (New Brunswick, N.J.: Rutgers University Press, 1953), p. 521 for the complete text of this letter.
5. Obtainable from Grossman Publishers, 125A E. 19th Street, New York, N.Y. 10003.
6. Mark Luca and Robert Kent, *Art Education: Strategies of Teaching* (Englewood Cliffs, N.J.: Prentice-Hall, Inc., 1968), p. 22.
7. Adapted and modified from *National Geographic*, November 1960, pp. 620–621.

8. Adapted from the experiences of Honora Samway, Estabrook Elementary School, Lexington, Massachusetts.

9. Drawn from suggestions made by Joseph Grannis, Harvard University Graduate School of Education, Cambridge, Massachusetts.

10. *The Anthropology Curriculum Study Project,* 5632 Kimbark Avenue, Chicago, Illinois 60637.

11. Many of these activities, since modified, have been adopted from the author's experiences in the team-teaching schools of Lexington, Mass., 1957–1966.

bug

This lady bug
has laeg and
has nine dits
and can flie
and walk.

Maria
Age 8

four

*Using Textbooks and Literature
to Personalize Learning*

A natural beginning point in decentralizing your classroom to permit open learning by your pupils is to institute learning centers on the basis of the programs, books, and materials that you currently use in your classroom. Although you may now be in tune with some of the ideas I have presented for the implementation of learning centers, it is understandable that you may still feel more comfortable using textbooks and related materials as your primary medium of teaching. Is it possible, then, to implement centers with textbooks and still provide open learning experiences in the form of self-paced activities by your pupils, the exercising of personal options by them, and on the basis of the other ingredients I have discussed in the preceding chapters? Not only is this possible, but it is often necessary. The textbooks you use, judiciously selected, are important in opening up experiences to your pupils. Indeed, a good many texts, in almost all subjects, typically introduce skills to be developed, demonstrate the skills, provide exercises for your pupils to master them, and often include reviews or tests to measure the extent of pupil achievement.

Consider how you could teach mathematics, for example. One way to start is to place one or more copies of the textbook you use in a mathematics center. Plan the use of the textbooks so that your pupils feel free to function at their own pace, have the opportunity to choose examples, exercises, and activities, work together, and evaluate their own progress. To accomplish this, it is necessary to include in the mathematics center, as in other learning centers:

Clear, legible directions
Comfortable atmosphere and space to work
Readily available materials
Multilevel activities
Variety in choice of work
Self-correcting keys

In instituting a mathematics center, the important thing to remember is that once it has been established, it should function without heavy reliance on your support. That is, it must be self-operative in that the pupils who use it do much of the work traditionally delegated to you. It is through this process that you will then be able to work with those pupils who may be in need of more directed teaching. The way your pupils function in the mathematics center is, of course, important. Let me now turn to an approach which has a built-in appeal to youngsters and has resulted in their achieving significant progress.

TEAM LEARNING IN MATHEMATICS

Team learning—two or more pupils cooperatively learning together—is a process that lends itself to personalizing experiences of pupils in learning centers insofar as it is based on varying the content and pace of learning according to specific needs of pupils. Recognizing that not all pupils need the same skills and that no one textbook adequately serves all pupils in the same classroom, I present the following approaches, not as classic procedures for individualizing mathematics, but as transitional steps to a more open, flexible, and personalized method of teaching mathematics which you may find useful.

It is likely that you will subsequently implement a plan of teaching that suits your own situation and in which your pupils will be encouraged to select the subject areas of their particular interests in mathematics and, in this way, undertake the scope and sequence of learning preferred by each. For example, given a list of offerings at a mathematics center, for instance, the history of numbers, sets, and set theory; the addition, subtraction, division, or multiplication of whole numbers, fractions, or decimals; arithmetic puzzles; "fun with arithmetic"; etc., your pupils may be given the option of selecting any one of the offerings, or perhaps will substitute one of their own. In the interim, inasmuch as you may lack the supplies, books, and instructional materials necessary to carry out a better program, a significant step forward can be undertaken by capitalizing on the textbooks you now have available in your classroom. To individualize, or better to *personalize*[1] the experiences of your pupils through the use of textbooks in a mathematics center, it is important that you initiate the process of diagnostic teaching.

INDIVIDUALIZING MATHEMATICS
THROUGH DIAGNOSTIC TEACHING

It is feasible to pretest your pupils' understanding of mathematical concepts and development of skills as a prerequisite to instituting new concepts and skills in the learning center. What do your pupils already know? One technique I have practiced successfully in the upper grades is to make use of the existing checkpoints, reviews, and tests found in the mathematics texts as diagnostic tools. A beginning step is to find the mathematical location of the pupils in your class. Ask that each arbitrarily open his book to any end-of-the-chapter review or test he wishes and do the examples and problems. The successful accomplishment of those problems will entitle him to move on to a subsequent checkpoint. If not successful, then obviously this is a segment of the mathematics program he must learn before moving on. An alternative approach is for you to designate the book test to be taken by the pupils. Some of you may prefer to use the first check point presented in the book; others may prefer to randomly select checkpoints from any portion of the book. This process of diagnosis is not fundamentally different from that utilized in the IPI (Individually Prescribed Instruction) programs practiced in many schools today.[2]

Plan on several days of pretesting until the appropriate mathematical location of each pupil is found. In some instances you may expect to find that certain of your pupils pretest themselves completely out of the book originally intended for their use. Should this occur, it is clear that experiences and materials more appropriately geared to their levels of competency need to be instituted in the mathematics center. These may be in the form of enrichment materials and projects, or that of the book traditionally found in the next grade level(s). In the latter case, your diagnostic procedure should continue until the pupils are properly placed in the scope and sequence of the mathematics program. Figure 4-1 shows a consequence of the diagnostic procedure described. Space, of course, limits showing the number and distribution of all the pupils in the program, thus only one segment is illustrated.

Look at Figure 4-1. Note that as a consequence of not doing satisfactory work in the end-of-chapter test on computation, pages 97–99, Frank and Sandy are placed at the point where the meaning of addition and subtraction is introduced in the mathematics continuum. Mary, Freddy, and José, having passed this test but unable to complete the next test on numeration successfully, are placed at that point on the continuum where base-ten numeration is introduced. As revealed in the figure, Jim and Bob's diagnostic test results are such that they are placed in the portion of the mathematics program where geometry is to be studied and practiced.

Observe that even in this small segment of the total pupil population in the classroom there are wide differences in the work to be undertaken by the pupils. When extended through the entire mathematics program, this diagnostic approach to learning permits children to work at their own rates and provides a

FIGURE 4-1   Placement of Pupils on a Mathematics Continuum*

	COMPUTATION								NUMERATION										GEOM.	
	Meaning of addition & subtraction Pages 79-81	Addition and subtraction Pages 82-85	Properties of addition Pages 86-88	Meaning of mixed numbers Pages 89-90	Involving three fractions Page 91	Addition & Subtarction (mixed numerals) Pages 92-96	End-of-Chapter Test Pages 97-99	Enrichment: Pascal's triangle Page 100	Base-ten numeration Pages 101-103	Expanded notation Pages 104-105	Other numeration bases Pages 106-108	Meaning of decimals Pages 109-111	Expanded notation for decimals Page 112	Changing fraction numerals to decimals Pages 113-114	Changing decimals to fraction numerals Pages 115-116	Addition & subtraction (decimals) Pages 117-119	End-of-Chapter Tests Pages 120-122	Enrichment: Base-twelve numeration Pages 123-124	Classification of angles Pages 125-126	Classification of triangles by sides Page 127
Albi, Frank	X																			
Brown, Jim																			X	
Carry, Mary						X														
Dune, Sandy	X																			
Eddy, Freddy						X														
Foil, Tanya																				
Garcia, José						X														
Jonas, Bob																				X

*From *Seeing through Arithmetic 6* by Maurice L. Hartung, Henry Van Engen, E. Glenadine Gibb, James E. Stochl, Lois Knowles, and Ray Walch. Copyright © 1968 by Scott, Foresman and Company. Reprinted by permission of the publisher.

wide range of experiences over all levels of achievement. However, page-by-page learning can be deadly. To give vitality to the single textbook approach presented here and to provide pupils with the opportunities to climb uniquely different progress ladders, you should break the programmed effect of this approach. This can be accomplished by interspersing projects in the skills sequence at appropriate points which invite your pupils to go beyond the book exercises to problems of application. These projects may be created by you, or suggested by your pupils.

The next step is to invite your pupils to work together. Carefully match them in teams of two and three to a team. Look at Figure 4-1 once again. Notice the grouping of children that occurs. Frank and Sandy, Jim and Bob, and Mary, Freddy, and José may be formed into three distinctive teams on the basis of their placements on the mathematics continuum. This paired partnership or team learning approach has strong advantages in that the pupils of the teams can share their mathematics work and problems, and compare their solutions. Your pupils are likely to stimulate, urge, argue with, and confront each other in the process. If they do not agree on solutions, they search for and correct the points of conflict immediately. Kids teach kids under this arrangement. Considerably less directed teaching by you is called for simply because the appropriate level at which each of your pupils can perform has been discovered. Instead, you will be called upon to function as guide, counselor, and interrogator.

This diagnostic procedure can be carried further. For example, once it has been determined that your pupils' entry points fall within a particular segment of the mathematics sequence, each may then be pretested in terms of each of the skills comprising each segment. Thus, if you look at the computation segment of Figure 4-1, it is conceivable that Frank's proper placement on the continuum is at that point where the addition and subtraction of mixed numerals are introduced, whereas Sandy's work commences at the point of properties of addition. This is shown as Figure 4-2.

FIGURE 4-2   Refined Placement of Pupils on a Mathematics Continuum

	Meaning of addition & subtraction Pages 79-81	Addition and subtraction Pages 82-85	Properties of addition Pages 86-88	Meaning of mixed numbers Pages 89-90	Involving three fractions Page 91	Addition & Subtraction (mixed numerals) Pages 92-96	End-of-Chapter Test Pages 97-99	Enrichment: Pascal's triangle Page 100
Albi, Frank						X		
Brown, Jim								
Carry, Mary								
Dune, Sandy			X					
Etc.								

Because, under this procedure, these two pupils are at different points in the continuum, you must make a decision as to the proper course of action. Should each be encouraged to work individually from the point of entry on the mathematics continuum? Or are they close enough in ability and achievement so that they might both benefit by working as a team? This extended approach to diagnosis, (Figure 4-2), although more precise in the appropriate placement of pupils on a learning continuum, may be construed as somewhat more difficult to implement. You may prefer to initiate the first approach (Figure 4-1) as a transitional step, inasmuch as it calls for considerably less pretesting and

FIGURE 4-3   *Directions for Implementing Team Learning at a Mathematics Center*

CONGRATULATIONS! Because your test results show that each of you are at different levels in the kind of arithmetic work you can do, you are invited to work with a partner. You may work as slow or as fast as you like. Can you measure up to such a responsibility? I feel each of you can! To help you (and me, too) keep a record of your progress, I'm going to give each team a job sheet. It will tell you just where to begin. The rest is up to you!

Job Sheet Directions

1. Note the assignments listed on your job sheet and the pages in your arithmetic book where you can find them. You will see that some have the letters RDS and WA tagged on. A RDS (Read, discuss, solve) assignment is work you can discuss with your partner(s). WA (Work alone) assignments are to be done individually. Note also that you have opportunity to choose the number of, and the specific examples you wish to do.

2. Observe that there are blank spaces in between some of the assignments. This permits you to substitute an activity or project of your own. To do this, you must agree as a team that you wish to do so. The project must be related to the arithmetic you are doing. If you can't think of anything interesting, select an idea from the list of projects found in the arithmetic center.

3. When you finish a RDS assignment, you and your partner need to see how well you have done. Pull out the proper answer key from its slot in the arithmetic center, and correct your work. If you have completed the assignment successfully (at least 90% correct), you may move on to the next assignment listed on your job sheet. If you score less than 90%, I'd like to look at your work and discuss it with you. We may decide that you need more practice on the assignment. If this is the case, I will direct you to an activity sheet that should help you, or I may have to work more with you and others who may have a similar problem in arithmetic.

4. When you finish a WA assignment, turn it in to me. I need to know how well you can work by yourself. You may need to switch partners once in a while if you need to work slower, or can work faster than your present partner(s), or if you've been absent.

5. Here are some important points:
   a. Don't be timid about arguing with your partner over a problem on which you disagree!
   b. Call me when you and your partner are stuck or can't agree on a procedure or solution!
   c. Be neat!
   d. Be accurate!
   e. Put all your completed work in your personal folder!

provides for a more stable team learning arrangement. Whatever you decide, it is important that you establish the climate for working individually or in teams at the mathematics center, that you prepare job sheets or contracts for the work to be done, and that you make available all the materials necessary for the pupils to work *independently* of you at the center. Should you wish to institute the team approach I describe here, directions for pupils working together are shown in Figure 4–3.

To the extent that places are available at the mathematics center, your pupils may proceed to work on their mathematics in designated teams, or singly, as determined by your diagnostic survey. At the same time, the remaining pupils in your class may function at other learning centers in other subjects, or participate in directed teaching experiences as needed. It may be necessary that you limit the amount of time in which your pupils are operative at the center so that all find it open to them on a daily basis. Should your pupils wish to continue their mathematics work rather than proceed to another learning center open to them, you need to provide space for this probability. This may be constructed in the form of carrels placed along the walls of the classroom, as in Figure 4–4, or at clusters of desks not designated as specific learning centers.

FIGURE 4–4   Individual Learning Stations Constructed of Easily Accessible Dividers

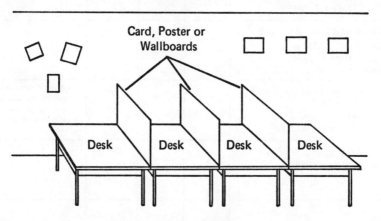

Since most team work at the mathematics center is self-directed, you must prepare job sheets as guidelines for your pupils. To a considerable extent the scope and sequence of the mathematics skills to be included in each job sheet can be excerpted directly from the textbooks in use. Figure 4–5, an extension of Figure 4–3, shows a representative job sheet. Note that it provides for pupil team work in the form of *read, discuss,* and *solve* (RDS) activities, individual pupil work in the form of work alone (WA) assignments, and supplementary activities such as projects and teacher-directed assignments, thus varying the stimuli and broadening the learning experiences of the pupils. Work alone assignments are designed to see how well pupils can perform without the assistance of their partners and to determine the compatibility of the team membership in terms of rate and level of work.

FIGURE 4–5   Record of a Pupil's Progress on a Selected Segment of a Mathematics
Program

Pupil's Name _____   Partner(s) _____

Job Sheet No. 5, Computation

SKILLS TO BE LEARNED	DATE STARTED	DATE COMPLETED	SUCCESS-FULLY DEMONSTRATED	ADDITIONAL PRACTICE NEEDED
Meaning of addition & subtraction, pp. 79-71 (RDS) Do any 4 to 6 of the 8 problems. Do any 2 of the 3 blocks.			No	You confuse adding rational numbers with adding natural numbers. Activity Sheet No. 4 will help you with this problem.
Addition & subtraction, pp. 82-85 (RDS) Do any 2 of the 4 problems. Do any 5 to 8 of the 10 "trys." Choose any 2 or 3 of the 4 blocks to do.			✓	
Properties of addition, pp. 86-88 (WA) Do any 2 of the 3 tables. Choose one of the blocks to do. Select from 8 to 12 of the 15 problems.			✓	
Select a project related to addition & subtraction from the list at the arithmetic center (RDS) Record its title in this space.			✓	
Meaning of mixed numbers, pp. 89-90 (RDS) Do any 10 to 15 of the 21 problems. Choose any 1 or 2 of the 3 blocks to do.			No	You have difficulty changing mixed numerals to fraction numerals. Practice interchanging fractional parts on the flannel board. If this does not help, see me.
Involving three fractions, p. 91 (WA) Select from 5 to 8 of the problems to do. Do from 6 to 9 of the 12 examples.				
Addition & subtraction (mixed numerals) pp. 92-96 (RDS) Do any page or pages of work you wish in this section.				
End-of-chapter test, pp. 97-99 (WA) Do all the exercises.				
Enrichment: Pascal's triangle, p. 100 (RDS) Do any amount of the problems you wish.				

Observe also that the pupils are not required to do all of the examples and problems in a designated assignment. This allowance for preferred choices of the pupils has the advantage of breaking the programmed effect of the textbook approach to learning, provides the pupils with decision-making opportunities, and enables them to choose those activities which they feel they can accomplish successfully. Blank spaces are interspersed throughout the sequence of the skills to be learned so that teacher- or pupil-initiated projects can be initiated to invigorate and enhance the development of mathematics skills that book assignments alone do not guarantee.

Although there are increasing numbers of textbooks that now provide inventory tests for the placement of pupils on a learning continuum, such as the text cited, they tend to confine the pupils to a strict usage of the one book. Consequently, teachers are apt to restrict children only to the scope, sequence, and treatment presented in the text, despite the fact that not all children learn mathematical skills in the same way. The job sheet, as shown in Figure 4-5, is designed to encourage both pupils and teacher to branch out from the programmed effect of the book through self-initiated and teacher-guided projects and related activity sheets. Should firm teacher control be indicated, it allows for the inclusion of periodic examinations and check tests without undue interruption to the skills sequence. Additionally, in a most important sense, the job sheet provides opportunities for interaction and self-pacing of pupils, peer tutoring, preferred choices of examples to do and problems to solve, and self-correction and evaluation of individual progress. It must be remembered that job sheets vary from child to child as a consequence of the diagnostic procedures advocated. This is to say that the placement of pupils on the mathematics continuum may involve textbooks of levels other than the one ascribed to a particular grade, thus more than simple rate (speed) progress is taken into account. Through this procedure, the mathematics program is gradeless in its scope and treatment.

Utilizing multilevel textbooks to completely individualize your pupils' mathematics experiences in this direction is both feasible and practical. Its justification is clear. For example, it has long been established that pupils within a single class vary widely in academic achievement and potential; that is, in a fourth grade class they are at least four grades apart in achievement; in a fifth grade class they are five grade levels apart, and so on. This knowledge of the disparities in pupil achievement can be put to use simply and effectively by you. Consider a fourth grade class where pupils range from third to sixth grade levels in their mathematics progression. A reasonable step would be to gather the texts ascribed to each of these grades, identify the skills components common to each, extract these clusters of skills from each book, and place them in sequence irrespective of grade levels. Clusters of skills that comprise the entire scope and sequence of an elementary school mathematics program (K–6) typically include such topics as set concepts, place value, operations, sequences, inequalities, notation, number facts, equations and solutions, number line, basic principles, processes (algorithms), rational numbers, and ratio and proportion as shown in Figure 4–6.

Note, in the figure, the sequencing of skills that are included in each of the set concept clusters extracted from textbooks used in Grades 3, 4, 5, and 6. Similarly, the other segments of skills which constitute the scope and sequence of the mathematics programs in grades three through six may be extracted from each of the respective grade level books and rearranged into clusters of related mathematical skills. Once this has been accomplished, pupils may then be pretested to determine which cluster of skills is essential to their immediate progress in mathematics. For example, those of your pupils who need work in addition and subtraction may function sequentially in a cluster which helps develop their computation skills; those who have difficulty with fractions may be assigned to a "fraction cluster"; others who need experiences with set theory may be placed in a cluster which provides opportunity for their skill development in this category; etc. Thus, your children are operative in various segments of the mathematics continuum and are not performing or demonstrating the same skills at the same time in the mathematics center. In addition to representative clusters of skills, Figure 4–6 shows the sequence of skills through which pupils progress in one of the clusters, the particular entry point of each pupil dependent on the results of pretesting.

FIGURE 4–6   Scope and Sequence of Skills Representative of Elementary School Mathematics Programs, Grades 3 to 6*

	Set Concepts	Place Value	Operations	Sequences	Inequalities	Notation	Equations and Solutions	Etc.
P U P I L	**GRADE 3** Sets, numbers & numerals Comparing sets Division and sets Intersection of sets Product sets Fractions and sets							
P R O G R E S S I O N	**GRADE 4** Sets, numbers & numerals Addition and sets Multiplication and sets Division and sets Product sets Sets of equivalent fractions							
	GRADE 5 Solution sets Union & intersection of sets Sets of equivalent fractions Sets of ordered pairs							
	GRADE 6 Sets of numbers Fractions and sets Sets of equivalent fractions Sets of ordered pairs							

*Excerpted from the Scope and Sequence Chart from *Elementary School Mathematics*, Teacher's Edition, Book 1 by Robert E. Eicholz, Charles F. Brumfiel, Merrill E. Shanks. Copyright © 1971, 1968 by Addison-Wesley Publishing Company, Inc.

To carry out this progression, the mathematics center you plan to establish must contain job sheets and materials essential to meeting the different entry points of your pupils in the sequence of skills comprising each of the clusters. As in the previous illustration for placing children appropriately on a mathematics continuum (Figures 4-1 and 4-2), this procedure also constitutes a natural step to completely eliminating grade level designations. Instead pupils progress from skill to skill within the appropriate cluster according to their individual competencies and rates of work, irrespective of their administratively assigned grade levels—in this illustration, that of the "fourth grade." In addition to multilevel, multiexperience job sheets and material, the center should include the necessary answer keys to encourage self-direction and self-evaluation by your pupils and a list of projects for their personal enrichment.

EXTENDING MATHEMATICS EXPERIENCES IN LEARNING CENTERS

It is important and necessary to extend the experiences of your pupils beyond those provided through textbook exercises, even though such experiences cut across grade lines. Another major step, therefore, is to equip the mathematics center with materials which capitalize on the learning styles of each pupil. A component of the center which focuses on fractions or a separate "fraction center," for example, might include:

Self-correcting, programmed texts
Cuisenaire-type rods
Teacher-constructed activity sheets
Fraction games (like Bingo and Lotto)
Electric board with corresponding fractions
Fraction wheels with appropriate cut-outs
Flannelgraph and manipulative fractional parts
Exercise pages torn from workbooks
Filmstrips and slides
Matching equivalent fraction lines
List of projects
Pupil-formulated examples, puzzles, and problems

Multiple materials such as these provide the teacher with access to pupils who are not turned on by books alone. For although some of your children may find more stability through work in books, others may prefer to work with games, manipulative materials, or other objects corresponding to their interests at various times.

It should be understood here that although I have stressed that children learn best when interested, this does not mean that they should not be required to work in areas that do not interest them. It is equally important that your pupils learn to cope with the frustrations and problems associated with tasks they dislike but which are essential to reaching their goals. In this sense, then, they *are* working toward their interests. It is pertinent to note, furthermore, that even though children are capable of making wise choices, as illustrated in an earlier chapter, this does not mean that all budget their time effectively. Should this occur, encouraging such pupils to log the time spent in the various activities of the learning center may assist them to determine and guide their own progress and to develop their responsibility for doing so. The log need not be complex. Note Figure 4-7, for example. Consisting of a form which lists the materials available at the fraction center, all it requires is checking the materials used under the dates each is used.

FIGURE 4-7   Checklist Useful in Identifying Pupil Selection of Materials and Their Frequency of Use on a Day-to-Day Basis

FRACTION CENTER

Pupil_____   Skill(s) to be practiced_____

Materials listed here are useful in helping you understand various ways to use fractions. To help you keep a record of your progress and keep me informed, please place a check (✓) to the right of the material you have used under the date you used it. Have fun!

ACTIVITY MATERIALS	Date	Date	Date	Date	Date
Programmed text					
Cuisenaire rods					
Filmstrip	✓	✓	✓	✓	
Bingo fraction games					
Electric board					
Fraction wheels					
Flannelgraph					
Workbook pages					
Activity Sheets					
Slides					
Fraction lines					
Project No. 1					
Project No. 2					
Etc.					

If a more precise recording of time spent by your pupils on activities is necessary, a form such as Figure 4-8 may prove useful to both the pupils and to you.

FIGURE 4-8   Checklist Useful in Identifying Pupil Selection of Materials and the Time Spent with Each During Periods of the Day

---

FRACTION CENTER

Pupil_____   Skill(s) to be practiced_____
                                      Date_____

Good use of your time is important! Checking the materials you use at this center will help to show you how much time you spend with each. Place a check (✓) opposite the material you use in the time slot you use it. Remember, some of your friends may wish to use the same material. Too many checks of the same material may prevent them from enjoying some of the same things you like. An elephant "never forgets." Do you?

ACTIVITY MATERIALS	8:45 to 9:00	9:00 to 9:15	9:15 to 9:30	9:30 to 9:45	9:45 to 10:00	10:00 to 10:15	10:15 to 10:30	10:30 to 10:45	Etc.
Programmed text									
Cuisenaire rods									
Filmstrip	✓	✓	✓	✓	✓	✓	✓	✓	
Etc.									

Record-keeping, as depicted in Figures 4-7 and 4-8, also has the advantage of keeping you informed as to what each pupil is doing when and provides information about your pupils' choices and pace of work. A look at the figures may suggest to you that the pupils involved are not selecting the most appropriate activities or making the best possible use of their time. Consequently, some redirection of a particular pupil's activities (Figures 4-7 and 4-8) may be in order so that a broadening of experiences beyond that of the filmstrip will take place. It is conceivable that you may decide in favor of the continuous use of the filmstrip if it turns the pupil on to developing the skill to be learned and practiced. Whatever the decision, the checklist serves two important purposes: (1) identification of materials which attract and sustain the attention of your pupils; and (2) direction for guiding you and your pupils to appropriate courses of learning.

Those of you who feel much can be gained by your pupils in the form of indirect exploration will find discovery-type activities particularly adaptable to use in learning centers. Consider using Cuisenaire rods, for example. Pupils who function in a center containing these invariably will take it upon themselves to construct castles, stairways, and arches, create designs such as rays and stars, and build trains and roads with little or no direction from you. In the process of this independent action, even the very youngest of your pupils is likely to learn number relationships. Should it be needed, more direct exploration may be invited through your questioning. For example, ask them to find as many different ways as they can to use the rods to make eight equal piles. Thus, even under directed exploration, your pupils are apt to discover relationships without your telling them.

Teachers who are not textbook-oriented may prefer to develop their own scope and sequence of skills to be practiced in a mathematics center. This approach may have important advantages for you in personalizing the mathematics experiences of your pupils, but it is difficult to implement successfully in learning centers. It is of worth in that it attempts to capitalize on the pupils' needs as they occur. Consequently, it requires a highly skilled and perceptive teacher who is completely flexible in approaches to teaching. The beginning teacher may find it more feasible to teach within a sequence with clearly defined objectives and directions and subsequently build into this sequence the flexibility essential to meeting the differentiated needs of pupils.

You can also develop, in similar fashion, team-learning procedures in the other subjects you teach. As described in this section on mathematics, plan on several days of pretesting your pupils in each of the subjects until you find their appropriate beginning points in the sequence of skills they are to learn. Once you establish the level of each pupil, it is a relatively simple procedure to match your pupils in teams so that they progress from skill to skill as a group.

PERSONALIZING INDIVIDUAL
READING EXPERIENCES

The teaching of reading is, of course, a primary concern of elementary school teachers. How applicable, then, is it to your plans for implementing learning centers in your classroom? I feel that informal reading experiences for your pupils in a reading center is particularly pertinent to those of you with classes of pupils ranging widely in their abilities to read and who feel that your basal reading programs are not meeting your pupils' developmental needs. I have previously illustrated one approach (Figure 1–8). Let me now turn to a more comprehensive procedure for personalizing the reading experiences of your pupils.

ESTABLISHING THE READING CENTER

To establish a reading center for the purpose of differentiated instruction and learning, gather roughly three times as many different books, magazines, and other reading materials as there are pupils in your classroom. The materials should vary as widely in reading difficulty and interests as do the reading abilities and interests of your pupils. They may be selected by you, solicited from your pupils, or gathered from outside sources. Place the reading materials in the center, preferably in a quiet corner or alcove of the classroom, along with pillows for your pupils to sit on or a rug to lie on, a table, bookshelves, card files of books, pupil records, and comprehension checks, and, if available, a tape recorder.

Your pupils' first exposure to the reading center should provide time for them to get used to freely selecting materials to read. You may wish to start with books alone and subsequently build into your reading center other important materials from which your pupils may select to read. Encourage them to browse freely among the books, knowing there are no questions to be answered, book reports to be written, etc. Allocate perhaps two to four weeks for this activity. The browsing period is particularly important for observing and noting the reading habits of your pupils under the pressure-free conditions of free reading. You may learn much about your pupils; for instance, the kinds of books they read, the extent of what they read, their degree of persistency in pursuing a topic of interest, and their capacity to share materials and ideas with each other. This period of time will also enable you to observe their reading habits in detail. You will note those pupils who are inclined to flit from book to book; those unable to use the card catalogue and survey topics of interest; those who select only one category of reading material, such as sports books; those who prefer to read by themselves; those who lip read, etc.

Finding your pupils' interests is, of course, the key to personalizing their reading program. You need to raise some important questions in this respect. Will the books selected by your pupils truly reflect their interests? Are your pupils in the best position to select readings that will fulfill their personal needs? Can your pupils direct their own learning and still have balanced reading diets? Obviously, some will be able to do so, and others will not. Your guidance may be in order; however, it should not be overdone. The opportunity you give your pupils to select their readings serves the immediate purpose of their discovering the relationship between their choices and the consequences of those choices. Consequently, the self-selection process is very important in developing your pupils' abilities to discriminate and judge intelligently.

READING INVENTORIES

You may find formalized reading inventories useful to you in assessing the reading interests of your pupils. Figure 4-9 illustrates one form which will help you determine the kinds of books you need to put in your reading center. As you can see in the figure, this particular inventory invites your pupils to respond in terms of their reading preferences.

Should you wish to add your own observations of your pupils' reading interests and behaviors, you may find the following form of record-keeping (Figure 4-10) useful to you.

Once you have established your reading center and have allocated reasonable time for free, no-strings-attached reading by your pupils for the purpose of capitalizing on their interests, you may implement procedures for continuous evaluation of your pupils' progress. To evaluate their progress, it is pertinent, although not absolutely essential, that you familiarize yourself with the books and materials placed in the reading center. Whereas this is feasible in the primary grades, it is difficult for those of you who teach in the upper grades because of the time and energy you must expend to read the literature utilized in your classes. Solution? Use pupils to take on much of the responsibility for evaluation generally delegated to you. The procedure I suggest here is an arrangement whereby you use your children as pupil teachers.

FIGURE 4-9   Reading Interest Inventory

Name of Student_____ Reading Level _____

Directions: Rank the following topics in terms of your reading preferences. Use a "1" to indicate your first choice, a "2" for your next choice, etc.

FICTION

Sports _____
Adventure _____
Fairy tales _____
Legends & folklore _____
Animals_____
Poetry_____
Other _____

NON-FICTION

Biographies _____
History_____
Sciences (Nature) _____
Sciences (Physical) _____
Adventure _____
Newspaper & Magazines _____
Foreign Lands _____
Sports _____
Space _____
Sea _____
Other _____

IMPLEMENTING THE PROGRAM

To explain, clarify, and put your reading program into action on the basis of pupil interests discovered and the utilization of pupil teachers, you need to take some preliminary steps. These include the preparation of book-title cards, pupil progress reports, and diagnostic profile charts. Begin by preparing book-title cards, preferably on 5 by 8" note cards. As shown in Figure 4-11, include the title and author of each book. Allocate space on the cards for recording the names of the pupils you will designate as pupil teachers. One card for each book

FIGURE 4-10   *Teacher Observations of an Individual Pupil's Reading Interests and Behaviors*

Student's Name _Tony Champion_   Reading Level _____

During a period of the month, beginning _____ and ending_____, _Tony_ expressed interest in the following topics when given opportunity to freely select his own reading materials.

Subject Topics	Books read	Teacher Observations
Adventure	1. 2. 3.	
Sports	1. 2. 3.	Enjoys football stories especially. I need to find more books on this subject. A word-by-word reader. (Note finger-ptg.) Can easy-to-read football stories be found? Have got to reduce his vocabulary burden. Vocabulary drill?
Science	1. 2. 3.	
Legends & Folklore	1. 2. 3.	
History & Biographies	1. 2. 3.	
Foreign Lands	1. 2. 3.	

Summary: Tony is a persistent, but struggling, reader. Tends to tackle books that are difficult for him. Something to "prove"? Interest focuses strictly on sports. At this stage, do I encourage this? Try to broaden his interests? How? I'll have to think more about Tony and his reading habits.

placed in the reading center should be prepared and placed in a file box accessible to your pupils.

FIGURE 4–11   Book Title and Pupil-Teacher Card

```
┌─────────────────────────────────────────────────────────────┐
│                                                               │
│   CALL IT COURAGE                         Armstrong Sperry     │
│                      Pupil Teachers                           │
│                                                               │
│   1. Tommy L.                                                 │
│   2. Susan                                                    │
│   3. ─────                                                    │
│   4. ─────                                                    │
│                                                               │
│                                                               │
│                                                               │
│                                                               │
└─────────────────────────────────────────────────────────────┘
```

The purpose of this card is to guide pupils who read books to the pupil-teacher responsible for evaluating their reading progress. The procedure is for the pupil to select from the book-title file box the title card of the particular book he has read to note the designated pupil-teacher of that book. If a pupil's name has not yet been recorded on the card, the reader of the book will know that he is the first pupil to have read it and should therefore confer with you. During the conference you evaluate the pupil's understanding of the material read, his mastery of its vocabulary and the fluency of his reading, while making notations on his strengths and weaknesses. Should remediation or redirection be indicated, you may suggest the appropriate reading experiences. If you feel his performance is satisfactory, enter his name on the title card as the designated pupil-teacher of the book.

Note in Figure 4–11 that Tommy L.'s name is the first name recorded. This indicates that he was the first pupil to read *Call It Courage* and is thus responsible for evaluating the progress of the next reader of this book, in this instance, Susan. As shown in the figure, Susan is the current pupil-teacher, having been evaluated by Tommy L. as a satisfactory reader of the book. This is to say that when a pupil goes to the title card file after reading a book and finds a pupil's name recorded, he goes to that pupil rather than to you for an evaluation of his reading. Under this arrangement, all *first* readers of a book in the reading center are evaluated by you and all subsequent readers of the same book by the pupil designated as the pupil-teacher. All performances felt to be unsatisfactory by the pupil-teacher are referred to you for action.

For purposes of record-keeping and your evaluation, it is advisable to have your pupils keep an account of the books they have read. Figure 4–12 illustrates a procedure you may wish to consider for this purpose.

FIGURE 4-12   Pupil Progress Report in Reading

Pupil's name _____*Peter*_____

Title and Author of Book Read	Conference Date	Teacher Comments
1. The Marble Fountain Valenti Angelo	9/4/73	Peter, you have a fine flair for reading. You quickly get to the nitty-gritty of a question. I like the way you get at the main points in your responses. I imagine you found this book a bit easy, too easy, for you as I did not pick up any words that you did not completely understand.
2. Rabbit Hill	9/19/73	Congratulations, Pete. You took on a tough book this time. Fun, though, wasn't it? You continue to read well orally and answer questions right to the point. Your vocabulary check suggests you need to spend some time on a few words. I have listed these on the back of this card. Look them up and show me how well you can use them.

You may well question the conference approach I describe here as one which negates the many mechanics of reading. On the contrary! Although I feel that too many teachers place too much emphasis on exercises calling for word attack, syllabication, word analysis, pronunciation, etc., at the expense of the time spent in which the pupils actually read, the approach illustrated does not necessarily discount these components of the reading process. Instead, it gives reason to teaching these skills *as the need for each arises.* Furthermore, I am convinced that a few well-spent minutes with each pupil in your classroom is immeasurably more valuable and results in greater reading progress than the more conventional approaches have presently proved. Note, for example, the countless numbers of remedial reading classes that currently exist in the schools.

You may also question the expenditure of time necessary to write comments on the pupils' reading progress. Is it worth your effort? Indeed, more than evaluating your pupils' reading is involved here. The approach I suggest builds confidence in pupils by communicating their strengths to them, allowing for personal decision-making, providing self-pacing opportunities, and encouraging your pupils' assumption of responsibility for subsequent learning experiences. Written comments, furthermore, help to personalize your contact with your pupils. True, the interaction that takes place in the conferences is verbal, however, writing salient points as a matter of record reinforces the teacher-pupil interaction and will help guide your pupils toward the realization of their reading goals.

Should you wish to emphasize the skills components of your reading program more extensively than thus far indicated, you may find the following procedure (Figure 4–13) helpful.

FIGURE 4–13   Oral Reading Diagnostic Profile Chart

Student's Name _____		Reading Level _____		
Skills needing improvement	Books Read			
	Johnny Tremain	Recommended Treatment	Winnie the Pooh	Recommended Treatment
Word-by-word reading			Does this frequently	Utilize tachistoscope with phrases and short sentences.
Finger pointing			Frequent use of index finger	Provide easy reading materials
Limited sight vocabulary	Does not use context clues	Provide reading passages in which context clues are readily noted		
Substitutions				
Reversals	saw for was	Possible semantic problem. Reduce detailed study of words. Get child to question the sense of what he's reading.		
Omissions				
Insertions				
Poor expression and enunciation				
Hesitation				
Volume too loud or soft				
Repetitions				
Comprehension			Responds correctly to less than 75% of questions	Encourage use of reading materials of less complexity.
Etc.				

As suggested earlier, you may not find it feasible to familiarize yourself with the books placed in the reading center. Consequently, it is necessary to prepare a series of questions pertaining to the books that may be used by your pupil-teachers to check the reading comprehension of their classmates. The questions may be prepared by you or by your pupil-teachers when advisable. Can your pupils prepare appropriate questions pertaining to books they have read? I think you will find some of your pupils are very capable of doing so. Others will need guidance and practice. It is well worth your time to explore with your pupils the art of asking open-ended, thought-provoking *questions*, as well as in finding the *answers*.

Those of you who are experienced teachers are, of course, familiar with questions concerning a book's main idea, its plot, setting, and sequence of events. Many teachers give equal attention to questions about leading book characters, their descriptions, those "liked" and "not liked," and the parts of books "enjoyed most" by pupils. However, considerably more attention needs to be focused on inferential thinking and its applicability to your pupils and on appraisal of their personal values. For instance, "What would happen if . . .? Why . . .? What do you think, feel, believe, etc., about the book you have just read?" It is likely that increasing your skills of questioning will lead your pupils to increase their own.

In formulating prepared questions to test your pupils' reading comprehension, it is reasonable to construct six or eight questions to assess their ability to identify and get at the meaning of words, recall events, and infer from the events that take place in the books selected by them. Perhaps two of these questions might consist of simple vocabulary checks, two or three may require recall, and the remaining may call for inferred knowledge. Utilization of this relatively unsophisticated, but very pertinent, procedure will enable you to identify key components of your pupils' reading skills. A card catalogue of prepared questions may subsequently constitute the nucleus of questions posed by both

FIGURE 4–14   *Representative Comprehensive Check Utilized by Pupil-Teachers to Check Understanding of Book Read by Classmates*

JOURNEY TO THE CENTER OF THE EARTH   Jules Verne

1. What was the purpose of the journey?

2. What did Arne Saknussen have to do with the journey?

3. What might happened if . . . . ?

4. Why did Arne try to .. . . . ?

5. What do you think about . . . . ?

6. Is there a particular reason why you chose this book?

you and your pupil-teachers in checking reading comprehension. Figure 4–14 shows a representative series of questions that may be utilized for this purpose in the reading center you establish.

Written directions at the reading center may serve to restate the guidelines you expressed orally in establishing the procedures of the center. Should you wish to utilize this procedure as well, Figure 4–15 is presented as an illustration.

FIGURE 4–15   *Directions Given Pupils in the Use of the Reading Center*

What Do I Do Next?

Dear Kids,

Welcome to the Reading Center! To make our Reading Center work, I need your help. We need to help check each other's progress. Once you have read the book of your choice, the following steps need to be taken. Can you take on this responsibility? Follow directions? I think you can!

Sincerely,
Mr. Thomas

1. When you have finished reading, or have gotten what you wished from the book you selected, select the title card of your book from the <u>Book Titles Box.</u>

2. To check your reading, we need to meet and construct a record of your progress. Bring your book and book title card with you. I'll ask you questions about what you've read, have you define and use some of the words in the book, and listen to you read.

3. If we are satisfied with your progress, I'll write a comment or two on your <u>Personal Record Card</u> expressing this. Should we pick up something in our conference that suggests you need further work in reading, I'll indicate this on your card also.

4. If I feel you're an "expert" on the book you have read, I will ask you to be the pupil teacher of this book, and record your name as such on the title card of the book. This means you will ask the next reader of the book questions about what he has read, check his vocabulary, and listen to him read much as I did with you. Questions to be asked and vocabulary to be checked are found in the <u>Comprehension Check File Box</u>. Remember, you are the teacher now.

5. If the pupil you are checking out does well, record his name under yours on the title card of the book. He will then become the pupil teacher of the book and will check out the next reader of the book as you did him. He now becomes the teacher.

6. If the pupil you are checking out does not respond well to your questions and does not seem to understand the vocabulary used in the book, ask him to see me. Your responsibility for his progress ends at this point.

7. When not busy checking out classmates on books you have read satisfactorily, you are free, of course, to continue your own individual reading and the same procedure with me. If a classmate has read the book you select before you have, he takes on the responsibility of checking <u>your</u> progress. OK?

Where do you go from here? Consider the following benefits to both pupils and teacher of this learning center approach to reading.

To the pupil . . .

Social stigma is virtually eliminated. There is no reward or embarrassment for pupils who read faster or slower. The pupil is not associated with a reading group. Instead, he reads at his own rate, in his own time.

The importance of. each pupil's background, tastes, and interests is emphasized.

Pupils progress at their own rates.

a. Less able readers gain more positive attitudes because they personally select books. Consequently, as their reading experiences are broadened, so are their interests, vocabulary, and knowledge.

b. More able readers move beyond graded materials. Consequently, as their reading experiences are broadened and uplifted, so are their interests, vocabulary, and knowledge.

A closer teacher-pupil relationship develops because of the frequent conferences necessitated.

Pupils are prepared to cope with things to be learned outside the classroom: i.e., independent search.

Pupils are provided opportunities to communicate new vocabulary, new understandings, and new materials read on the basis of their freely selected experiences.

Pupils identify places for themselves in the general scheme of classroom life.

Pupils gain in poise, self-reliancy, and ability to make wise choices. Consequently, they increase their desire to read.

More reading takes place.

To the teacher . . .

The teacher's interests in reading increases because of the wide varieties and levels of offerings.

A closer teacher-pupil relationship develops because of the frequent conferences necessitated.

The teacher spends more time helping pupils in the area of reading.

Essential skills, vocabulary, and generalizations are taught as needed—at that point when the pupils themselves seek the skill, word, and understanding essential to communicating.

The teacher is encouraged to use diverse approaches to teaching pupils of different abilities.

The teacher is provided a more intimate and exact picture of the pupils. Consequently, they are given better guidance.

Doubtless there are other advantages for teacher and pupils. But what about the disadvantages of such an approach? Among those pronounced by critics of individualized reading programs are the following:

1. Not all pupils assume the responsibility for wise selection of materials.
2. Pupils frequently pursue only one or two types of reading materials.

3. Teachers must acquaint themselves with a great variety of reading materials.
4. Sequential teaching of skills is neglected.
5. Vocabulary is not controlled.
6. Scheduling of essential individual conferences is difficult.
7. A large amount of record-keeping is required.

These are serious charges. However, in my opinion, they are debatable generalizations. In fact, according to research findings on child development accumulated by the University of Michigan, pupils choose materials to fit their needs as well—or *better*—than do a good many teachers.[3] Furthermore, the matter of pupils choosing only one or two kinds of reading—certainly not true of all children—is not necessarily negative, particularly if these are pupils who normally resist reading. Isn't it better to give them this opportunity than to force them to function in a reading program where they have *no* choice? Should you feel this does constitute a problem, appropriate guidance to judicious selection of books may be in order. Indeed, this is a primary function of teaching and learning.

As already noted, you need not be acquainted with all the materials necessary to implement a program of individualized reading. Although desirable, it is not imperative. Much can be gained by utilizing your pupils' knowledge of the materials they have read to evaluate each other's reading progress. The criticism that sequential teaching of skills is neglected and that vocabulary is not controlled is a correct statement but not a valid complaint. There is little or no evidence that reading skills should be taught in sequence or that vocabulary control is essential to reading progress. This is a key issue, for the reading program presented here is based on the premise that both the sequence of skills to be taught and the vocabulary to be developed varies from pupil to pupil.

Is scheduling difficult? Record-keeping excessive? Only if you make them so! Start on a small scale with pupils who can take on the responsibility of working on their own with a minimum of direction. Keep record-keeping down to its lowest possible level, otherwise the very important advantages ascribed to the learning center approach to the education of your pupils will erode. Utilize simple checklists. Engage your pupils in the process of essential record-keeping. Do not teach anything that kids can teach kids as well or better than you can!

The opening to better achievement in reading lies in highly differentiated and enriched reading experiences. This is the essence of the procedure described. The learning center approach presents these experiences as the most important media of *learning* and *thinking*. Therefore, you must not construe the approach presented as one in which a number of simple skills are taught in a few informal conference situations. I present, instead, the beginnings of a *total* reading program designed to develop children's capacities to discriminate, reason, judge, evaluate, and solve problems in connection with *all* classroom activities. Skills associated with developmental reading are not ignored, but are taught *as needed*.

Word recognition and study, speed reading, skimming, note-taking, outlining, distinguishing between fact and opinion, drawing conclusions, using reference materials and the library, reading newspapers and magazines, etc., may all be built into the personalized reading program of each of your pupils.

A wide variety of activities may also be integrated into the program, a few of which are listed here. Your pupils may . . .

Present a puppet show to illustrate a story.

Construct a diorama or miniature stage setting to represent a scene or setting in a story.

Dress as one of the characters in a book and tell about his role.

Paint a picture to depict an event in a book.

Compose an advertisement, make a poster, or decorate a book jacket to attract pupils to a book.

Write a book review for a classroom, school, or town newspaper.

Write a script based on a book and dramatize it.

Construct models and objects on the basis of information and directions derived from a book.

Tell or pantomime a story to the accompaniment of music.

Model characters with soap, clay, or wood.

Write and draw a rebus for a story to develop skill in interpreting words into pictures.

Institute a panel discussion on the same book or with the purpose of comparing different books and different authors.

Create new incidents, new characters, and new adventures to add to a book.

Institute a book fair to attract readers.

Try a book by jury or in the form of a debate.

Utilize postcards, cartoons, pictures or one's own artistic endeavors to illustrate accounts of the material read.

Create word games, puzzles, and quizzes about a book.

Tape excerpts or reports on a story read.

Construct charts, displays, and bulletin boards centered around books.

Create a conversation in dialect between two characters.

VARYING THE DIRECTIONS IN READING

The direction that individualized reading programs may take varies widely. I have presented only one procedure applicable to the implementation of learning centers. As indicated, reading experiences for your pupils may be provided on the basis of pupil interests in a diversified program and on the development of their skills as the need arises. An alternate approach is to narrow the focus of your pupils' reading experiences, yet still to capitalize on their interests within the boundaries of a particular focus. For example, you may hold it more desirable and feasible to center activities on certain segments of the total reading program and implement your reading centers on this basis. Under this plan of action, a biography center, a historical center, a pupil specialties center, a folklore center, a poetry center, a newspaper and magazine center, etc., may be established, each for a period of time, for instance, six weeks.[4] Although, under this plan, the focus may be prescribed by you, such as in the reading and study of folklore, your pupils may select the particular reading they wish to pursue in the content area established. The evaluation of your pupils' reading progress may follow the pattern previously described which utilizes pupil-teachers, or it may take a more structured form under your direction. That is, a center which focuses on the reading of folklore may include your guidelines for the purposes of evaluation. For example, you could invite your pupils to explore the origin and meaning of folktales; the humor, symbolism, and exaggerations utilized; the writing and illustration of original folktales, the creation of conversations in dialect; the feelings elicited; and other related aspects of folklore.

A biography center may include guidelines which focus on your pupils' abilities to explore the influences which helped shape an individual's personality and talents; his training and education; his aspirations; his successes, obstacles, and failures; and the setting, people, and events of his era. Pupils might also be encouraged to examine the sources of the biographer's information and his treatment of the material.

Your pupils may enter a world full of exciting events through a learning center which pivots on the reading of historical fiction and, at the same time, search for authenticity in the form of fair, unbiased, objective historical facts true to place, period, and people. Through the activities of such a center, they can be given opportunities to enhance their imaginations with research and writing skills. They may catch the flavor of life at sea, the grimness of the slave trade, the nobility and suffering of people, the heroic and the decent as well as the barbaric and cruel acts, and the picturesque dialogue of other times and other places. Dodge City in the 1880s, Salem in the 1770s, Walter Reed in the 1900s, and England in the Bronze Age come to life! Your pupils explore the setting of the story, the architecture in vogue, the means of transportation and communication, the dress and speech of the characters, and the general flavor of the times. Responding to the directness and realism portrayed in historical fiction, your pupils may come into contact with the climate and geography of a region; the industries, occupations, and education of its people; the food the people produce and eat; their ideas, inventions, and contributions; and the changes that have evolved. They may find dialects in books and learn how to speak them, utilize recordings and tapes of earlier speech patterns, and note the spelling and writing patterns that have changed.

Always effective, a pupil specialties center opens pupils to as wide a variety of topic selections as there are books available. Your pupils may read about a subject of their choice to the extent that they become the recognized experts in the field selected. They may elect to read about dinosaurs, spiders, the human heart and brain, horses, unusual plants and strange animals, snakes, space, or rockets. Anything goes! If interested in music, they may select materials about composers, opera, jazz, folk ballads, and musical instruments. Some of your pupils may opt for the study of countries—any country in the world! Others, interested in art, may wish to read about famous artists, painters, sculptors, and architects. This is only a partial list. Before making a firm decision on their topic of interest, it may be necessary to teach your pupils the use of a card catalogue to acquaint them with the many kinds of materials useful in pursuing interests. It may also be important to teach them the format for a bibliography, citing references, notetaking, and organizing the information gathered. These should be taught in conjunction with their expressed interests as the need for each develops, and not as skills completely separated from the pupils' endeavors.

A variation of the multilevel, multiexperience pupil specialty center approach described is one in which a number of sub-centers are integrated into the total learning center as implemented by Mrs. Sharon Meier in her classroom. This is shown in Figure 4-16. Observe that most of the materials in each of the sub-centers are familiar to and are already utilized by many of you in your classrooms. The point is that those of you who wish to decentralize your classrooms already have much of the material needed to construct and implement your learning centers.

As shown in the figure, dividing a comprehensive learning center composed of a wide range of activities has the advantages of: (1) minimizing clutter, and (2) providing the elbow room needed by pupils to carry out the diverse activities. It also has the added advantage of separating the more "noisy" activities from those which require greater concentration and privacy. Therefore, when constructing a learning center, it is important that you consider the amount and types of activities to be included before deciding the most appropriate physical arrangement.

Note the skills involved! There are times when I have been bombarded by the question, "When do I teach the 'skills'?" A look at the figure clearly reveals that the pupils who function at the various sub-centers are called on to listen, read, write, hypothesize, create, construct, and report. I have repeatedly made and illustrated the point that skills essential to the intellectual, social, psychological, and academic growth of your pupils will not be ignored through the implementation of learning centers in your classroom. In fact, the development of those skills will be enhanced.

PUPIL READINESS FOR READING

Some teachers feel that the open, learning-centered classroom is predicated on pupils' capacities to read and, therefore, may not be an appropriate learning environment for those who are unable to read. Let me assure you that this is not the case. Most open education movements underway in the schools are, in fact, occurring in the primary grades where a good many of the pupils have not yet learned to read. In my opinion, the so-called non-reader is likely to develop more quickly his ability to read in greater depth in a learning-centered classroom. This, I feel, will take place because of the multiple experiences open to him that may not be available in more formalized settings. He will learn to read, furthermore, not at some arbitrary point on a reading continuum as in a traditional classroom, or at a specific time during a "reading period," but when he is ready to read.

FIGURE 4–16   *Integration of Materials and Activities in a Learning Center*

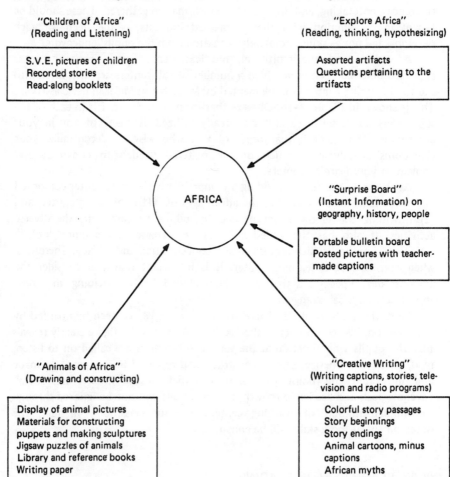

This readiness to read, of course, varies from child to child. Reading difficulties stem from many sources. For example, given the fact that your non-reading pupil has good eyesight and hearing, and falls within or above the normal range of intelligence, it may be that he has perceptual problems at the visual and/or auditory level. This may make it difficult for him to work in the activities of the various learning centers you plan to establish. The more knowledge you have concerning these conditions, the better you can plan experiences beneficial to him. Often such children's reading difficulties may be a result of:

1. Slow development of the motor skills required to speak, write, and handle skillfully the materials prerequisite to learning to read.
2. Inability to grasp, integrate, and recall letter and word patterns.
3. Inability to memorize.
4. Disorientation of space and direction.
5. Inability to discriminate between similar words and letter sounds.
6. Poor eye control and function.

Understanding these characteristics is important, for pupils who exhibit them will likely pose challenges to you. Such children are usually identifiable. Typically, they tend to reverse and invert letters; consequently, they come up with all kinds of bizarre letter combinations. They are often confused by too many symbols in print. They find it difficult to discriminate between letters that look alike, such as b-d, n-u, and p-q. The direction in which the hands of a clock move may bewilder them. Variances in spatial dimensions are equally puzzling to their eyes.

Knowing your pupils' specific learning disabilities, such as the few I mention here, will assist you in planning appropriate learning center activities for them. In planning the activities of your centers, for example, it is important that you keep the number of symbols and words you use to a minimal level. Provide opportunities for extensive kinesthetic practice in manipulation to help develop the right-left orientation necessary for them to learn to read. Help them to develop their power to discriminate visually and auditorily through extensive experiences which require them to listen carefully, observe sharply, and respond accurately. Keep the directions you use at your centers on a very simple level to compensate for their inability to memorize. Considerations such as these are necessary if you are to meet successfully the challenges posed to you by these very special children.

Other non-readers you may have in your class simply cannot be categorized as having specific learning disabilities. It may be that they have not yet learned to read because they lack the many prerequisite experiences necessary to their learning to read.[5] Initially, then, it is important that you avoid teaching them skills of reading in the form of traditional "lessons." The key to their learning to read will rest on the diversity of the experiences and on the extent of the contact with their classmates you provide them, rather than on a particular method you use to teach them to read. Developing their confidence is a necessary first step. Discover their stage of development and build on it. The greater their contact with the materials you place in the learning centers of your classroom, the more likely they will learn to explore the materials, to choose those of interest to them, and to make use of those they choose.

Imagine that one of your "non-readers" is at the reading center you have established. What might you include there that is not based on his ability to read, yet will subsequently help him learn to read? Books in which to look, puzzles to put together, pictures to be placed in a story sequence, or to be used in making a picture book, recorded stories for him to listen to, and objects and pictures to sort out and classify may be of use. The keys of a typewriter invite him to touch and explore. A microphone to talk into and a receiver to feed back his voice interest him in words. Empty food boxes and labeled jars show familiar words. A "television set"—perhaps constructed in partnership with more able readers—encourages him to turn a dial, name a channel and its call letters, and to tell about the picture sequence illustrated. With paints, crayons, and clay he can express a story tape recorded by you or read to him by a classmate. In short, you can establish your reading center, as well as the other learning centers, on the basis of experiences which are apt to cause him to want to read. Most likely those of you who are preschool and primary grades teachers already have in your repertoire literally hundreds of reading readiness activities applicable for inclusion in the center. On the other hand, the student preparing himself to teach perhaps is unaware of the prerequisite skills necessary to children learning to read and of the activities appropriate to their development. Centered largely on their capacities to discriminate visually and auditorily, such skills develop the children's abilities to:

Note similarities and differences in objects, signs, and symbols.

Perceive differences in orientation (left, right, above, below, short, long).

Note differences in size of objects which are similar (little, big).

Hear rhyming words (can clap hands when they hear a word that rhymes with one you present).

Note differences in sounds, rate, and pitch (low, high, fast, slow, loud, soft).

Hear words which begin with same letters (big, boy, bag).

Hear words in a mixed group of words which begin with same letters.

Match objects with pictures.

Supply rhyming words (girls and boys, things and _____).

Match letter or word from a group with a printed isolated letter or word.

Reproduce a simple geometric figure.

Arrange a picture story in correct sequence.

Answer questions about a story read to them.

Retell in simple words a story told or read to them.

Recognize the colors of the spectrum.

Express ideas with paints or crayons.

Recall letters flashed to them.

Find designated objects from several flashed simultaneously.

Talk about personal experiences to a group or class.

Know the reading readiness skills essential to your pupils' learning to read. Use them as specific objectives and guidelines for constructing the activities to be implemented in your learning centers. To construct the appropriate activities, first pretest your pupils to see where they stand in relation to each of the skills. Then establish priorities for activities on the basis of the diagnostic results. It is a relatively simple matter, for example, to find which of your non-readers have difficulty recognizing colors, recalling letters flashed to them, reproducing geometric figures, hearing words which rhyme, etc. Your next step, then, is to put this knowledge to work. For those pupils who are deficient in recognizing colors, include activities in your centers which will help them to overcome this inability. Those who find it difficult to recall letters similarly can be provided with experiences in the centers to help them develop their capacity to do so. There are many activities designed specifically for children who can't read that are applicable for inclusion in your learning centers.

Note the reading readiness skills listed. Obviously, for your non-reading pupils to learn and to practice skills necessary to their learning to read, you need to implement activities in your learning centers which focus on these skills. Included here are activities which require them to locate, arrange, match, and classify materials; differentiate sounds and colors; and recognize, recall, and reproduce letters and symbols; as well as other skills that need to be developed. Keep in mind that the development of these skills need not be restricted to the activities of the reading center. The ability of your pupils to read is more likely to evolve out of the multiple and varied experiences they undergo in the total range of the learning centers you establish in your classroom. However, permit me to illustrate a few activities that you may find useful for implementation in your reading center to develop the skills listed. The activities are grounded in the assumption that the pupils who experience them are able to speak and to understand your instructions. Also, although there are two other approaches you can use in the work of the center, your directed teaching or peer tutoring, the activities illustrated here are predicated on the use of materials and devices that can be operated by the pupils themselves.

In order for your pupils to work without direct supervision by you, it will be necessary for you to first prepare and record the directions they are to follow in advance, along with the associated materials to be included in the center. Following this, you will need to orientate your pupils to the kinds of devices available for their use, how they are operated, and what they are to do with the products of their activities when their work has been completed. Subject to your imagination and experience, all kinds of materials not requiring your pupils' ability to read can be included in the reading center you establish. These may range from assorted pictures, scraps of cloth, letters of the alphabet, ideographs, puzzles, and home-made tachistoscopes to the more commercial learning laboratory systems which include articles such as audio and flash card readers, language masters, reading accelerators, micro-projectors, and eye-span trainers.[6] Learning laboratory systems tend to be costly. If available, however, they are useful for inclusion in your reading center. Because they are easily operated, they do not require your direct supervision, thereby freeing you to carry on other teaching responsibilities. By simply pressing a button, your pupils can listen to your recorded instructions, respond to you, record and listen to their own voices, and replay the results as many times as they wish. To sharpen and extend their auditory and visual discrimination, you can paste simple words, pictures, and drawings on computer-sized cards for this purpose. Your pupils may subsequently learn to read words, phrases, and simple sentences through the association of words with pictures, words with words, and in general, sound with sight.

A cassette or tape recorder, microphone, headphones, and the easily obtainable materials mentioned are sufficient for implementing in your reading center the following activities. In fact, they may be more suited to your own specific circumstances and more flexible in that they do not restrict your activities to prescribed spaces as do the programmed and blank computer-type cards of the learning laboratory systems. Imagine one of your non-readers at work in the reading center you have implemented. He inserts a cassette tape, presses the appropriate button on the tape recorder, and listens to your recorded directions.

> See the picture of the lion in the city! How did he get there? Where will he go? What will he do? What will happen to him? Use the microphone to tell me about it.
>
> Look in the brown envelope marked "SS." Pull out the pictures. Put those that begin with the same sound in a pile (bug, bottle). Show me your pile when you have done this.
>
> Look in the alphabet tray. Pick out all the letters that are made with straight lines. Put these in the box marked "SL." Pick out the letters made with curved lines. Put them in Box "CL." Show me what you have done. If I am busy, select another tape to listen to until I'm free.
>
> Pull out the pictures from the envelope marked "ST." Place them in a row so that they tell a story. Tell the story you have made into the microphone. Perhaps you'd like to listen to your story? Rewind the tape and play it back so you can.
>
> Words that sound alike! (Boat, coat.) Look at the pictures in the envelope marked "SA." How many can you put together that rhyme?
>
> Pick up the different pieces of cloth from the ice cream bucket. Use the microphone to tell me how each piece feels.
>
> How good are you at building a house? Select the pictures from Box "HB." Which comes first? Second? Third? Show me the house you have built with the pictures.
>
> Listen to the sounds I make! Look at the objects on the table. What do you hear? (Spoon stirred in a cup, guitar strings being plucked, roar of a train, pages of a book being flipped, etc.) Pick a friend. See if the two of you can agree on matching the sounds you hear with the objects on the table.

Select a picture from the envelope marked with a "CC." (Dog chasing a cat, two boys fighting, etc.) Why is the dog chasing the cat? What do you think happened before? What will happen next? Why are the boys fighting? How will it end? Pick up the microphone and tell me what you think.

Look in the puzzle box. How many pieces can you put together so that they fit? (The pupil learns to match colored paper with the corresponding word.)

Can you find a bird (squirrel, lizard, etc.) in the forest picture? Look in the envelope marked "FP" for the picture. Show me what you find.

Draw a picture of a creature from outer space. What's his name? Where does he live? What does he like to do? Talk into the microphone and tell me your story. Play it back and listen to it. Perhaps a friend would like to listen to it, too.

Look at the pictures in Envelope "M." Which of the things you see in each of the pictures (flag, cheese, lamp, giraffe, jello, fruit, etc.) would you take to the moon if you were an astronaut? Make two piles of pictures. In one pile put those showing the things you would take. Put those you would not take in the other pile. Show me what you've done when you are ready. I'll be interested in hearing what you have to say.

I trust that the activities listed here for inclusion in your reading center only begin to stir your imaginations. Many of you, I'm certain, are even more imaginative and will create new and novel ways for working with pupils who experience difficulty in learning to read. If you are a student or beginning teacher about to get underway, you will do well to develop a file of activities useful in developing the skills necessary to learn how to read. Given a list of reading readiness skills, one approach is to take each and search out as many activities as you can applicable to its development. You may wish to type these on index cards and file them for use as needed. The idea is to accumulate, for your reference, sets of activity cards, each set appropriate to the particular reading readiness skill to be developed.

Figure 4-17 illustrates one such activity. In this instance, pupils are invited, through letter association, to construct the words listed by placing the letter blocks in the appropriate tray receptacles. Or, if they prefer, they may select words from other sources, or spell those they already know. A primary typewriter may also be used for this purpose.

Perhaps your non-readers have not yet developed their natural abilities to read. To stimulate them, plan to throw a lot of spice into your reading center. Insofar as it is possible, make the experiences of the learning center enjoyable for them. In fact, this may well be the quickest route to their learning to read. Include in your center objects familiar to them and provide activities that invite them to create, invent, and build. Keep in mind, however, that although exposure to the real world is important in arousing their interests, nothing can be more deadly than your restricting the activities of your reading center to facts, reading readiness exercises, and the like. Once your pupils are on the road to reading, expose them to the colorful language and beauty of expression found in books, for example, "the great grey-green, greasy Limpopo River," immortalized by Rudyard Kipling in one of his *Just So Stories,* "The Elephant's Child." Vocabulary-controlled books, when used as steady diets, are apt to dull your pupils' senses and discourage them from reading. Substitute, instead, books that offer your pupils new sounds and words, vivid impressions, and the fresh presentation of ideas.

FIGURE 4–17   Representative Letter-and-Word Association Activity for Implementation in a Reading Center

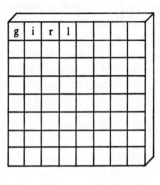
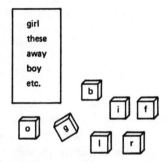

Weigh carefully the literature to which your non-reading pupils are to be exposed. Style, content, and illustrations are important. Frequent repetition of sounds and words, such as those found in the well-known Dr. Seuss books, often provide built-in appeal and are valuable in helping pupils distinguish between words that sound alike and those that are sharply different. Books with numerous illustrations may be helpful to those pupils who have not yet learned to read. Those who have taken their first giant steps into formal reading may find it comfortable to pick up books containing familiar words, brief sentences, and short stories. Even the very smallest of your youngsters may be influenced by the size and weight of the books you place in your reading center. Books for preschoolers, in particular, need to be small and light enough to handle.

The reading center you plan should provide your pupils with the opportunity for free and continuous use of the books you place in it. This is a central factor in helping your non-readers learn to read. Note, when provided a reading environment, preschool children identify and select books they want to have read to them long before they have learned to read. Out comes *Go Dog Go, Hop on Pop,* and other Dr. Seuss books, along with assorted books on dinosaurs, "Sesame Street," rain and snow, Pinocchio, the birth of a baby, and whatever else is made available to them. Constant exposure and complete accessibility to the books as well as no-strings-attached opportunities to select them appear to be the keys to this very important step of identification. Similarly, you will find that through your pupils' association and contact with the books you place in your reading center, that they will see in them something relevant to their own interests and want to read.

PUPIL-INITIATED READING

Procedures for implementing personalized reading programs in classrooms, of course, vary. You may wish to implement a completely informal program based on books and materials largely selected by your pupils, or one in which informal reading activities are undertaken in conjunction with your directed teaching. The experiences of Mrs. Maria Luna, a first year, sixth-grade teacher in Anthony, New Mexico follow the former. I now draw heavily on her experiences because they illustrate and reinforce many of the points made throughout this section on personalizing the reading activities of pupils.

Why pupil-initiated reading? All you need to do is ask your pupils why. Mrs. Luna's present reading program grew out of her pupils' dissatisfaction with their basal readers. Certainly numerous other elementary school pupils, wherever they may be, harbor many of the same feelings. Perhaps some of your own, given the opportunity, will express themselves like Mrs. Luna's students:

"The book is too easy."

"The book is too hard."

"I like football stories."

"It's impossible for us all to like the same stories."

Clearly, statements such as those expressed by Mrs. Luna's sixth-graders, are familiar to those of you who are experienced teachers. The differences in pupil reading needs and interests expressed within these very few statements are apparent. Recognizing, then, that similar needs and interests may well exist in your own classroom, how do you begin to personalize the pupils' reading experiences?

The obvious first step is to invite your pupils to bring in their own materials. The beauty of this step is that you will probably learn things about your pupils you never realized. Consider, for example, Mrs. Luna's thirty-five, predominantly Spanish-speaking children. Although most came from economically impoverished circumstances, they somehow managed to scrape up as many as one hundred books within the first week alone. The reading materials brought into the classroom included such personal preferences as *Sports Illustrated Magazine*, the *Readers' Digest*, *TV Guide*, *National Geographic Magazine*, *McGuffey's First Eclectic Reader*, *Ripley's Believe It or Not*, the *Guinness Book of World Records,* Spanish language newspapers, assorted novels, all kinds of comic books, and various true confession and romance-type magazines. You can see, I'm sure, the wide range of reading interests reflected in this partial list of materials brought in by the pupils.

Once the reading materials have been brought in by your pupils, the transition to autonomous, pupil-initiated reading experiences can be made by inviting each pupil to talk about the material he has brought in. Subsequently, the material may be placed in a center for other pupils to read. It is important, at this point, to let your pupils decide for themselves the amount of time each wishes to spend reading. During this time, you may plan to record your observations of reading problems and meet with your pupils as needed and as requested by them.

Mrs. Luna reports some interesting results under this arrangement. Her pupils instituted their own library system, in the process of which they made subject cards, author cards, and noted cross references. They suggested and made charts to show the number and kinds of books and other materials read. They constructed "summary books," which included the title of each book, its author, the pages read, and a synopsis. They instituted panel discussions of books read. They debated. They taped and wrote reviews which required the reader of a book to respond to class questioning. The pupils evaluated each other's performance on book comprehension. Full-length, written book reports virtually disappeared, the pupils preferring to make travel posters such as "Come to the Land of...." They designed jackets for books for the school's library, illustrated with drawings and slogans such as "Why not the Giraffes?" They drew book characters, wrote skits, gave plays, wrote poems, made dioramas, and created "talking book" reports.

It is interesting to note the progress in reading made by Mrs. Luna's class during the course of the 1972–73 school year. In September 1972, according to results of the McGinnis Reading Test, only five pupils out of thirty-five read at grade level or above. In May 1973, after having undergone the informal reading program described above, thirty-three pupils read at grade level or higher, eleven of these being above grade level. Two pupils who had heretofore been classified as non-readers had improved to the point where they read at approximately the third-grade level.

More important than the standardized test results is what happened to the pupils in the process of their informal reading program. They *learned* rather than were taught the skills of reading. In other words, they utilized these reading skills to learn more about their particular interests. Included were the skills of alphabetizing, skimming, and summarizing, along with the skills of using dictionaries, extending their vocabularies, and writing creatively. They read more. No one pupil read less than fifteen books during the course of the year. One read over one hundred books, and most of the pupils read from thirty to forty books. Still more important were the changes in behavior that took place. The pupils' attitudes were broadened and their interests expanded. They learned, furthermore, to accept each others' viewpoints through the argumentation and debate that took place in their classroom. Above all, they learned to enjoy reading.

The informal reading program I describe in this chapter is not intended to be a panacea for all the reading problems you may face in your classroom. Indeed, no one approach to the teaching of reading is. Experience shows, however, that informal reading in the elementary school classroom is feasible, workable, and productive. The primary grades are no exception. In fact, the importance of the reading options provided children in their primary years of schooling under this arrangement has been clearly demonstrated:

> We have actual evidence that a child's use of books may decrease to almost a zero level over the period of the primary years if his teachers do not behave in a manner that moves him to increase the range of options he selects.[7]

Earlier in the chapter I briefly outlined the advantages of an informal reading program. I hope you agree that it is good for your pupils and, equally important, good for you.

In my opinion, the literature and activities you informally add to your reading center cannot help but attract, hold, and sustain your pupils' interest in reading. Unlike basal reading programs which are built largely around vocabulary, the literature presented in the reading center exposes pupils to situations, plots, themes, ideas, events, and knowledge as well. Inasmuch as literature is not typically restricted to grade levels, is there a better way to stimulate and meet your pupils' interest in reading? Surely you will agree that your use of funny, informational, adventure, science, travel, nature, mystery, sports, and other books in your reading center will more than likely provide the personalized reading experiences necessary for your pupils to achieve their individual goals.

POINTS TO REMEMBER

- Team learning provides opportunities for wide ranges of experiences over all levels of pupil achievement.
- Diagnostic teaching is a necessary process to differentiated learning.
- Discovery-type activities are particularly adaptable for use in learning centers.
- Finding pupils' interests is the key to personalizing their learning experiences.
- Achievement in reading rests on highly differentiated and enriching reading experiences.
- The self-selection process is very important in developing pupils' abilities to discriminate and judge wisely.

NOTES

1. The term "individualize" is subject to a number of interpretations. It is often used to suggest a one-to-one teaching experience between a teacher and an individual pupil or a learning experience which involves an individual pupil with a set of learning materials, as in programmed learning. The term "personalize" goes beyond these interpretations to include the preferred choices of individual pupils for learning.

2. Individually Prescribed Instruction (IPI) programs were initiated in 1963 by the Learning Research and Development Center at the University of Pittsburgh and the Oakleaf Elementary School.

3. From a packet of materials on the Cross-Age Helping Programs developed by the University of Michigan's Center for Research on the Utilization of Scientific Knowledge. These materials include a reprint of Peggy Lippitt's article, "Children Can Teach Children," published in the *Instructor*, May 1969.

4. Adopted and modified from a plan implemented by Team Kappa, Lexington, Mass. under the direction of Mrs. May Reinhardt to whom major credit is given for this approach.

5. A useful discussion of pupils' experiences prior to school entry is found in Chapter 6. See the section subtitled "The Physical Arrangement."

6. Possibly the best single source of information on learning laboratory systems is obtainable from the National Audio-Visual Association, Inc., 3150 Spring Street, Fairfax, Virginia, 22030. If interested, you may wish to write for their 20th edition (1974–75) of *The Audio-Visual Equipment Directory*, which pictures and describes them.

7. R. W. Henderson, "Accountability and Decision-Making in Open Education: Tucson Early Education Model," *Childhood Education*, 41 (April 1973), 368–372.

Convey the need for his assistance—by you and by his classmates. Promote his feeling that he belongs by expressing that you like him, that you're glad he's in your room, and that his contributions are useful, and by giving him the responsibility of directing his own learning. Create a team spirit as a transitional step to your pupils functioning well in learning centers. Lay the groundwork for this through emphasis on group work, cooperative projects, and paired learning experiences, thereby giving the pupils opportunity to plan, share, cooperate, and work together. How else can they learn what to expect from each other?

Help each pupil feel important through his participation in multiple experiences which require that he formulate, express, and implement his ideas. Smile, and touch and praise him frequently, but in a natural and real manner. Point out his assets and the uniqueness of his position in your class by providing opportunity for him to lead as well as to follow, to explain as well as to listen, to show as well as to watch. Take this a step further by teaching all your pupils to give attention to, praise, and display approval of each other's work and progress; for example, "Mrs._____ , see what Billy has done!" "Look at Armando's and Jennifer's experiment."

There is little argument that a child's degree of motivation for learning on his own depends on the way he sees himself. Inasmuch as the open environment you plan calls for much independent learning by your pupils, the development of their self-esteem and acceptance of themselves as persons with control over their growth is central to the establishment of a positive climate in your classroom. A conjunctive relationship with each of your pupils is important in this development. In building this relationship, it is important that you go beyond your own individual ideas. "What do *you* think, Albert?" "How do *you*, Charlie, feel about this experience?" "What are some of the problems *you* see, Dolores?" To develop your pupils' self-awareness, awareness of others, and their feelings of mastery, try establishing a specific time of day, *everyday*, when they can talk about their feelings, when they can be themselves, with opportunities for their expression of positive and negative feelings. Encourage them, also, to transcend their personal feelings to think of something that would make someone else in the class feel good. Bring into the discussions their accomplishments so that each pupil thinks in terms of "I am. I can do. I'm appreciated. I'm good. I'm liked. I am me!"

Equality.   Closely related to your pupils' acceptance of each other is their practicing of the Golden Rule. "Do unto others as you'd like done to you!" Your pupils' recognition of each other's similarities and differences are the necessary ingredients. Teacher-pupil planning and evaluation sessions are important vehicles in this process and provide practice in democratic participation. Invite and encourage your pupils to help determine the objectives of their classroom experiences and to help implement them. Balance their freedom to do so with the order needed to maximize their time for instruction and learning. Dare to be equal with your pupils, not in the sense of maturity, experiential background, and knowledge, but in terms of confronting a mutual task, problem, or idea head-on as equals.

Mutual Respect.   Good teaching demands built-in sincerity between you and your pupils, devoid of all sham. Most beginning teachers have a running start here in that they've been attracted to teaching as a profession in which honest and sincere relationships are the rule rather than the exception. Build on these relationships through open and free discussion uninhibited by the sting of judgments regarding success and failure, right and wrong, and best and poorest so that your pupils can learn to recognize their own capabilities, feel their impact on each other, and accept the responsibility for their own behavior. First, they must have self-respect, then, respect for others. Once this mutual respect has been established, you may reasonably expect that your pupils will behave responsibly in classroom activities.

Encouragement.   The crucial component in encouraging your children to learn is that you communicate your sincere desire to help. In fact, children "will gladly accept a harsh and explosive act if they sense the sincere desire to help behind an openly expressed anger."[2] How, then, is this desire communicated? Providing a healthy emotional climate in which your pupils can function openly and freely is, of course, the foundation on which to build. Shoot for spontaneous pupil effort and results which lead to their self-esteem. Stimulate divergent thinking and expression. Institute problem-solving situations which emphasize scouting, scouring, and scrimmaging and not necessarily the "right" answers. Get away from cookbook formulas for teaching. In my opinion, such formulas do not work because what is important to some pupils is not so for others. Lessen the staccato marks of the red pencil, the "X's," and the "You can do better's!" Substitute written marginal comments and verbal responses which reinforce the pupils' contributions; for example, "A fine comparison, Larry!" "That's clear reasoning, Loretta!" "You express this point sharply, Sam!" Eliminate references to "don't," "shouldn't," "poor," and "never." Try, instead, "That's a very interesting idea, Jerry!" "Isn't Lolly's hobby fascinating, boys and girls?" "That's all right, David, have you tried . . .?" Accept your pupils as they are and then work with them in terms of what they hope to become. Let *their* objectives become your objectives. Build on what they have going for them, rather than on what you think they should be.

Help your pupils to teach themselves. Provision for choice-making opportunities is central to this process because this conveys to your pupils that you feel they are capable of making choices and that learning is an intensely *personal* affair. What your pupils believe about themselves affects every aspect of their lives. Who would argue the fact that children have their own set of values? To help them, you need to know what these values consist of. It is through opportunities for self-selected learning experiences that you can come to know their preferences, interests, and attitudes, and give time to them as individuals.

This is a crasy cattes in the desert   you can see one in the desert if you go it is green if you can go you better watch out Our you can step on it and it can go all the way in your foot. It will he art a lot.

Mary Helen
Age 9

five

*Ingredients Essential
to Getting Underway*

The first four chapters have focused strongly on the dimensions, character-istics, and ingredients essential to opening up the classroom. The response to the oft-asked question, "How will I know it when I see it?," should now be clear to you. It is characterized by the free movement of pupils, flexibility of time and curriculum, multilevel texts and teaching aids, spontaneous and diversified activities, the absence of grades, individual and small-group independent learning experiences, pupil input and operational involvement, teacher-pupil planning and mutual decision-making, kids teaching kids, and opportunities for pupils to self-select, self-direct, and self-evaluate their academic and personal progress. You are, hopefully, finding the form, shape, and substance of the open classroom less of an enigma than it may have first appeared. What may still prove puzzling to some of you, however, is the transition to and subsequent total implementation of the above characteristics in the classroom. I now turn to this challenge.

ESTABLISHING THE CLIMATE:
PREREQUISITE TO OPEN LEARNING

In my opinion, the most important, most imperative single ingredient necessary to open up the classroom so that children express their freedom to learn is the relationship between teacher and pupils, and pupils and pupils. This cannot be stressed enough! The way you prepare your classroom environment and establish

171

the climate for this relationship in large measure will determine the shape, substance, and direction your open classroom will take. In opening up your classroom so that this freedom to learn is subsequently woven into the fabric of a learning-centered environment, it is important that you first practice the ingredients of this freedom in your present classroom insofar as they are possible and manageable. As you do so, keep in mind that each pupil's freedom in your classroom is limited only by the rights of his classmates to behave similarly. This constitutes the heart of the matter. For the type and extent of your pupils' progress and self-fulfillment will be shaped by the conditions of learning under which they are to function.

STARTING WITH THE TRUTHS

How, then, do you begin? Without question, an initial step in establishing the climate for open learning is to get to know your pupils as *individuals*, not as a class. Know the interests they express, the ways they speak, the questions they ask and how they ask them, the ways they feel, their reactions, the books they read, the things they do, how well they do them, and even *how* they learn. Go beyond cumulative records and conferences with parents to frequent observations of and talk with your pupils. Infiltrate their playground activities, games, and conversations. Record their communication—their ideas, concerns, likes, dislikes, favorite television programs, colloquialisms, speech difficulties, and conversational patterns. In this way you start with the truth about what the pupils are. Extend these to what you already know about children. Focus strongly on their individuality and initiate activities on this basis as a preliminary step to subsequently decentralizing your classroom in the form of learning centers. By accepting and using the fact that each of your pupils perceives differently and thereby learns differently, you create the environment which encourages each to explore his individuality. At the same time, you expose and open yourself up to the pupils by the ways you look, speak, feel, act, and respond, so that they see in you some relationship to them.

Secondly, to help your pupils feel free to learn, you must eliminate, inasmuch as possible, all conditions and situations they view as threatening. It is important that you diminish any existing anxieties your pupils may have lest they add to those that may naturally evolve in moving from the traditional to the open classroom. Central to this crucial preparation are elements long advocated by figures such as the eminent late psychiatrist Rudolph Dreikurs. Among these are acceptance, equality, mutual respect, encouragement, independence, and the natural and logical consequences of these behaviors in the classroom.[1] A good start would be to build upon these as essential prerequisites to opening up your classroom.

Acceptance.   Try to encourage each of your pupils from dependence to independence so that each accepts himself for what he is and for his potential.

independent pupil experiences in your classroom through provisions for free reading, group work, individual and cooperative projects, bulletin board construction, reading circles, peer tutoring, game playing, running of projectors and recorders, "helping hands," and other activities that do not require your direct supervision. If you have not already built independent experiences such as these into your classroom, it is essential to do so as a prerequisite and transitory step to decentralizing the classroom experiences to more open activities. Start with a few such activities, increasing their number and frequency as your pupils demonstrate their ability to work independently and responsibly.

Fourth, educate the more responsible pupils in the use of audio-visual and self-instructional materials that are available for classroom activities. They, in turn, may then assume the responsibility of teaching other pupils to handle these materials independently. Once all your pupils are proficient in doing so, you are free to pursue more important matters than running a projector or record player, directing games, and supervising assorted learning aids.

Fifth, implement peer tutoring. An initial step would be to pair off children. Match pupils who work well independently of you with pupils who find this difficult so that the latter may take on some of the work and study habits of the former. Begin simply, first by encouraging each pair to work together on relatively easy tasks such as examining each other's papers, comparing answers, and sharing knowledge. Gradually build up to the point where they initiate and formulate learning contracts of mutual interest, create activities for learning centers, and carry on projects which require autonomous input.

FIGURE 5-1   Pupil-Constructed Device for Teaching Arithmetical Facts

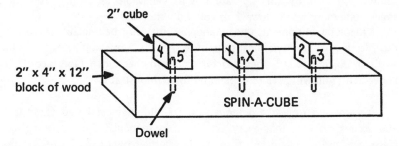

You may wish to work more specifically with designated tutors in terms of what is to be taught. Pin-point their teaching targets. Zero in on what they are to teach partners needing their help; for instance, "Here are some words your partner can't read, spell, or doesn't understand." "Leon has some difficulty with two-place divisors, do you think you can help him?" Encourage the tutors to develop their own strategies for teaching. Given this opportunity, kids often come up with unique techniques. They are especially adept at creating and utilizing puppets, games, puzzles, riddles, graphics, and word play. They sometimes surpass teachers in the effective use of these for teaching purposes. In fact, Bill Mayhall, a staff member of New Mexico State University's Regional

Resource Center for the Handicapped, relates that slow-learning, handicapped children, after a period of training, frequently do a better job of directed teaching in tutoring sessions than do a good many knowledgeable teachers! Should your school be blessed with videotape equipment, and should you wish to educate pupils to tutor in a positive fashion, you might consider the following procedure.

1. Videotape the teaching of a task to a pupil, e.g., vocabulary drill using flash cards.
2. Use positive reinforcement throughout the demonstration as called for, e.g., "Excellent," "Fantastic," "Attaboy," "Now you're moving!"
3. Replay the videotape to selected tutors.
4. Encourage the tutors to count the number of times you praised the tutoree.
5. Stop the replay at appropriate points to emphasize the techniques used.

It is hoped that the pupil tutors you have selected will emulate the good teaching and reinforcement techniques demonstrated.

The next step in the training program is to videotape each tutor as he works with a classmate. As he teaches, try flashing a sign behind the tutoree to remind the tutor to use reinforcement; for example, "Look for things to praise!" Upon completion of the session, replay the tape for the tutor to note his teaching. Ask him to count the number of times he said something which made the tutoree feel good and to note the degree of enthusiasm he projects. A word of caution—praise must be believable to the pupil being taught. Expressions such as, "Billy, you're really smart!," are not as believable as, "Billy, you correctly spelled one more word today than you did yesterday!"

Videotape equipment, understandably, may not be available to you. A tape recorder is a good economical substitute. At least your pupil-tutors will be able to listen to, if not see, their teaching performances. If a tape recorder is not convenient, you will have to depend on live demonstrations.

Natural and Logical Consequences.   Children must be educated to know and accept the idea that every act has a consequence. Since opening up your classroom makes your pupils responsible for their own behavior, it is important that they learn to accept the consequences of that behavior. These may result naturally from their own actions, or from those *logically* determined by you and the class as a whole. Take, for example, the pupil who persistently does not listen to directions or explanations of an assignment or the explanation of activities at a learning center, yet continually asks what he is supposed to do. You, reasonably, do not have time to reexplain. The consequence of his behavior is natural. He simply will have to find something else to do! At least two advantages occur from this *natural consequence:* (1) you give the pupil reason for listening the next time, and (2) your time is better spent with pupils who have listened.

Consider, also, the pupil who breaks a mutually agreed upon ground rule established by the class that requires each pupil to remove his personal effects from a learning center when he has completed his work so that other pupils are free to use it. To free the center for future use, his personal materials are placed in a lost and found box by the pupils wishing to use the center. The *logical consequence* of his behavior is that he must then take time to search for and sort out his belongings—time that might be better spent doing something else. He will learn to accept the logic of this consequence because, as a member of the class, he participated in the establishment of the rule regarding this behavior. It is important to note here that in both illustrations you are not punishing the pupils. They are, instead, learning to conform to the guidelines of living, which makes the work of your classroom manageable.

Dreikurs and Grey[4] make the valid point that logical consequences express the "reality of the social order"—the rules of living, so to speak. To function effectively in a decentralized learning environment, whatever its form, shape, and direction, "rules of living" are necessary. Freedom and order must balance in an open environment if it is to function on the basis of democratic principles.

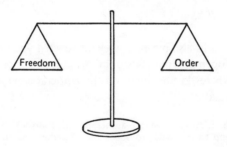

Educating your pupils to accept the consequences of their behavior is a necessary ingredient of this balance. Build as few rules as needed and always in open discussion with your pupils. Avoid the construction of rules with moralistic overtones because these are self-defeating. Encourage, instead, the formulation of rules which regulate the logistics of the classroom so that time for instruction and learning is maximized. Open discussion should accompany the institution of rules. Let your pupils express their ideas on what the objectives and functions of their classroom should encompass. Explore the consequences of each with them so that a mutual understanding is reached. The rules of living that evolve should clearly define the consequences of acts and be formulated so that your pupils understand and respond to the logic of the consequences. Children, of course, are not always temperate. Therefore, it is your function to insure that the rules drawn up by your pupils are sound, reasonable, and fair. Otherwise, the pupils are not likely to accept the logic of the consequences of the rules should they be broken.

A smooth, cooperative functioning of activities and interrelationships in your classroom is not apt to occur without joint planning by you and your pupils since each pupil is involved in his own needs, interests, and intentions and not necessarily those of the classroom as a whole. As is true in any family, it is essential that all children are encouraged to discuss and expand on the means for the effective realization of these attributes. Create, then, a classroom atmosphere in which each pupil has a *constructive* role. Do this *before* you attempt to decentralize your classroom in the form of differentiated learning centers. That is, begin opening up your classroom through democratic participation in the environment of your classroom as it now exists. Establish the climate for this by integrating the class in terms of "one for all and all for one." That each child contributes to the welfare of the group and to the individual progress of each other child is the important goal. You and your pupils are partners in this respect. Invite pupils to pose problems, outline objectives of learning centers, suggest activities, clarify interpersonal relationships, evaluate their own and each other's progress, assume behavioral responsibilities, and take on an equal share for the shape, format, and function of the classroom. Teacher-pupil planning, a long-ignored process in the classrooms of the United States, is necessary for this pupil participation to take place.

TEACHER READINESS

Starting with the truths also means you examine what you know about yourself. Are you ready to open up your classroom? What are your preferences, attitudes, and intentions? Where do you stand on the autocratic/democratic continuum? Rudolph Dreikurs states:

> Wherever children move from an autocratic environment into a democratic setting, they tend to run wild, to abuse their freedom, because they have not learned to rely on their inner restraint when the outside pressure failed to force them into submission.[5]

Do you dare to look at yourself, as a teacher, in terms of this continuum? Certainly, we can agree that even though it is difficult to categorize a classroom as strictly autocratic or democratic, Dreikurs places the responsibility for the classroom environment on you. There can be little argument that the extent to which you are autocratic or democratic will determine the degree of your success in opening up your classroom. How prepared are you to provide open learning experiences for pupils in your classroom? How do I look at me? Recall Figure 1–2. How many of the open characteristics in how many of the selected dimensions do you currently practice? How many of the "traditional" characteristics? To what extent do you practice each of the characteristics shown in the figure? If you find yourself mostly exhibiting open characteristics, you're ready to go. In fact, you may already be there!

If you need further assurance on where you stand, you may wish to respond to some twenty-nine assumptions closely related to open education postulated by Barth,[6] with the view of examining your attitudes and beliefs about motivating children, conditions for learning, intellectual development, evaluation, and knowledge. There are still other instruments available to help you assess your feelings about, and disposition towards, education. These are fine as far as they go. However, I feel it is more important to examine what you are *actually doing* in your present classroom by evaluating your *teaching* practices because this procedure goes beyond assumption and commitment to reflect more clearly the extent of your readiness to open up your classroom. I provide a set of criteria in Chapter 8 (Figure 8-18) by which you may assess your teaching practices. Most of you will find, I'm certain, that you practice both open and closed education in your classrooms, and also that you are probably more open in your teaching practices than you perhaps realize.

What about your role and function in a completely open, learning-centered classroom? How well do you understand these very important components? Will they differ from your present practices? The next section of this chapter will help you to understand better the position you will need to assume in making the transition from a traditional classroom to one which focuses on open learning.

THE TEACHER'S ROLE AND FUNCTION

Too often the role and function of the teacher in the open classroom are misunderstood. Your role is pivotal. Even though you plan to develop the unique and very special capacities of your pupils and allow them to choose their own goals and some of the experiences essential to their achievement, you should in no way feel that your influence and function as a teacher are diminished. Quite the opposite is the case. The fact that you plan to place considerable emphasis on your pupils knowing their own needs, making their own decisions, and choosing their own courses of learning does not mean that you are merely to stand by while these are occurring. Nor does this mean that your pupils are to have equal voice in all the actions they undertake. The kind and extent of their decision-making power will depend on the particular activities to take place. In some instances, it may be important that they have a greater voice than you do. In other instances, it may be in their best interests that they have less voice than you in decision-making.

If you still have doubts regarding your role and function in an open classroom environment, rest assured that they will be more important than ever. Your pupils will continue to turn to you for leadership, guidance, direction, and instruction. However, your role in carrying out these important functions will take on a very different pattern. I have never read about or heard the teacher's role in the open classroom better expressed than by the Frobelians:

> ... the teacher actually has a more active directing part to play than on any planned instructional programme through which pupils are processed in an almost routine way. But the part to be played is of course a very different kind. It is based on not *imposing* anything on children, but on so closely co-operating with

their native interests and drives that whatever they are led to do is felt as
something that comes out of themselves. The teacher provides starting experiences which produce that result; invites questions and discussion; raises questions
of his own; puts out suggestions; indicates possible lines of activity; introduces
provocative new stimuli; makes thought-arousing comments, etc. Some of these
"take," others do not; those that do, get adopted and what then follows is the
child's own response.[7]

What you personally bring to the classroom you plan to establish is
especially pertinent to its formulation. Your behavior will set the tone. To what
extent, for example, do you feel you must control your pupils' learning? Should
those pupils who come into your classroom with different backgrounds and
perceptions be provided with different learning opportunities? The same
opportunities? Some of each? How do you plan to work with pupils who find it
difficult to interact with their peers? What about those pupils who aspire to new
experiences but are reluctant to leave the security of more formalized
experiences? What will you do with pupils who seem to learn best in highly
structured, teacher-directed activities? Your outlook is uniquely important.
Your view of teaching, curriculum, and children, without question, provides the
key to the kind of classroom you will establish. The way you prepare the
environment of your classroom is a primary factor in this establishment.

PREPARING THE CLASSROOM ENVIRONMENT

Children, we know, are blessed with a wonderful capacity to learn. However,
mere possession of this innate gift is no guarantee that they will learn, or that
they will learn in productive and positive ways. Social stimulation is necessary
for this to take place. The thesis of this book is that open learning is more likely
to evolve in a decentralized classroom environment because it provides for
greater social interaction than does the conventional classroom. This is not to
say that open education cannot be practiced in a traditional row-by-row
classroom setting. Indeed it can! But it is less likely to occur because the
traditional classroom does not utilize the rich and varied settings of the open
classroom. The climate for learning in the decentralized classroom, building as it
does on the children's spontaneity and openness to experience, is shaped by
their personal initiative and involvement. I am not suggesting here that if only
you leave your pupils alone, they will educate themselves. Far from it—your
guidance and help are important factors.

Also, an important component of this climate is the physical structure of
the classroom you plan to establish. Physically decentralizing your classroom is
necessary because of the diverse needs and interests of your pupils. For you to
accomplish this successfully, you will need an abundance of materials to provide
the flexibility necessary to your classroom's organization and the implementation of its activities.

GATHERING THE MATERIALS

Teachers in many public school classrooms are trapped by a predetermined and prearranged physical space which leaves little to the imagination. Unfortunately, the space of your classroom does not have the advantages of the innovative, multilevel classroom structures increasingly prevalent in independent primary schools. Nevertheless, you can do much to build learning environments on a child-sized scale based on their interests in your present classroom. Even though catwalks, towers, easily assembled and disassembled modular components, and other architectural innovations are not available in the immediate future for most public school classrooms, you can turn to cardboard carpentry,[8] fabrics, screens, carpeting, portable furniture, and other assorted materials to create a learning environment in which things happen *to* your pupils.

In constructing your total classroom environment, it is pertinent to note that what your pupils are to find and experience there will shape their thinking, behavior, spirit, and aspirations. What the pupils find in your classroom teaches them what you, as their teacher, think of education, and even more importantly, what you think of them! Tables or desks clustered together suggest to them that dialogue is important. Readily available science equipment implies that experimentation is invited. Assorted and differentiated art materials signify to them that artistic and creative expression takes many forms. Multilevel, diversified textbooks signify that the pace of learning is not rigid and routinized. Tools for construction and materials for invention express to them that construction and invention are encouraged. Questions and problems posed denote the importance of inquiry and of clear and logical thinking. Diverse, rich literature and music present the range of human experience. Opportunities for decision-making by your pupils suggest that you expect them to take responsibility for their own learning. Materials for study mean just that to the pupils—study is expected. Self-correcting devices imply that self-evaluation is encouraged. Open space denotes freedom of movement and expression to your pupils.

I am afraid that too many teachers use "lack of materials" as their chief reason for not moving into more open teaching practices. This is unfortunate. As presented in Chapter 3, many materials are available to you without cost. Start now! Commence gathering your materials *in advance* of your attempt to open up your classroom. Become a "junkie"! Scour Salvation Army stores; church bazaars; print shops; stationery stores; supermarkets; lumber, rug, electrical, and phone companies; clothing, box, and electronic factories; and railroad and junk yards. In short, tap the resources of your local community. What is to be gained? Here's a partial list of materials attainable *without cost* from the following sources.

Manufacturers and Assorted Companies

cloth remnants	cartons and boxes
yarn	rug swatches

buttons	damaged bricks
tape	tile samples
plastic scraps	used computer cards
styrofoam packing	large cable spools
broken cinder blocks	linoleum
wood curls	plexiglass
leather	wire scraps
sheet metal scraps	scrap wood
cardboard tubes	sawdust

Stores, Markets, Restaurants

sample food packages	cardboard display cases
used ice cream containers	outdated catalogues
used posters	used plastic cups
empty cigar & candy boxes	wallpaper ends
refrigerator & freezer cartons	can cartons
packing boxes	discarded plastic spoons
fruit crates and trays	discarded menus

Reach out further! For the price of stationery and stamps you can obtain free materials from a multitude of sources on a multitude of topics. Listed are a few topics and addresses for your interest.

Airplanes
Cessna Aircraft Co.
Air Age Ed. Division
Wichita, Kansas 67201

Aluminum
Aluminum Co. of America
1501 Alcoa Building
Pittsburgh, Pa. 15219

American Industry
Educational A.B.C.'s of
    American Industry
Niagara Falls, N.Y.

Americans
Famous Americans
John Hancock Life Insurance Co.
Boston, Mass.

Animals
First Aid & Care of Small Animals
Animal Welfare Institute
P.O. Box 3492
Grand Central Station
New York, N.Y.

Aquarium
The Aquarium as a Hobby
Metaframe Corporation
87 Route 17
Maywood, N.J. 07607

Astronomy
Consolidated Edison Co. of N.Y.
4 Irving Place
New York, N.Y. 10003

Aviation
O'Hare International Airport
P.O. Box 8800
Chicago, Ill. 60666

Banks
Manufacturers Hanover Trust
New York, N.Y. 10015

Bees
Dadant & Sons, Inc.
Hamilton, Ill. 62341

Blood
American Red Cross
325 East Washington Street
Muncie, Ind. 47305

Boating
National Association of Engine
and Boat Manufacturers
420 Lexington Avenue
New York, N.Y.

Camera
How to Make a Camera
Eastern Kodak Co.
343 State Street
Rochester, N.Y. 14650

Carpenter Tools
Simple Explanations of
Carpenter Tools
The Stanley Works
New Britain, Conn. 06050

Cars
Automobile Manufacturing Assoc.
320 New Center Building
Detroit, Mich. 48202

Coal
National Coal Association
1130 17 Street, N.W.
Washington, D.C. 20036

Compasses & Orienting
Silva, Inc.
LaPorta, Ind. 46350

Copper
Kennecott Copper Co.
Nevada Mines Division
McGill, Nevada 89318

Cotton
National Cotton Council
P.O. Box 12285
Memphis, Tenn.

Craft Ideas
Indiana State Board of Health
State House
Indianapolis, Ind.

Dairy Animals
The Story of Dairy Animals
Swift & Company Agricultural
Research Division
Chicago, Ill. 60604

Dentist
A Visit to a Dentist
American Dental Association
211 East Chicago Avenue
Chicago, Ill. 60611

Dog
Care of Your Dog
Massachusetts S.P.C.A.
180 Longwood Avenue
Boston, Mass. 02115

Ear
Human Ear
Sonotone Corporation
Elmsford, N.Y. 10523

Farming
Tommy Looks at Farming
Public Relations Department
The B. F. Goodrich Co.
Akron, Ohio

F.B.I.
United States Department of
Justice
Federal Bureau of Investigation
Washington, D.C. 20535

Flags
Flags of All the States
State Mutual Life Assurance
Company of America
Worcester, Mass. 01605

Flight & Aviation
United Aircraft
East Hartford, Conn. 06108

Florida Animal Tracks
& Poisonous Snakes
Game & Fresh Water Commission
Tallahassee, Fla. 23204

Forest Products
American Forest Products
Industries, Inc.
1835 K Street, N.W.
Washington, D.C. 20006

Fort Ticonderoga
The Library
Fort Ticonderoga
Ticonderoga, N.Y. 12882

Fresh Fruits & Vegetables
United Fresh Fruit & Vegetable
    Assn.
777 14 Street, N.W.
Washington, D.C. 20005

**Gas (natural and
    manufactured)**
American Gas Assoc., Inc.
605 Third Avenue
New York, N.Y. 10016

History of Measurement
Ford Motor Co.
The American Road
Dearborn, Mich.

How Gas Is Converted to Power
Ford Motor Co.
The American Road
Dearborn, Mich.

Granite
Barre Granite Association
Box 481
Barre, Vermont

Leather
Leather Industries of America
411 Fifth Avenue
New York, N.Y.

Lumbering
Weyerhaeuser Co.
Tacoma, Washington 98401

Meat
Swift & Company Advertising
    Supply Department
41 and South Laflin Street
Chicago, Ill. 60609

Medical Scientists
Metropolitan Life Insurance Co.
One Madison Avenue
New York, N.Y. 10010

Model Railroading
Kalmbach Publishing Co.
1027 North Seventh Street
Milwaukee, Wisc. 53233

Molds
Pfizer Laboratories
Division Charles Pfizer
232 East 42 Street
New York, N.Y.

Money
The Story of Money
Chase Manhattan Bank
One Chase Manhattan Plaza
New York, N.Y. 10015

Music
Fun with Music Booklet
H. & A. Selmer, Inc.
Box 310
Elkhart, Indiana 46514

**National Parks, Forests,
    Monuments and Camping**
The National Parks Association
1300 New Hampshire Ave., N.W.
Washington, D.C. 20202

**Oil, Story of
Oil and Gas**
Phillips Petroleum Co.
Bartlesville, Oklahoma 74003

Paper Making
Southern Pulpwood Conservation
    Assoc.
1365 Peachtree Street, N.E.
Atlanta, Georgia 30309

Paul Revere
Revere Copper and Brass, Inc.
230 Park Avenue
New York, N.Y. 10017

Plants & Poultry, Story of
Swift and Co.
Agricultural Research Division
115 West Jackson Boulevard
Chicago, Ill. 60604

Police & Fire Fighting
Fire Enterprise Education Corp.
Merchandise Mart Plaza
Chicago, Ill. 60654

Railroading
Association of American Railroads
Transportation Building
Washington, D.C. 20006

Ranger 'Rithmetic
U.S. Department of Agriculture
Washington, D.C. 20250

Rayon
D.R.C. Fibers Division
Midland-Ross
P.O. Box 580
Painesville, Ohio 44077

Rubber
The Rubber Manufacturers Assn.
444 Madison Avenue
New York, N.Y. 10022

Projects for the Poor
International Bank
1818 H Street, N.W.
Washington, D.C.

Salt
Morton International, Inc.
110 North Wacker Drive
Chicago, Ill. 60606

Sheep
American Corriedale Assoc., Inc.
P.O. Box 896
Columbia, Missouri 65201

Ships
U.S. Department of Commerce
Maritime Administration
Washington, D.C. 20235

Solar System & Stars
General Electric Co.
Schenectady, N.Y.

Space Exploration
National Aeronautics and Space
Administration
Washington, D.C. 20546

Steel
United States Steel
Public Relations
71 Broadway
New York, N.Y. 10006

Stories of Science & Invention
General Motors Corporation
General Motors Building
Detroit, Mich. 48202

Textiles
American Textiles Manufacturing
Institute
1510 Johnston Building
Charlotte, N.C.

Timber & Forestry
United States Department of
Agriculture
Washington, D.C. 20250

Trademarks, Story of
National Biscuit Company
425 Park Avenue
New York, N.Y. 10022

Trains
Great Northern Railway
Public Relations
175 East Fourth Street
St. Paul, Minnesota

Transportation, History of Land
General Motors Corporation
Public Relations Staff
General Motors Building
Detroit, Mich. 43202

Tree, Growth of a
American Forest Products
Industries, Inc.
1835 K Street, N.W.
Washington, D.C. 20006

Uranium
Union Carbide Corporation
Marketing Services
30–20 Thomson Avenue
Long Island, N.Y. 11101

Volcanoes of the U.S.
Washington Distribution Section
U.S. Geological Survey
1809 South Eads Street
Arlington, Virginia 22202

Washington, George
Washington National Insurance Co.
Evanston, Ill.

Water
American Water Works Assoc., Inc.
Two Park Avenue
New York, N.Y. 10016

Water Transportation Resources
The American Waterways
Operators, Inc.
1250 Connecticut Avenue
Suite 520
Washington, D.C.

Wildlife Management
Wildlife Management Institute
709 Wire Building
Washington, D.C.

Most of the material received from sources such as those listed here will be up-to-date literature. Space does not permit cataloging the many additional sources of information available to you. Keep in mind, however, that practically all states and most countries have travel and information divisions and tourist offices that will send you much material including pictures, maps, and facts and figures without charge. City chambers of commerce are also a good and cooperative source.

The *Elementary Teacher's Guide to Free Curriculum Materials*, published annually by Educators' Progress Service, Inc., Randolph, Wisconsin 53956, is invaluable. If your school does not have this volume, convince your principal to order it. It includes almost 2,000 items available to you at no cost! Ranging from topics on airplanes and marine life to teaching tools and world cooperation, it's little wonder there are any sources left to find for free materials available to you. The guide goes as far as to provide free sample units on the use of free materials. In one issue alone, units on economics, desert life, communication, conservation, shelter, the seas, and letter writing were included. The same company also publishes the yearly *Educators' Guide to Free Films* and the *Educators' Guide to Free Filmstrips*.

There are other valuable sources you may wish to explore for ideas on getting and using free materials. *A Useful List of Classroom Items That Can Be Scrounged or Purchased*, available from Early Childhood Study, EDC, 55 Chapel Street, Newton, Massachusetts 02160, categorizes "junk items" under subject headings and lists low cost games, toys, puzzles and science aids useful in opening up your classroom. The use of common community and home materials for purposes of art, crafts, and construction is covered in *Beautiful Junk*, written by Diane Warner and Jeanne Quill, and available without charge from Project Head Start, Office of Economic Opportunity, Washington, D.C. Care to invest one dollar? Try Sue McCord's *Trash to Treasure*, a well-illustrated source for using castoff materials in your classroom. It's obtainable from Project Change, State University of New York at Cortland, Cortland, New York.

If you really want to go on a spending binge, you can subscribe to *Big Rock Candy Mountain* for four dollars. Like its parent publication, *The Whole Earth Catalog*, it will provide you with useful sources of classroom materials and some really good ideas for teaching. It can be purchased from the Portola Institute, 1115 Merrill Street, Menlo Park, California 94025. *The Yellow Pages of Learning*, at $1.95, is a must! Edited by Richard S. Wurman and published by the Massachusetts Institute of Technology Press, Cambridge, Massachusetts 02142, it proclaims the city is an education—a virtual classroom without walls. Rife with indispensable learning resources, it guides pupils to any city and town. The *UNESCO Sourcebook for Science Teaching* ($5.25), UNESCO, United Nations, New York, N.Y., eliminates the teacher's lament, "I can't teach science because I don't have the materials I need!" This sourcebook is loaded with ideas for making science equipment and conducting experiments, which are useful in the institution of science centers. In fact, the UNICEF division of this organization has even more to offer in terms of the "do-it-yourself" approaches provided by their educational materials. Send for their free publications list, basic brochures, and bibliographies of visual and printed materials. Materials obtainable from them at minimal cost include books on how to make folk toys of different countries, children's art and writing around the world in both the native language and English, festival dolls and figures in authentic dress, color display sheets and photographs of children in schools of various countries, teachers' kits, and slide sets and filmstrips depicting life around the world.

Also helpful to you in establishing learning centers is a series of handbooks published by Educational Service, Inc., P.O. Box 219, Stevensville, Michigan 49127, costing from $4.00 to $5.00 each. *Spark* is full of ideas easily adaptable for inclusion in social studies learning centers. *Spice* deals with the language arts and contains many worthwhile activities for use in language arts centers. Similarly, *Probe* (science), *Plus* (arithmetic), *Anchor* (vocabulary), and *Rescue* (remedial reading) are chock-full of practical ideas, techniques, games, and activities that can be used for the construction of learning centers which focus on each of these subjects. Other books in this series are also available. If you are interested in career education as a focal point of study, write for the book; *Career Education: An Idea Book*, Portland Public Schools, Portland, Oregon.

The beginning teacher may not be aware of the many sources of materials and information available because little attention is given to acquisition of materials in most education courses. The United States government is an excellent source. Subscribe to its monthly announcements (free), or purchase the Monthly Catalog of U.S. Government Printing Office Publications ($4.50) from the Superintendent of Documents, Government Printing Office, Washington, D.C. 20402. It is loaded with activities appropriate for inclusion in your learning centers. While exploring government sources, include the many embassies located in Washington that can provide you with first-hand information and contacts with their countries. Closer to home, touch base with the various government agencies in your own community. Listed in the phone book, agencies such as the Social Conservation Service of the U.S. Agricultural Department and the Fish and Wildlife Service of the U.S. Interior Department have many free materials on a wide range of interests to include in learning centers.

Are your pupils interested in environmental education? Have them write for *A Starter Catalog of Free Materials* from the Resource Center for Man-Made Environment Education, Department of Architecture, North Dakota State University, Fargo, North Dakota 58102. Or do they want to learn about birds, snakes, sharks, alligators? Encourage them to write the Louisiana Wildlife and Fisheries Commission, Information and Education Section, P.O. Box 44095, Baton Rouge, Louisiana 70112. The commission will send, free, any one of several dozen bulletins ranging in size from eight to sixty pages on various wildlife in Louisiana. Multiply this by the amount of wildlife materials available from the other forty-nine states, and you can readily imagine the wealth of information obtainable, without cost, on that one interest alone!

It should be increasingly clear to you that sources of free and inexpensive materials are extensive. Books on open education will put you in touch with still other sources. Open education workshops and university summer courses often provide lists of sources as well. *The Scholastic Teacher*, 50 West 44th Street, New York, N.Y., is a good vehicle for obtaining information about workshops, as is the Association for Childhood Education International (ACEI), 3615 Wisconsin Avenue, N.W., Washington, D.C. Centers such as the Mountain View Center for Environmental Education in Colorado and the Workshop Center for Open Education in New York City (6 Shepard Hall, City College, Convent Avenue and 140th Street, New York, N.Y. 10031) are also good sources of information.

For a comprehensive bibliography on open education, contact the Advisory For Open Education, 90 Sherman Street, Cambridge, Massachusetts 02140. The compilers of this bibliography ($1.25), Roland Barth and Charles Rathbone, list books, films, periodicals, and materials applicable to your classroom. It is also available from the previously mentioned Educational Development Center under the title *A Bibliography of Open Education*, as is the booklet, *Analysis of an Approach to Open Education* (free), by Anne Bussis and Edward Chittendon. Simultaneously, you may wish to ask for the center's free monograph, *Open Education at EDC*, which lists its entire stock of films and publications for purposes of rental and purchase. You'll find much of value therein, including a set of three monographs on the characteristics of open education.

How far do you want to go in gathering materials? Citation Press, a division of Scholastic Book Services (50 W. 44th Street, New York, N.Y. 10036), has published a series of twenty-three paperbound booklets on informal schools in Great Britain. Although not dealing with American education, there is much to be gained in exploring this material that is applicable to open education practices. The National Froebel Foundation, 2 Manchester Square, London, W.1., England, also has published a series of short pieces on elementary education which may prove helpful to you. Hopefully the places listed will assist you to get started in gathering materials and information useful to opening up your classroom. Now, dig in and you're on the way!

In the interim, while waiting to accumulate materials from outside sources, reach inward. Ask the parents of your pupils to contribute materials to the activities of your classroom. Prepare to be inundated, for almost all parents will cooperate in donating throw-away items which can be put to use in the learning centers you plan to establish. To expedite this process, you might prepare a list of materials along with a statement which invites parents to contribute any of the items posted for their attention. Team Omega, one of three teaching teams of Franklin School in Lexington, Massachusetts, did precisely this. Strapped by insufficient materials to carry on diversified science experimentation, we initiated "Operation Shoebox," which involved our pupils in filling up shoe, cigar, candy boxes, and other containers with scrap or junk material their parents were willing to give to the team. You can imagine the results! Within a period of a very few days, we had accumulated enough materials to make storing them a problem. Needless to say, "lack of materials" never again became our excuse for not attempting more imaginative approaches to teaching.

Some of the items parents are willing to contribute to your classroom are listed here. Many, many more are available to you, even broken-down television sets, typewriters in need of minor repair, and various small engines such as those on lawn mowers. Occasionally, in fact, people will go as far as to *pay you* for hauling off an old upright piano!

Materials Obtainable from Homes

used egg & milk cartons	ice cream containers
popsicle sticks	stuffed toy animals
used paper cups	flashlight bulbs
clothes hangers	discarded toy blocks
beads, buttons, ribbons	fragmented erector sets
macaroni and noodles	extra golf tees
strainers	used sponges
screens	unused flower pots
flour	discarded clothing
plaster	pipe cleaners
oil	cheese cloth
vinegar	string
salt & sugar	muffin tins
coffee cans	empty thread spools
TV dinner trays	needles & thread
used light bulbs	discarded shoe laces
throw-away pie pans	dominoes
toothpicks	checkers
dry cells & batteries	games & toys

plastic & paper bags	puzzles
jars and bottles	dolls
bottle caps	bell wire
candle stubs	emory cloth
used straws	used toothbrushes
empty cereal boxes	assorted gears
nails & screws	discarded funnels
nuts, bolts, washers	sandpaper
marbles	mirrors
cancelled stamps	paper towel tubes
playing cards	measuring cups
old books	discarded food utensils
old photographs	pots & pans
books & magazines	barrels
clothespins	plastic dishpans
old seed packages	

Now what about storage space for the items brought in by the pupils? You may continue to use the original shoe, cigar, and candy boxes for this purpose, or you may wish to separate and classify the materials for better accessibility. Some teachers find it expedient to use ice cream buckets; others utilize discarded wine bottle boxes; still others use assorted empty can containers. A variety of cardboard boxes in all sizes and shapes are easily obtained from supermarkets. Those used to pack bottles, in particular, provide ready-made compartments for storage. You can use the ice cream buckets, individually labeled, in upright positions. If this poses the problem of spillage or if they are too deep for your pupils to reach into, you may prefer to lay the buckets on edge and glue them side-to-side (see Figure 5–2) so that the contents of each are visible and accessible to your pupils. Or, if you prefer, you can construct a cabinet of side-to-side boxes as shown in Figure 5–3.

FIGURE 5–2   Storage Center Composed of Empty Ice Cream Buckets

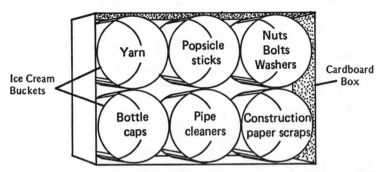

Note the various sized compartments in the cabinet. The wine bottle box (B), for example, may be used to store items such as toothbrushes, pipe cleaners, and clothes pins, along with bottles, light bulbs, and jars that fit snugly into each of the divided spaces. Larger materials such as funnels, measuring cups, and

FIGURE 5-3   Storage Cabinet Composed of Cardboard Boxes Set Side-to-Side

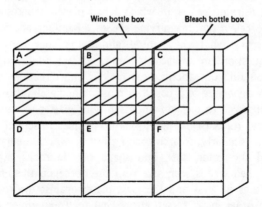

packages of flour, salt, and sugar can be stored in the box designated "C." Still larger items, which include boxes of games, toy animals, and pots and pans may be placed in the completely open cartons (D, E, F) for safekeeping. Flat materials are easily stored in carton "A" once the upright cardboard dividers are removed. You may also find it expedient to use plastic wash basins or vegetable bins for storage. Should you substitute tables for desks, these boxes are particularly useful for the storage of pupils' personal belongings. They are also useful as tote trays when pupils find it necessary to move their materials from learning center to center.

Why the emphasis on gathering materials? The answer is clear. What do you want your pupils to learn? To value? To become? Learning begins with a question. The greater the abundance and variety of materials, the greater the likelihood your pupils will find something to interest them. The most accessible materials are found in nature. Just think of the questions that are apt to arise when the pupils come into contact with animal bones and skins, driftwood, rocks and minerals, pine cones and needles, leaves, sand and soil, vegetation of all kinds, bark fragments, sticks and twigs, seeds, acorns, unprocessed wool and cotton, feathers, mineral and plant pigments, clay, pebbles, flint modules and flakes, fossils, and other primary source materials.

MAKING USE OF NATURAL OBJECTS

Materials found in nature have a strong appeal for most youngsters. Capitalize and build on this natural interest by instituting learning centers which make use of these materials. Use imaginative approaches and experimentation. Much can be accomplished that is applicable to the subject content of your classroom. The development of skills need not be ignored. In fact, the teaching of science, arithmetic, and the language arts can be enriched through the use of natural objects. Earlier, in Chapter 3 (pp. 84-85), I made reference to the attraction rocks had for my pupils and cited the natural consequences of this attraction.

In my classrooms, for example, I found it intriguing to watch my pupils function at a learning center in which I had placed squares of glass, pennies, portions of porcelain tile, magnifying glasses, a hammer, and rock specimens for them to discover what they could about the specimens. Other than an open-ended question on a placard used to attract pupils and initiate action: "What can you find out about these rocks?," no directions were given to the pupils on how they were to proceed. Almost immediately, those attracted to the center were observed to pick up the magnifying glasses to study the specimens, hold diaphanous rocks to the light, pick up pennies to scratch the samples, use their fingernails similarly, scratch rock against rock, use the hammer to chip off pieces, record the color, feel, and shape of the rocks, weigh the various specimens in their hands, rub them on the porcelain tiles, scratch the rocks against the plates of glass and the glass plates against the rocks, all the while engaging each other in conversation on what their experimentation revealed to them.

I'd like to think that the natural questioning attitudes of the pupils had found an outlet through the opportunity presented in the learning center. I can readily imagine each of my pupils confronting the materials in the center and asking, "I wonder why the glass plate, porcelain, magnifying glass, and penny are here. Can I somehow make use of them? These rocks look different. Is there some way I can lump those that look alike together? And, if I do, will I find something out?" The almost immediate result was that each child developed his own classification system through his own procedures, yet emerged with many of the same observations as those made by professionals in the field. Their observations, for example, that rock specimens vary in hardness, cleavage, feel diaphaneity, shape, composition, and streak are much the same as those of geologists and mineralogists.

Contrast this approach with that used in my earlier teaching days which invariably took the pattern, "Today, boys and girls (the entire class, no less!), *we* are going to learn how to classify rocks and minerals, first by determining the hardness of each, then by. . . ." This was done in spite of the individual interests expressed by my pupils.

The learning center approach went beyond the initial stimulus and response. Within hours of their experiences with the rock and mineral specimens, my pupils proceeded to enrich the materials and expand the activities of the center. They gathered books and source materials for further exploration, collected rock samples, investigated the composition of buildings made of stone, looked into the production of cement, observed the construction of a dam, and studied the way roads used to be laid and how they are now. From this start, some of the pupils went into a more extensive study of the earth sciences.

You can carry this further. Consider still other experiments that can be done with rocks, stones, and pebbles. Place a variety of stones and other appropriate materials at a "rock center." Encourage your pupils to experiment with different sizes and shapes. Let them find out dissimilarities in the volume and weight of the stones. Rather than describe the procedures that are necessary, place a tape measure, containers of water, and empty containers and basins in the center. Invariably, I think you will discover that your pupils will develop their own strategies for accomplishing this task, no matter what their grade level. Some of your pupils will take it upon themselves to measure the length, width, and circumference of the different rocks with the tape measure you have provided in the center. Others will likely experiment with principles of displacement by dropping rocks into a container of water and measuring the differences in the rise of the water to determine which specimens are heavier and lighter. Still other pupils may catch and measure the extent of spillover of water. The very youngest may simply arrange stones in order of size to determine the smallest to the largest. Consequently, you can expect most of your pupils to be involved with counting, seriating, estimating, weighing, and measuring. Contrast this approach to arithmetic with the textbook approach. Note that much more than arithmetic is involved. Pupils inquire, investigate, infer, and invent. They also discover, diverge, and demonstrate. Continuous evaluation takes place as they group, sort, and classify, deriving scientific concepts and generalizations in the process of their experimentation.

Do rocks sink or float? If the former, what is the rate of descent? Do rocks burn? Change color? Crumble? How are fossils imprinted in the rocks? Why are rocks different in color? Where does soil come from? Can you make soil here at the learning center? Why is the color of desert sand different from that of the soil in the mountain? Children find a natural outlet to the study of geology, the study of the earth on which they live and the plant and animal life which sustains it. Imagine, if you will, the quantity of the self-directed activities you can expect to emanate from their experimentation. There is simply no end to the possibilities. Natural transitions to the study of geography, history, ecology, and man-made shelters and edifices are likely to be made by your pupils.

Extend the "rock center" further. Encourage your pupils to search for and create expressions which involve rocks and stones. Help them to get started by listing a few idioms, phrases, and sentences. Expressions such as "stone cold," "rock bottom," "heart of stone," and "a stone's throw from here" may be enough to stimulate pupils to search the literature and invent brand-new expressions to be added to the list, thus enriching their language and possibly leading to further exploration of colloquial and dialectical speech patterns and the study of the people who use them. Who are the people who use such expressions as "a stone's throw from here"? Where do they live? What do they do? Do they go to schools similar to ours? What is the origin of the expression? This is a fascinating approach to the study of people. Present your pupils with other expressions to consider. "Sticks and stones may break my bones," "Rolling stones gather no moss," "Gravel Gertie," "hard-rock music," "rock and roll." Your pupils will explore the origins and meaning of each of these expressions.

The "rock expressions" formulated may be artistically enriched. Paint a rock face! Create an animal! Construct an insect! Place plaster of paris, paints and brushes, and materials such as pipe cleaners in the center. Invite your pupils to create and construct new forms of animals, insects, plants, and mosaics out of the stones available. Or, for those who wish, encourage their making fossil imprints.

Extend the rock center further. The vocabulary development of your pupils is a natural consequence of their contact with stones at the center. Your pupils will explore size, texture, color, cleavage, and shape, as well as comparatives (heavier, smoother, lighter, shorter, longer, rougher than). Encourage pupils making use of the center to develop and extend the vocabulary associated with characteristics of the stones.

A representative list might include:

Size	Texture	Color	Cleavage	Shape	Other
large	soft	white	straight	pointed	opaque
small	rough	rose	curved	regular	translucent
area	smooth	yellow	break	uniform	transparent
measure	rounded	red	plane	proportionate	heavy
volume	sharp	black	sever	symmetrical	light
diameter	crumbly	brown	split	flat	porous
magnitude	silky	pink	fracture	round	igneous
mass	greasy	gold	well-defined	cube	sedimentary
dimensions	composition	silver		cylinder	metamorphic
tiny	arrangement	copper		oblong	basalt
little	structure	green			erosion
	grain				strata

... Plymouth Rock ... Mt. Rushmore ... The Rosetta Stone ... The Great Wall of China ... Easter Island ... Stonehenge ... Gibralter ... Camelback Mountain ... The City of Rocks ... Jerusalem's Wailing Wall ... The Blarney Stone ... they intrigue and pique the interest of children. People, places, and events! Place pictures of these historic rocks in the rock center. What stories do they tell? Geography and history are studied. Maps are explored, location skills are developed, and history is recaptured by your pupils.

Most children enjoy discovery-type learning experiences. Some of your pupils, however, will likely prefer and need to be directed by you. Thus, instead of encouraging them to learn on their own at a rock center, your initial lesson plan to involve them in learning experiences built around rocks might assume this pattern.[9]

ROCKS! ROCKS! ROCKS!

Note the rocks in this center. Pick them up. Look at each carefully. Any one of these is either an igneous (IG-nee-uhs), a
sedimentary (sed-uh-MENT-uh-ree), or a metamorphic (met-
uh-MAWR-fik) rock. To learn which is which, do the following:

1.   Select one rock
    a.   Does it look glossy?
    b.   Is it made of shiny grains?
    c.   Do you see streaks or "veins" running through it?
    d.   Can you see crystals in it?

    If you can answer yes to each of these questions, you
    probably have found an igneous rock. If you are not
    sure of your answers . . .

2.   Look at the rock again
    a.   Is it made up of layers?
    b.   Does it look like hard clay?
    c.   Is it soft enough for you to scratch with a penny?
    d.   Does it split into thin pieces?
    e.   Is it brown, or red, or black, or grey, or white?

    If you can answer yes to each of these questions, you
    probably have found a sedimentary rock. If not com-
    pletely satisfied with your answers . . .

3.   Look at the rock once again
    a.   Is the rock made up of layers?
    b.   Is it real hard? So hard that you can't scratch
          it with a penny?
    c.   Does it have many colors?
    d.   Can you see shiny bands or streaks of black
          and white running through it?

    If you can answer yes to each of these questions, you
    probably have found a metamorphic rock.

Now, how many of the rocks can you identify as igneous, sedimentary,
or metamorphic? Show me when you see me free. What kinds of
rocks can you bring in to help our rock center grow?

Similarly, learning centers may be created with other natural objects and the various throw-away or discarded items you have collected. Many approaches to learning are invited. In a "button and bead" center, pupils may classify buttons according to size, color, shape, and number of holes, or may design patterns of beads. In a "bottle and lid" center composed of assorted bottles, jars, and lids, they may be given opportunities to match and screw lids to the appropriate bottles and jars. Your pupils have cellophane to crinkle, newspapers to crunch, magazines to cut up, and objects to touch, smell, taste, hear, and see. They classify smells and tastes, describe sounds and sights. They wonder, imagine, and ask questions. What can I make with the clay? What can I build with the sticks and twigs? Sticks, poles, and logs? How many ways can they be used? *Read* to find out. They read about spears, bows and arrows, teepee frames, log cabins, rafts, baseball bats, dugout canoes, ships' masts, fence posts, telephone poles, parking signs, brooms, fishing rods, "witches" on stakes, Joan D'Arc burned at the stake!

Coupled with some of the almost overwhelming amount of commercial materials that may be available to you, more imaginative teaching and learning are likely to take place. When constructing your learning centers, it is important to utilize the materials of which they are to be composed as *means*, rather than as ends. They must consist of more than displays of materials. *Why* the learning centers? Are they to be established for purposes of motivation, diagnosis, prescription, or enrichment? The purpose of each center must be clear. Once this has been accomplished, you are ready to get underway.

POINTS TO REMEMBER

- Preparing a positive climate for learning is a necessary prerequisite for opening up the classroom.
- The relationships between teacher and pupils and pupils and pupils are the most important ingredients of the open classroom.
- To open up the classroom, begin with the truth—what we know about children and about ourselves.
- Communicating a sincere desire to help is a crucial component in encouraging pupils to learn.
- Too sharp a transition to self-initiated learning experiences may increase the anxieties of children.
- What the pupils find in their classroom teaches them what you think of education and of them.
- Materials for open education are readily available.

NOTES

1. See: Rudolph Driekurs, *Psychology in the Classroom* (New York: Harper and Row, Publishers, 1968), and Don Dinkmeyer and Rudolph Dreikurs, *Encouraging Children to Learn: the Encouragement Process* (Englewood Cliffs, N.J.: Prentice-Hall, Inc., 1963) for more extensive treatment of these topics.

2. Dinkmeyer and Dreikurs, *Encouraging Children to Learn: The Encouragement Process*, p. 122.

3. Carl Rogers, *Freedom to Learn* (Columbus: Charles E. Merrill Co., 1969), p. 105.

4. For a thorough and profound discussion of logical consequences, see: Rudolph Dreikurs and Loren Grey, *Logical Consequences: A New Approach to Discipline* (New York; Hawthorn Books, Inc., 1968).

5. Dreikurs, *Psychology in the Classroom*, p. 73.

6. Roland S. Barth, "So You Want to Change to an Open Classroom," *Phi Delta Kappan*, October 1971, pp. 97–99.

7. National Froebel Foundation, *Children Learning Through Scientific Interest*, London, 1966, pp. 141–142.

8. *Building with Cardboard* ($ .60) and *Building With Tubes* ($ .60) are obtainable from *Advisory for Open Education*, 90 Sherman Street, Cambridge, Massachusetts 02140. *Our Catalog* can be purchased from the Workshop for Learning Things, Inc., Watertown, Massachusetts. The Education Development Center (EDC) in Newton, Massachusetts, also supplies monographs on cardboard carpentry.

9. Adopted and modified from a plan submitted by Phyllis Bucholz and Doris Burress, Mesa Verde Elementary School, Farmington, New Mexico in my workshop course on learning centers/open classroom, San Juan College, New Mexico State University, July 8–26, 1974.

..... Recently
my Grandmother came. I hate her. She seems to think she knows everything. She is always praising herself and denouncing me. I also don't like religion, talk, talk, talk. Always the supremacy of our religion. Always miracles. Always the truth of the bible. And always the greatness of God and his great doings, doings that have no evidence. And always services, Sunday School and donations to the house of God, all to remind us of that fathomless nothing, this supposed great ruler, formed out of the imagination of man, and basking in the shallow light of a long, perhaps snobbish reign of being a big religion.

— Eddie, Age 10

six

Getting Underway:
Preparations for Decentralizing
the Classroom

Thus far, I have attempted to introduce you to the ingredients necessary for opening up your classroom. I trust you are now familiar with the different forms of learning centers and the media for their implementation. Furthermore, it is hoped that you also recognize the very important preparatory steps needed to establish the climate for open learning in your classroom. These include:

1. Knowing your pupils as individuals
2. Discussing the management of the classroom with your pupils
3. Encouraging your pupils to select, manage, and evaluate their learning experiences
4. Developing your pupils' interpersonal relationships through activities which require cooperation and consensus
5. Personalizing your pupils' learning

This chapter discusses the various preparations you need to make to organize and get your classroom activities underway. The commencement of your organization is, of course, predicated on the assumption that you have acquired the support you need to decentralize and open up your classroom. That is, you should have presented your plans for doing so to and gained the support of your principal, the school system's administration, and the parents of your pupils. Equally important, you should have acquainted your teaching colleagues with your intentions and have also received their encouragement. It is, then, reasonable to expect that you are ready to organize your classroom for implementing your learning centers.

ORGANIZATION OF THE CLASSROOM

Central to opening up your classroom is the assumption that your pupils are creative, constructive, cooperative, and responsible boys and girls who are capable of directing themselves toward their personal and social goals. This assumption is tied closely to the direction you wish your classroom to take for there is little question that the learning environment you formulate will, in some way, shape your pupils' capacities to be creative, constructive, cooperative, and responsible. The richer and more varied the organization of your classroom, the richer and more varied will be your pupils' responses.

How, then do you want your classroom to be shaped? How carefully should you plan? Too often, real learning is least effective when it arises from carefully planned situations which are strictly organized by teachers. If you agree with this point of view, you may need to think twice about rigidly prescribing learning centers for your pupils. At times this may be necessary, but if too often practiced, it may lead to negative reactions by your pupils. Announcing just what is to be done and precisely how it is to be done may result in your pupils becoming unimaginative and uncreative, bored, irresponsible, and even hostile. Some researchers, in fact, believe this is the primary reason for the negative behavior of pupils. I tend to agree that it is *one* of the reasons. I feel, therefore, that in organizing your classroom to provide for open learning experiences, it is necessary that you subscribe to theory Y rather than to theory X of the "self-fulfilling prophecies" shown in Figure 6-1.

Look at Figure 6-1. Study its components. Working on the assumption that you wish to include the components of theory Y in the organization and operation of your classroom, how do you set them into motion? What form will your classroom take as you put them into practice? Should you completely decentralize and diversify the activities of your pupils? Or should you use a more gradualistic approach to the establishment of your learning centers? How do you guide your pupils to open learning centers? How do you guide your pupils to open learning experiences of benefit to them? Indeed, your task is a challenging one!

Directly related to this task is your outlook on children and the assumptions you hold about educating them. Note in Figure 6-1 the contrasting assumptions about pupils. Examine those listed under theory Y. Clearly, they will guide you to relationships and practices with your pupils that will help them realize their full potential. Note the key words in the theory which call on you to trust in, plan and cooperate with, encourage, and guide your pupils. Their self-fulfillment

FIGURE 6-1   *Educational Assumptions and Practices*

THEORY X		THEORY Y	
Pupils are . . .	Therefore I must . . .	Pupils are . . .	Therefore I must .
Passive	Motivate them	Active, changing	Guide them
Short-sighted	Plan for them	Far-sighted	Plan with them
Unimaginative	Prescribe for them	Creative, inventive	Foster inquiry
Dependent	Direct them	Independent	Encourage self-direction
Conformists	Routinize their activities	Growing	Open alternatives to them
Irresponsible	Check up on them	Responsible	Trust them
Against you	Guard against them	With you	Cooperate with them

will, in large measure, hinge on whether or not you practice these very important elements.

How will your pupils fulfill themselves? This, too, is your challenge! Treat your pupils as inquisitive, curious young people and, most likely, they will become so. Given opportunities to create and invent, they are apt to become creative and inventive. Given responsibility, they tend to become responsible. To meet this challenge, then, it is necessary that you establish some guidelines. You will need to consider (1) what your pupils have already learned, (2) what your pupils would like to learn, and (3) what your pupils need to learn. Given this information, you may then proceed to determine the measures essential to implementing the necessary learning centers. Among these are the following:

The sequence and scope of the learning to take place

The amount and kind of materials needed to set this learning into motion

The difficulty levels of the learning materials

The rates at which the selected learning materials are to be processed

The physical and social context in which the learning experiences are to take place

The kind and extent of supervision necessitated

The amount, kind, and frequency of evaluation needed to guide your pupils' progress

Genuine pupil participation in the organization of the classroom is needed to implement these measures. Invite their participation *before* you attempt to diversify their learning experiences. You should plan the organization and activities of your classroom with your pupils frequently. Some teachers prefer this to be done two or three times a week. The staff of the S. Y. Jackson School in Albuquerque, New Mexico goes as far as to conduct family group planning with its pupils four times a day, each day. Whatever your particular circumstances, the very first step you need to consider in determining the objectives, organization, and direction of your classroom is the institution of teacher-pupil discussions at least once a day and preferably more often. In my judgment, you cannot possibly diversify the activities of your classroom in terms of democratic principles and functions without regular discussions with your pupils. Their full participation, in fact, is necessary to ensure the stability of the classroom.

TEACHER-PUPIL PLANNING

Why teacher-pupil planning? A smooth, cooperative functioning of activities and interrelationships in your classroom is less likely to occur without it, since each of your pupils is wrapped up in his own needs, interests, and intentions. It is important that all your pupils be given the opportunity to discuss and elaborate on what is needed for the effective progress of each in the classroom. This, I suggest, is a natural transition to the establishment of a learning environment in which each will tend to feel he had a *constructive* role, thus integrating all of their needs, interests, and aspirations. Learning in the environment you plan to develop is not necessarily easy. Cooperation, therefore, is central to its success. To gain, each of your pupils must learn to give. Hopefully, their participation in the planning of your classroom will lead them to practice the behavior needed for it to function well.

In planning with your pupils, it is essential that you encourage them in the pursuit of their own education. Solicit their ideas on the operation of the classroom, the objectives of the learning centers to be established, the evaluation of the work to be undertaken, the problems that may arise, their interpersonal relationships, and their responsibility for the management of the classroom. As a consequence of this participation, you may expect to find your pupils increasingly thinking of the classroom as *their* classroom—a good place in which to learn and to express themselves.

Consider the following important aspects of planning with your pupils. In my opinion, teacher-pupil planning is necessary in opening up your classroom because it:

Clarifies directions, procedures, management, and limitations of learning experiences

Increases pupils' knowledge and understanding of each other's contributions

Opens interrelationships between teacher and pupils, and pupils and pupils

Invites sharing of pupil responsibility for the purposes, procedures, and activities of the classroom

Develops pupils' capacities to make decisions
Stimulates the teacher and pupils to help each other
Develops the teacher and pupils' feelings of self-acceptance and adequacy
Develops mutual trust, respect, and cooperation of teacher and pupils
Builds classroom unity, cohesiveness, and togetherness.

Thus, feelings are aired; problems are discussed; solutions are projected; attitudes are clarified; values are supported or modified; doubts are alleviated; assistance is offered. I hope you agree that teacher-pupil planning is an important forum for determining the organization and practices of your classroom.

How ready are your pupils to function in an open classroom environment? What do you do with the pupil who destroys other pupils' work? What about children who bring in their hostilities from the outside or those who start fights? How would you handle pupils who bother others? What about the boys and girls who get so excited about projects at learning centers that they disturb others? How do your pupils find out what is required of them? What might they expect in the way of choices available to them? What about the pupil who is inclined to do nothing when given more freedom than he has been used to? How are you going to handle grading? These very important questions provide all the more reason for your instituting teacher-pupil planning on a daily basis. It is a necessary vehicle for pupils to learn about themselves, their feelings, their relationships with each other, and what is expected of them by you and by their classmates.

I do not imply here that open discussion will solve all the questions and problems that may arise in your classroom. Nor do I claim that the learning center approach to opening up your classroom is a panacea for the misbehaviors and problems that may exist in the more conventional classrooms. However, it is fair to say that when questions and problems are brought into the open for examination, evaluation, and action, misbehavior and ineffective learning are less likely to occur than if they are not. I do not look at teacher-pupil planning through rose-tinted glasses. I do suggest, however, that it is a *necessary practice* for putting your pupils, time, and materials to their best possible use. Your function is most important in this respect. You can help your pupils to determine and clarify their goals, provide the resources needed for them to carry them out, suggest courses of action, guide their progress and, at the same time, invite their input in the decisions that have to be made in order for them to achieve their goals. Furthermore, full participation by your pupils in formulating the guidelines within which they are to function and in planning the activities for the classroom will naturally lead to their interest in following through on their plans.

For example, witness the introduction to the study of the local community as planned by one of my student teachers and her seven- and eight-year-old pupils. Soliciting their input as to what their city was made up of, the student teacher received responses such as streets, parking lots, schools, fire stations, jail, hospital, and people. While recording their answers on the blackboard, the student teacher invited further comments about procedures for constructing a "city." The pupils responded:

"We could make it like a map with streets and buildings."

"We could make buses out of match boxes."

"We could make buildings out of shoe boxes."

The student teacher, capitalizing on the pupils' involvement, then proceeded to implement each pupil's contribution:

"Diana wants to make a map with streets and buildings. Who would like to work with her?"

"Tony wants to make buses. Who'd like to help him?"

"Gloria would like to construct some buildings. Who would like to do this with Gloria?"

You may not agree with this particular approach used by the student teacher to initiate interest in community planning. It does, however, illustrate an attempt to invite pupil input into the learning experiences. From the responses that evolved, learning centers based on the specific interests and contributions of the children were set into motion; for instance, those pupils interested in constructing a map, in making buses, or in constructing buildings were encouraged to work in the area of their interests.

You never know what may emerge from teacher-pupil planning sessions. I once witnessed one in which the pupils suggested they group themselves back-to-back so that they did not face each other. It was a rather strange arrangement to view, but this was the pupils' choice and was respected as such by their teacher. Needless to say, it is through this kind of trust and respect for your pupils' decisions that you can develop their awareness and appreciation of their own powers. Consequently, you can expect that they will create something out of their learning experiences that they consider good.

It is important that the operational guidelines of your classroom be authentic, manageable, and constituted so that your pupils are able to function within their framework. That is, the operational guidelines must be both believable and liveable. In establishing them, you may find that a good many of your pupils will tend to parrot rules, perhaps as a result of earlier home and school indoctrination. Younger children especially, may express rules of behavior in a negative manner, such as "no fighting," "no talking," "no tattletales." Or, also because of previous conditioning, their expression may take on the closed, authoritarian, somewhat artificial form of an editorial "we," for instance, "We will work quietly at the learning centers. We will finish our work each day. We will be fair with everyone." You may surmise, consequently, that sensing the artificiality of the "we wills," your pupils are apt to attach little or no meaning to them.

FIGURE 6-2   Behavioral Guidelines for Working in Learning Centers

Conduct at Learning Centers

Negatively Stated	Positively Stated
1. Be quiet at each center.	1. Talk softly when you need to.
2. Don't crowd.	2. Provide room for others.
3. Don't touch other pupils' things.	3. Respect other pupils' things.
4. Don't fight.	4. Cooperate, work together.
5. Don't work on top of the paper.	5. Keep inside the margins.
6. Don't copy.	6. Try to do the work by yourself. If you can't, ask a classmate or M. _____ to help you.
7. Don't take other pupils' places.	7. Wait your turn.
8. Don't run around the room.	8. If you must leave the center, have a good reason.
9. Mind the teacher.	9. Listen carefully to directions.
10. Don't tease.	10. Listen to each other's opinion.
11. Don't waste time.	11. Use your time wisely.

Figure 6-2 illustrates a set of rules formulated by primary school children regarding their behavior at learning centers to be established in their classroom. Note the oft-stated "don'ts." I wonder if this emphasis may have led these particular children to think of their classroom in terms of "do not's" rather than "do's." It is important to appreciate that guidelines such as these, stated "negatively" as they are, nevertheless have meaning to the pupils in that they are the rules to which they have been accustomed—at home, in school, and elsewhere. Thus, what your pupils have to offer must not be rejected or ignored. Instead, build on this foundation. Negatively stated guidelines will provide an opening for you to present the other side of the coin. You can provide a good learning experience for your pupils by introducing the positive experiences to be found in the classroom. In Figure 6-2, positively stated behavioral guidelines are presented alongside those suggested by the pupils to illustrate how you may encourage your pupils to move from negative to positive action. I do not suggest here that guidelines for your pupils' behavior be posted. In my opinion, it is far better to discuss them with your pupils so that they are subsequently internalized by them.

Teacher-pupil planning is closely tied to classroom management. An important first step is to discuss your role and that of your pupils. Inasmuch as the pupils may not have had previous experience with open education, they will likely need to learn both their privileges and their responsibilities. What you expect of them and what they expect of you must be communicated. What is tolerable and what is not must be clear. Directions for moving to learning centers need to be made explicit, the whereabouts of essential materials needs to be understood, and the tools of evaluation to be used by your pupils must be readily available to them. You may need to instruct your pupils in the use of projectors, tape recorders, record players, programmed machines, games, science equipment, self-instructional aids and kits, and other media to facilitate classroom management. You may also need to teach them how to work together for maximum results.

To help you further in your classroom management of the learning centers you plan to establish, a list of criteria pertinent to their implementation is shown in Figure 6-3. Specific guidelines for the construction of each center, you may recall, were introduced on page 112. The criteria shown in the figure are by no means conclusive. They are, instead, representative of the kinds of management decisions you will have to make to help you effectively implement learning centers in your classroom.

Your putting into practice the criteria shown in Figure 6-3 is, of course, no guarantee that your classroom will function smoothly. Nor is orientating your pupils to their responsibilities, providing the materials necessary for them to meet their objectives, teaching them to use these materials, and educating them to work independently and with each other any guarantee. As in any classroom, you can expect that problems will arise in yours from time to time, including the problem of classroom management. Among the management decisions that you will have to come to grips with is the physical arrangement of your classroom.

THE PHYSICAL ARRANGEMENT

As previously stated, the open classroom has no unique or particular physical form, and its shape may change from day to day as the needs and interests of the pupils change. Perhaps too much emphasis is currently being placed by advocates of open education on the physical arrangement of the classroom and not enough on the processes of learning that take place in the classroom. Getting rid of desks, setting up refrigerator cartons, installing area rugs, and utilizing all kinds of material for partitioning and for storage are useful only if they are intended to maximize children's learning and to capture their interest. Otherwise, they are of minimal importance. This is not to say that the arrangement of space and materials in the classroom does not shape the character and direction of the learning that takes place. Certainly, a prepared physical environment full of

FIGURE 6-3   *Criteria for Planning and Implementing the Total Classroom Environment*

Criteria	Yes	No
My learning centers are:		
1. Planned so that the purpose of each is clear to me.		
2. Planned to "fit" into the scope and sequence of the curriculum.		
3. Planned and implemented with sufficiently diverse learning experiences to meet the wide range of interests and academic needs of the pupils.		
4. Implemented, where appropriate, with directions which clearly inform pupils on the purpose of, and the procedures for, the activities to be undertaken.		
5. Instituted to help pupils develop appropriate study and work habits, as well as to develop their academic skills and conceptual understandings.		
6. Planned and constructed to expose pupils to new and challenging experiences, experimentation and exploration, and to successfully extend and enrich experiences with which they are familiar.		
7. Constructed so that immediate short-term and continuous long-term activities and projects are feasible.		
8. Formulated to provide a balance between individual work and group activities.		
9. Constructed and implemented for the purpose of developing the interpersonal relationships of the pupils wherever appropriate.		
10. Planned and constructed to give pupils opportunity for selecting as much of the experiences of the classroom felt to be appropriate.		
11. Planned to be adequately stocked with easily accessible materials in good condition, stored in clearly designated places.		
12. Implemented, where appropriate, with self-correcting keys and instruments for the pupils' self-assessment of their progress.		
13. Arranged sufficiently insulated from each other in terms of their specific purposes so that learning without interference is maximized for the pupils.		
14. Implemented so that pupils are given opportunity to stand at some centers, sit at others, work on the floor and move freely from center to center as needed.		
15. Planned and constructed with the view of holding pupils responsible for the cleanup and storage of their materials in the places designated for this purpose.		
16. Planned and constructed with the maximum number of pupils permitted to work at each center clearly posted or indicated.		
17. Defined and located so that pupils clearly understand where they are to function.		

experiments that challenge, games that excite, materials to puzzle over and manipulate, and many books and resources to select from is without question better than a classroom devoid of such materials. However, for you to surmise that a curriculum *for* kids will automatically and naturally evolve from a classroom environment that you designed with a wealth of materials is stretching the truth. It is possible, but not likely. The previous experiences of your pupils are the most important factors in the kind and extent of their involvement. Sharon Meier, the former head teacher in New Mexico State University's open classroom, describes the pupils' first reaction to the richly prepared environment:

> The kids were over-awed at such a magnificent set-up. They had never had so much material at their immediate disposal in their entire lives. They had had little if any experiences to build upon so that they could begin to utilize the discovery techniques we had so hoped they would use. Because of their immediate reactions to such a set-up, they seemed to bounce from place to place. The room was in one constant state of movement. We were disappointed because the kids wouldn't even look at a book, much less open one and read it.[1]

Although the teaching staff I cite here had implemented eye-appealing learning centers and provided exciting materials for their interesting mix of third- and sixth-grade pupils, the pupils were clearly not ready to function in the classroom described above. Having come from traditional classrooms that provided them with little previous opportunity to move about, plan, select learning experiences, work independently, and interact with each other, they found the sudden freedom thrust upon them simply too much to handle. Obviously, retrenchment was required. Consequently, classroom meetings were quickly instituted in which management problems were openly discussed, curricular directions were examined, likes and dislikes were aired, and diagnostic testing and individual conferences were undertaken to find out what the children were interested in and what they needed in order to pursue their interests. As a result, a gradualistic approach to the implementation of learning centers was instituted. A narrower range of activity choice was provided for the pupils. Individual contracts with them were drawn up; tutoring experiences were undertaken; pupils were taught and encouraged to work with each other. Subsequently, as the pupils demonstrated greater capacity to assume more and more responsibility for autonomous learning, their access to materials, to multiple activities, and to each other was correspondingly increased to where they were able to take on a major share of creating and implementing learning experiences in the classroom.

The point illustrated here is that although you personally may be ready to decentralize your classroom for open-access learning experiences, there are constraints of varying degrees placed on you by your pupils' previous experiences. As you organize your classroom for this purpose, you can reasonably expect that you will be faced with barriers to the implementation of your learning centers. However, these barriers are not insurmountable. Let me now turn to some of the more formidable obstacles you will need to come to grips with in making your preparations for getting underway.

BARRIERS TO IMPLEMENTATION

Recognizing the barriers and constraints against a decentralized classroom is, of course, a necessary first step in getting underway. The solution is to identify them, accept them, and meet them head-on. Along with the constraint placed on you by your pupils' previous experiences, additional restrictions that must be taken into consideration include the materials you have to work with, space for activities, time allocation, state and school regulations, and the various opinions of professional colleagues and parents with whom you are in contact.

THE CONSTRAINT OF PUPILS' PREVIOUS EXPERIENCES

The manner in which your pupils have previously functioned at home and in classrooms, including your own, has an important relation to the conduct you may expect from them in more open situations. If they come to you with considerable home and school experience in group activities and projects, working with peers, and in autonomous learning, consider yourself fortunate. The chances are they will function well, with minimal direction by you, in the learning centers you plan to establish. However, this may not be true of all your pupils. Certain of them may come from homes where they are given little opportunity for input and decision-making, even on a very simple level such as planning their activities, selecting clothes to wear, and choosing toys they want to play with.

Other children, particularly those from socially and economically disadvantaged backgrounds, may have had and continue to have very little access to toys, tools, books, pictures, and pets. Prior contact with these materials is important in that it is likely to set the stage for your pupils' successful experiences in your classroom. Often, children lacking such contacts may enter your classroom deficient in language, conceptual and reading abilities, and in competency for social interaction. For example, they may not have the ability to pace their learning because their conception of time may be at variance with that practiced in your classroom. They may be unprepared to respond to your system of rewards and punishment, and success and failure, if these differ from those experienced in their homes. Consequently, when you provide them with freedom of movement, activity, and pace of learning, those pupils who have significant disparities between the expectations of their home and neighborhood and that of your classroom may tend to withdraw or to exhibit uncontrolled behavior.

Pupils with this kind of background are not likely to be prepared for schooling and, as a result, sometimes suffer from the shock of changing environments. This is particularly true of impoverished children who sometimes have had no access to materials such as books, crayons, and games, and to no conversation in the home beyond that of "yes," "no," and "uh-uh" in response to their many questions. Knowing their home background, then, will enable you to understand their reluctance or inability to participate, to listen, and to converse with others. The materials and activities you provide, in fact, may be so unfamiliar to them that they may find them exceedingly difficult to cope with. Thus, these children are likely to offer a strong challenge to preschool and primary school teachers who attempt to get them ready for successful classroom experiences.

Additionally, those of you who teach in the intermediate and upper grades are likely to have pupils who may not be ready to function openly in your classroom because of their previous experiences in other classes. If, for example, they have had no prior opportunity for personal input, interaction, and decision-making, have had their activities strictly assigned and taught, or have some confusion on their part if you suddenly give them unaccustomeed freedom. As is the case with primary school children not prepared to function in an open environment, you will need to modify the extent to which you should provide open learning experiences for these pupils. It is important to provide the materials and related experiences in your learning centers necessary to this modification.

THE CONSTRAINT OF MATERIALS

The amount and different kinds of materials you have at your disposal and the ways they are used also limit the degree to which you can open up your classroom. The preceding chapters have acquainted you with materials you may find useful in the implementation of your learning centers. More important, however, is the way you use these materials. If you are a primary school teacher faced with children who lack the ability to remember things, to discriminate objects and letters of the alphabet, to function at abstract levels, and, in general, who lack the ability to visually and auditorially discriminate, it is important that you provide materials in your learning centers that help them develop these essential abilities.

Economically impoverished children, for example, may find it difficult to explore shape and size, weight and volume, and hardness and softness. They may find it difficult to derive concepts of time, speed, and ratio useful to their learning of arithmetic skills if they have had little exposure to real and toy clocks, cars and trains, and gears, pinwheels, and cooling fans. They may not know how to differentiate colors if they have had no access to crayons, paints, and pictures or the opportunity to purchase and wear colorful clothing. They may lack a three-dimensional perspective because their parents are not able to afford to buy them such items as Tinker toys, erector sets, Lincoln logs, play dough, interlocking plastic bricks, blocks, and other materials for construction and manipulation which help to develop this perspective. Children from impoverished environments, furthermore, may not have developed an awareness of the commonplace elementary principles of science, such as turning a nut on a bolt or hammering a nail, if they have had no previous contact with these experiences.

Perhaps you will find children from these environments reluctant to converse and interact with other children in your classroom. This may also be a reflection of their home life. Persistently exposed at home to conversations that focus on being poor, living in a slum, joblessness, and discrimination, it is likely they have learned to tune themselves out at will. Consequently, they may carry this behavior over to your classroom. This is to say that the ability of economically destitute and impoverished children to learn and to associate with other pupils in your classroom may be minimal at first because they have not received necessary stimulation.

Because of the various stages of readiness exhibited by your pupils and their diverse outlooks, you may find it necessary to adopt a modified plan for opening up your classroom. Directed teaching may be in order for some of your pupils and independent learning experiences for others. Obviously, you will need to spend time teaching pupils who lack the prerequisite skills necessary for them to function openly in your classroom. This does not mean, however, that all directed teaching must take the form of your presenting and explaining and the children listening. Learning centers can be established for the purpose of developing these prerequisite skills along with the directed teaching that may be necessary.

To pave the way for those pupils unable to use the symbols necessary to their speaking, reading, and writing, you can establish learning centers with multiple objects for them to handle and manipulate. In this way, you can provide them with the sense experiences for which the words are symbols. For example, to help them learn to distinguish between words such as heavy and light, rough and smooth, square and round, and hard and soft, you can place objects that clearly suggest these differences in a "feel box," bag, or on a table for your pupils to touch, weigh, and examine. Chalk, crayons, and finger paints may be placed in a center to help pupils distinguish colors and textures. All kinds of gadgets and the simplest of materials may be included in a learning center for your children to sense, sort, and build in order to develop their skills in comparing, estimating, relating, measuring, and counting. Corn kernels, beans, beads, popsicle sticks, buttons, and countless other easily attainable objects can be used for these purposes.

The important prerequisite skills of identifying and matching objects may be learned by experiences with geometric figures, pictures, puzzles, letters, and form boards in a learning center. Primary school pupils, in particular, and others in need of reading readiness experiences may be encouraged to fit geometric figures into slots on a board, or into drop-in openings in a container. They may be called upon to match pictures, letters, parts of words, whole words, and phrases as they progressively develop the skills of identifying and matching. Puzzles, ranging from simple two-piece to multiple-piece puzzles, may also be used to develop these skills. Commercial products commonly used in schools, such as the Letter Form Board, can be placed in a center to provide pupils with the experience in placing letters of the alphabet in the appropriate slots. Boards such as these are typically devised so that each letter provides the pupils with the correct feedback. For example, the letter "A" can only be placed in the "A" slot of the board.

As previously mentioned, those of you who are experienced primary school teachers are acquainted with literally hundreds of materials that can be included in centers for independent learning that do not require your directed teaching. Student and beginning teachers are increasingly aware of ways in which some of those materials can be put to use. For example, pegboards consisting of pegs to hammer with a mallet, oversized screws to turn with a wooden screwdriver, and large plastic nuts and bolts to be connected are very useful in developing primary school pupils' finger dexterity, small muscle coordination, left-to-right progression, and awareness of scientific principles. Transition to the use of professional tools is a subsequent step to developing these skills further in the intermediate grades and extending them to those that are involved in construction.

You may establish various other learning centers for the development of still other skills. Consider a "telephone center" to encourage conversation among youngsters reluctant to communicate. Set up a "dress-up center" consisting of clothing and mirrors to help your pupils see themselves as potential grown-ups and to encourage them to interact socially. A "blackboard center" or a "bulletin-board center" that cries out for decoration ("I feel so empty, boys and girls. Won't you please help brighten me up?") will help your pupils to plan and organize materials.

If you teach or are preparing to teach a kindergarten or first grade class in a middle-class neighborhood, you can be reasonably sure that most of your pupils will learn to read *without any formal instruction* simply because they have been exposed to the source materials necessary for reading to take place. Before entering school, for example, most have been given the opportunity to select their own books to look at, the records they want to play, and perhaps magazines to cut pictures from. They have become aware of numbers on clocks and watches, numbers and names on mailboxes, doors, and on television programs, and they have been exposed to names on many varieties of food boxes and packaged materials. They have observed multiple numbers and names on store signs and those encountered on family travels. At home, they have been encouraged to bring in from the mailbox the newspapers and magazines that mom and dad read and by doing so have learned to identify each by configuration, color, and format. They have perhaps learned to recognize the handwriting on correspondence from an older sister in college, a brother stationed overseas, or possibly from a friend or relative who lives elsewhere. This is real learning, even though they may not be able to read formally a single word.

Extensive opportunities for observation by these children cause them to want naturally to emulate what they see. Seeing dad and mom read, for example, makes them want to read, too. This desire tends to motivate them towards its satisfaction. As a result, they are apt to demonstrate readiness to read by picking up a book, a newspaper, a magazine, or other printed material. Should this take place in your classroom as well, you can establish a reading center for the purpose of expanding their interest in reading. The greater the variety of reading materials you include in the center, the greater is the likelihood that your pupils will take the steps leading to formalized reading. In Chapter 4, I discussed a preliminary procedure suggesting you invite pupils to bring in their own books, magazines, photograph albums, scrapbooks, picture cards of athletes, comic books, and other materials that may aid in the development of their reading skills.

To attract the pupils further, you may widen the mix of materials in the center by including travel posters, brochures, newsletters, library books, pictures, filmstrips, records, and other related materials. Wherever appropriate, be sure to include natural materials in the form of realia. Artifacts not typically found in your pupils' homes are likely to stir their imaginations, and may possibly lead to their wanting to find out more about the artifacts and what they represent. Wanting to find out, in turn, will often give your pupils the reason for wanting to read. This process of learning to read is summarized in Figure 6-4.

As can be seen in the figure, your central task is to capitalize on your pupils' readiness and desire to read by providing the materials, procedures, and practices in the reading center that enable them to reduce and overcome their obstacles to reading. To accomplish this purpose, it may be necessary for you to give formal instruction to certain pupils in addition to what they will experience at the reading center.

Most of you now teach, or will teach, heterogeneous groups of youngsters with varied experiences and different styles of learning. It is important, therefore, that you diversify the materials you intend to use in your learning centers so that they serve the needs of every pupil. Some of your pupils will need to be directed step-by-step in the use of these materials. Others will benefit by being invited to advance on their own accord. Behavior modification may be necessary for some; extensive freedom may be right for others. You may need to guard against a too hurried use of materials by certain pupils and against too slow a progress by others. Getting the right materials in the right places at the right times for the right pupils is a tall order to fill. This is one of the problems that will require your attention as you open up your classroom.

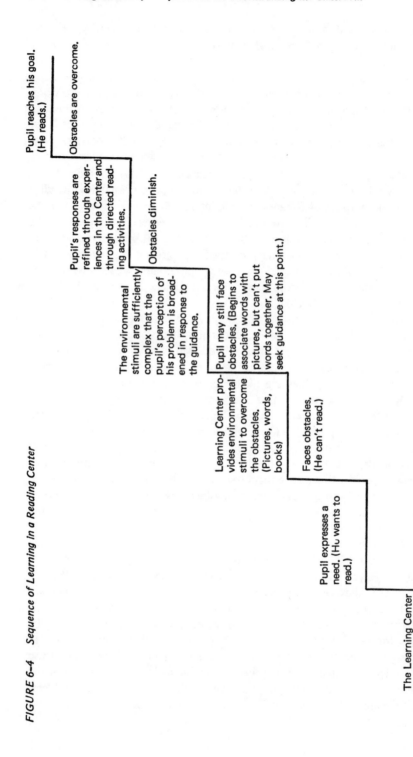

FIGURE 6–4   Sequence of Learning In a Reading Center

THE CONSTRAINT OF SPACE

Opening up your classroom may physically liberate your pupils' mobility but will also make it difficult to manage the various activities you plan to implement unless space is carefully defined and designated. How your learning centers are spaced, where they are located, and under what conditions they function will affect the manner in which your pupils learn. The extent of their absorption in the activities of the centers is important not only for purposes of instruction and learning, but also for your classroom management.

Sufficient space for your learning centers may pose a problem to those of you who teach under crowded conditions. How, then, can you maximize the space available to you? One procedure is to simply cluster your desks so that they abut in groups of, for instance, two to six. In this way, each cluster may be used as a learning center as well as for the traditional use of storage for each of your pupils' personal items. The number of desks you place together, of course, will vary with the purpose of each learning center. In my opinion, more than six in a cluster will prove too unwieldy. Figure 6-5 shows the space gained through this clustering process.

FIGURE 6-5   Clustering Desks to Achieve Greater Classroom Space

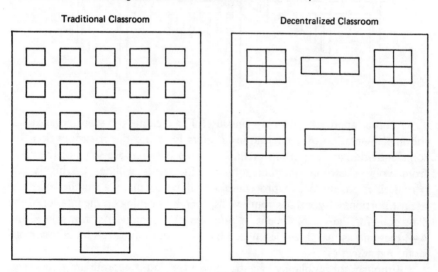

Clustering desks provides another important advantage. Unlike tables, they need not be fixed in number and size and are more readily moved as needed. The decentralized classroom pictured in Figure 6-5, for example, is likely to change from week to week or even from day to day as the activities change. Should you desire a more permanent arrangement, you can substitute tables for clusters of desks, an arrangement usually preferred by teachers in open classrooms because of the informality it invites and the stability it provides for table-top activities.

However, it raises the question of where to store the pupils' personal effects, books, and classroom materials. This is usually resolved by using deep-set trays, basins, shoeboxes or other containers for this purpose, but additional space is required for storage of these containers. A variation is to construct tables by attaching plywood, laminated wood, or formica tops to each of the clusters (Figure 6-6), thus maintaining the advantages of table surfaces and storage facilities. This construction was colorfully illustrated at the White Mountain Elementary School in Ruidoso, New Mexico, whose staff utilized metal panels obtained from a razed building as surfaces for clusters of desks. The identification of the learning centers was based on the various colors of their table surfaces, for example, the red center, the yellow center, etc., a setting which primary school children would find visually appealing.

FIGURE 6-6   Learning Center Constructed of Desks and Plywood Top

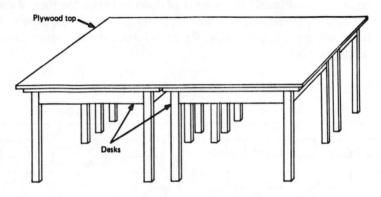

Another approach you may find useful in creating the space necessary to the implementation of your learning centers is to use the classroom floor for some activities. An important preliminary step is to remove some of the desks from your classroom—if your school principal is willing. If this is not permissable, an alternative procedure would be to place a number of desks against portions of your classroom walls, thereby opening up the interior of the classroom for the establishment of your learning centers. As shown in Figure 4-4, these desks may then be utilized by your pupils as carrels for autonomous study and activities.

Although not absolutely essential, you may find it appropriate to use rugs, pillows, carpets, drop-cloths, blankets, or paper for the floor activities you plan. The need for such would, of course, vary with the activities. In implementing these activities, you will likely discover that primary school children in particular will typically respond positively—at least that has been my experience and that of the teachers with whom I am associated. However, those of you who teach older children may run into pupils who will respond aggressively and noisily to activities taking place on the floor. Some may find the experience so unusual in a classroom setting that they do not know what to make of it. Others may view it as "kid stuff." And still others may subconsciously associate the activities that take place on the floor with previous experiences in gymnasiums, in their homes, or outdoors such as wrestling, tumbling, physical exercise, action games, and "horsing around." Obviously, if these behaviors take place in the classroom, such children need to be provided with other options or redirected to other experiences until they are ready to respond more positively. Certain children excepted, elementary school pupils of all ages when given the opportunity will usually enjoy floor activities inasmuch as they reflect natural life-styles. My own children, ranging in age from three to seventeen years, like those in most families read sprawled out on the floor, paint while lying on the floor, and construct gadgets, solve puzzles, play guitars, listen to records, and converse seriously while sitting on the floor. I personally rarely read while sitting at my desk. This is perhaps also true of you. The learning center approach, because of its emphasis on decentralizing and diversifying activities, is especially appropriate for continued encouragement of these kinds of activities in the classroom.

I present Figure 6-7 to help you visualize the space you can create by the removal of some desks, the clustering of others, the placement of still others against the walls of the classroom, and the substitution of tables for desks.

FIGURE 6-7   Representative Space-Saving Arrangement of Classroom Furniture

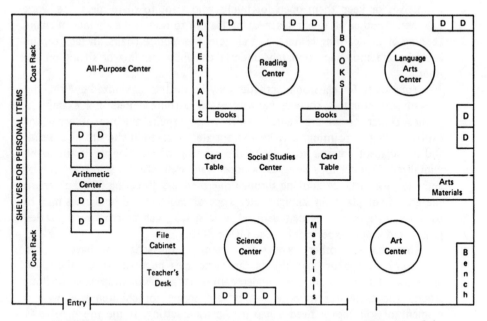

Dimensions, other than the space created in the physical arrangement of the classroom furniture, are also pictured in Figure 6-7. Note the use of the teacher's desk and file cabinets as a learning center. Reflect on how often you use your desk for your own personal use during the school day. I believe you will agree that most of your time is spent circulating from pupil to pupil and group to group and teaching in areas of the classroom away from your desk. Under this space-saving arrangement, you can continue to store your personal items and books in the desk and file cabinet for use as needed and, at the same time, use them as learning centers.

Observe, also, in Figure 6-7, the use to which you may put bookshelves and storage cabinets. Interestingly, I have discovered that many of the bookcases built alongside walls of traditional classrooms are removable. If this is the situation in your classroom, placing them in the proximity of the learning centers appropriate to the books and source materials they contain will provide immediate accessibility to them, thereby increasing the manageability and stability of each center. Bookshelves and storage cabinets, along with moveable screens, blackboards, and home-made partitions of cardboard, are also useful as dividers in separating your learning centers. This arrangement provides you with the added benefit of clearly identified and designated areas for activities, thus helping you to locate your pupils and to manage any excessive activity within each center. The use of furniture as partitions also provides some insulation from noise and interference by pupils among the centers. Note, additionally, in the figure, the space-saving placement of desks against the walls for use as study carrels. You may wish to partition these off for pupils who prefer to work by themselves or keep them open for pupils who want to share ideas and work together. Another pertinent space-saving feature to note is the absence of chairs at some of the learning centers. Not all activities require chairs. In fact, certain activities are more appropriately undertaken while standing or sitting on the floor.

Your space for classroom activities may be further maximized by using the tops of your counters, shelves, and cabinets as learning centers. For example, a science center or an art center, which often require the use of water for experimenting or painting, may be appropriately located at the site of the sink and its adjacent counter tops where the problem of cleaning up is apt to be minimized. Counter tops alongside window walls are useful for stand-up kinds of activities; for instance, looking through microscopes, dissecting frogs, observing the growth of plants in sunlight, etc. Tops of cabinets and bookcases may be used for many activities that demand little space, such as crossword puzzles, games, and simple experiments. (See Figure 3-16.)

There are still other avenues for extending the space you have in your classroom. Storage or coat closets can sometimes be used, as can the space underneath tables. Use the space underneath tables as it is or wrap paper or cloth around the table legs to provide a private corner for children who wish a moment of solitude or need a nap in a private setting. If the fire marshal is willing, spill over into the corridor. You should use materials that can easily be removed from the corridor each day so as not to conflict with fire regulations. Whatever the procedures you employ to make space for learning centers, the important thing to remember in planning the physical arrangement of your classroom is that not all of your pupils are likely to be sitting at the same time in the same activities. As illustrated in the very first paragraph of this book, some will be sitting, others standing, and still others may be sprawled out on the floor. Consequently, you do not need a desk and a chair for every single pupil in your classroom. Simply removing a number of these should help provide the space you need to implement your learning centers.

Figure 6–8 illustrates another variation of a physical arrangement of a classroom with a minimal number of desks and a maximum use of wall space.

FIGURE 6–8   *Extending Classroom Space Through Utilization of Tables, Counter Tops, and Wall Areas*

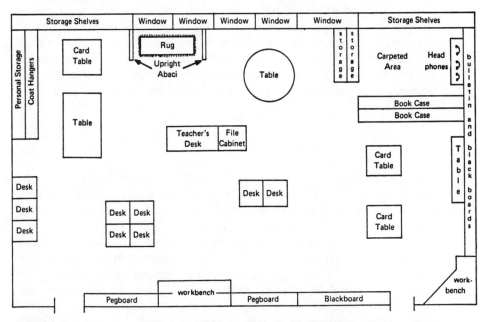

Witness in Figure 6–8 that tables have largely replaced desks to create needed space. In arranging your learning centers with this emphasis, a variety of tables of different heights and different shapes is useful for at least three reasons: (1) to account for the physical comfort of your pupils who vary greatly in height, (2) to serve the variety of activities you plan to institute, and (3) to take advantage of the classroom's construction. For example, a small round table is more conducive to learning experiences calling for pupils to interact than is a long rectangular table. On the other hand, the rectangular table lends itself better to placement against a wall than a circular table does. Observe also, in the figure, the ways bookcases and storage cabinets are used to partition off some of the learning centers. Note, particularly, how the back-to-back placement of the bookcase serves two centers, thereby eliminating the need for pupils in one center going to the other center for books and materials they may want. The point of this arrangement is that boundaries need to be established if the rights of pupils in each of the learning centers are not be impinged upon by constant pupil movement from center to center to obtain materials. Placing the materials in the learning centers in which they are to be used will help make your classroom activities more manageable than if materials were scattered throughout the room. Back-to-back and strategic placement of bookcases, storage cabinets, and other moveable furniture serves this very important purpose.

Other features to look at in the figure include the use of the shelf space above the coat hangers for storage of the pupils' personal effects, since most of the desks have been removed from the classroom; the utilization of wall space for pegboards on which to hang tools, sponges, and other items best stored in this manner; and the placement of some tables and desks against the walls to open up the interior of the classroom, thereby providing greater space for pupil movement. Notice, also, the imaginative use of the oversized, upright abaci as dividers to create the setting for an arithmetic center. Similarly, portable blackboards, if you have them, can be put to use for purposes of partitioning and instruction.

THE CONSTRAINT OF TIME

"My principal says I can teach no more than 90 minutes of science, and no less than 250 minutes of arithmetic each week. I'm up a creek. Here I have been planning to get learning centers underway in my classroom, and now this!" How many of you have been required to teach so many minutes in each subject, and no more or less? It is a highly debatable approach to the education of young children. Certainly, stipulating so much to be done under a prescribed amount of time does not fall within the spirit and scope of open education. You may feel that it is a constraining influence on the plans you have for opening up your classroom. Is it possible, then, to implement open learning experiences for your pupils under the constraint of time allotments? I think it is. A beginning step would be to decentralize and diversify the activities of your classroom in the form of subject centers and vary the scope of the activities within each center to account for the stipulated time requirements. If your principal insists on 90 minutes of science instruction per week, 250 minutes of arithmetic instruction each week, etc., simply build these time allocations into the structure of your learning centers as shown in Figure 6-9.

Figure 6-9, you realize, does not illustrate the best possible approach to the organization of your classroom inasmuch as time dictates the activities. However, you may consider it as a transitional step which provides open mobility for your pupils and, within the prescribed restrictions of time set forth by school policy, makes possible the implementation of your learning centers on the basis of open practices I have presented in this volume. That is, you may plan the activities in each of the subject centers shown so that autonomous, self-paced, and differentiated learning by your pupils is carried on in pressure-free settings. They will have the opportunity to decide what to do, how to do it, and when. Your pupils may plan activities for the centers, choose the centers in which to work, and determine the amount of time to be spent in each center so that the weekly time allocation for each is met. The constraints of time, furthermore, need not prevent you from diversifying the activities from center to center and within each center on the basis of your pupils' needs and interests.

FIGURE 6–9   *Learning Centers Based on Regulated Weekly Time Allotments Per Subject*

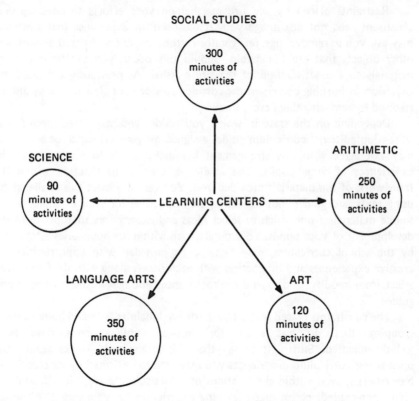

THE CONSTRAINT OF SCHOOL AND STATE REGULATIONS

State-adopted texts, curriculum guides, grade-level maintenance, homogeneously assigned classes, fire regulations, recess bells, and the school custodian are a few of the additional constraints you may have to deal with in providing open-access experiences for your pupils. The point is, you can! Consider, for example, the custodian who may feel it is more difficult to clean around the clusters of desks and tables you have arranged for use as learning centers than it is to clean in between the traditionally straight rows to which he has been accustomed. One custodian, in fact, told me exactly how I should arrange my classroom furniture to expedite his cleaning. Should this be your situation, try to win him over. See to it that chairs are placed on desks and tables at the close of each day to help him sweep the floor. Encourage the general cleanliness of your classroom by establishing procedures for storing materials not in use, picking up items from the floor, stacking books, cleaning blackboards, dusting counter tops and shelves, and emptying wastebaskets. It never hurts to have the custodian as a friend. Indeed, as experienced teachers well know, you may find him most useful in obtaining all kinds of source materials when you need them.

Restraints placed by the fire marshal on your efforts to open up your classroom need not discourage you. It has been my experience that a marshal may ask you to remove rugs, refrigerator cartons, paper-constructed devices, and other objects that are flammable. Should this occur, you can fire-proof the materials to the satisfaction of the fire marshal. As previously indicated, his objection to learning centers in the corridor outside your classroom may also be resolved by removing them every evening.

Depending on the state in which you reside, you may be required to use state-adopted texts, curriculum guides assigned by your principal, or both. You may not agree with this arrangement because it tends to predetermine the experiences of your pupils. The challenge, then, is to function within the framework of the materials provided you. You can also meet this challenge by using texts and guides, not as step-by-step directives for your teaching, but as source materials from which to select ideas and experiences appropriate to the development of your pupils. Your pupils, even within the boundaries established by the school curriculum, may likewise be provided with opportunities for creative experiences and interaction with each other, along with the freedom to select from, modify, and extend the experiences outlined in the textbooks and guides.

The constraints placed on you by grade-level maintenance and homogeneous grouping that do not allow for vertical pupil progress have been well-documented. Suffice it to say that this arrangement works against the open-access curriculum experiences you may plan to institute in your classroom. Nevertheless, even within the confines of a particular "grade," it is feasible to effect non-graded, personalized learning experiences for your pupils. Although you may not be provided with materials other than those ascribed to the particular grade you teach, it is important that you do not let this constraint negatively affect the implementation of your learning centers.

There is little or no reason why the experiences you provide in the centers for pupils, regardless of their grade designation, cannot focus on important processes such as inquiry, systematic investigation, innovation, confrontation of conflicts, and consideration of alternatives. Consider, also, as you formulate the activities of your learning centers, that there is no such thing as "first-grade art," "fourth-grade knowledge of science," or "sixth-grade music." Your time, additionally, may still be devoted to the diagnosis of your pupils' positions relative to the objectives of the grade level in which you teach, the learning style of each of your pupils, consideration of which classmates may assist them in their progress, the reward systems to which your pupils may respond, and to the learning centers that best facilitate their development. Also, as already pointed out in previous discussions of the constraints placed on your efforts to open up your classroom, your pupils may still be provided open education experiences in spite of the "graded" setting.

Minor school routines, such as the ringing of recess bells, announcements from the principal's office, and scheduled school events sometimes serve to constrain your pupils' learning by the untimely interruptions of their individual pursuits. This is a part of school life that you must live with. Consider, then, the advantage provided by your implementation of learning centers. Unlike the arrangement of the traditonal classroom, where desks have to be cleared and personal effects put away to get ready for recess, lunch, an event, or the next subject, the open, learning-centered classroom is not governed by timetables. Your pupils can go to recess or to lunch and on returning to your classroom continue their experiences in the learning centers you have established because the materials of the centers are constantly available for their use.

THE CONSTRAINING INFLUENCES
OF PROFESSIONAL COLLEAGUES AND PARENTS

Unfortunately, there still exist schools where changes in procedure undertaken in classrooms are frowned upon by school teachers and administrators and laymen alike. Hopefully, this situation does not exist in your particular situation. If it does, chin up and grin! Communication is important here. Your effectiveness as a teacher in the open classroom may initially depend on how well you have prepared your administrative and supervisory personnel and your fellow teachers to accept your proposed changes. You may need to clarify your objectives for them. Who knows, if you're lucky, some of your colleagues may wish to join you in your attempts.

Parents, too, may pose problems in opening your classroom. It is important that you make them aware of the changes you are contemplating. This communication may take the form of newsletters, personal conferences, neighborhood "coffees," back-to-school nights, and, somewhat more imaginatively, workshops on open education practices. Above all, it is important that you keep your classroom open to them at all times. Indeed, invite them to visit and work if they want to.

Doubtless there are other constraining influences that may affect the direction and scope of open learning in your classroom. Only a few of the more obvious have been discussed to show that obstacles are not necessarily insurmountable. The first step would be to accept them as facts and then to meet them head on. The types of limitations will vary from school to school. It is clear that the way your particular school is organized and administered will affect the amount and kinds of constraints under which you will have to function. This, in turn, is bound to help determine the particular steps and approaches you take to implement learning centers in your classroom.

POINTS TO REMEMBER

- Central to opening up the classroom is the premise that pupils are creative, constructive, cooperative individuals capable of directing themselves toward personal fulfillment.
- Genuine participation by pupils in the organization and learning expriences of the classroom is essential to its stability and is a necessary ingredient for open learning.
- The physical environment of the classroom helps shape the character and direction of the learning to be experienced by pupils.
- Pupils' previous experiences in homes and school affect the degree of open learning that can be successfully practiced in the classroom.
- Carefully utilized classroom space, furniture, and materials maximize the pupils' potential for learning.

NOTE

1. Sharon Meier, *"How It All Began"* (Unpublished paper, New Mexico State University, April 20, 1972).

at The First oF The year I was kindoF worid about school NoT The work or Teachers but my speling I hadent bene abile To spell as Fare as I caN remember I have never Liked speling and I Never will.

Virginia, Age 11

seven

Approaches to Implementation of Learning Centers

The particular approach you plan to use in organizing your classrooms for the implementation of learning centers depends on your own unique circumstances. The extent of your preparedness, the constraints placed on you, the degree of support you may expect, the views of teaching and learning you hold, the objectives you hope to attain, and the magnitude of your pupils' responsiveness all will bear on your approach. Clearly, there is no single standard procedure to decentralizing your classroom. The kinds of centers you implement will also affect the direction you take. In Chapter 2, various learning centers were presented, some of which you may find useful in determining the particular approach you wish to take in putting your plans into practice. Do you, for example, plan to use your centers for motivational, diagnostic, prescriptive, or enrichment purposes? Do you envision your centers as functioning singularly or simultaneously for these purposes? Since your pupils will have different needs, it is likely you will try to motivate some to learn, find out what others need in order to learn, prescribe activities for still others, and broaden the learning experiences of all.

The extent to which you plan to institute learning centers will vary with each of you. Some of you will find it more expedient to implement your learning centers gradually. Others may feel comfortable with a moderate approach. Still others are perhaps ready for the total conversion of your classroom. Let us now turn to these different approaches.

IMPLEMENTING LEARNING CENTERS GRADUALLY

Moving from a traditional classroom environment to one which completely embraces open learning, experiences, and interaction is likely to pose challenges to those of you who contemplate this move. A partial and gradual transition may be advisable, even when you have thoroughly set the stage and established the necessary climate for opening up your pupils to the different roles, relationships, and performances required of them. In implementing your learning centers gradually, you need to first consider the following three organizational points: (1) the number of centers to be established, (2) the amount of time to be allocated to the activities of the centers, and (3) the number of pupils to be involved.

THE NUMBER OF CENTERS

Initially, you may prefer to begin with only one learning center in which all of your pupils will have the opportunity to participate during some portion of their school day. Start slowly. Include a self-directed activity in the center with clear-cut guidelines for what your pupils are to do so that you may continue your work with those pupils who are not occupied at the center. To encourage your pupils' responsiveness to the center's activity, it is very important to include material that will hold their interest. The activity may focus on a single subject, an idea, or a skill to be developed. Blaze the trail with an experiment for your pupils to do, a puzzle to solve, or a gadget to invent! Or, if you prefer, you may try a more subtle approach by simply scattering books and magazines for them to browse through, records to listen to, or art materials to express themselves with. Subsequently, as greater interest in the center is shown, you may find it appropriate to sustain their interest in the center by increasing the number and variety of its activities. At this point you can also take steps to provide options for your pupils, first in the context of one center, then in others as they are implemented. Start with a very few options. Include, for example, opportunities for your pupils to select *some* of their experiences and make decisions pertinent to the experiences they select, to manage *some* of their own time in carrying them out, and to evaluate *some* of the experiences undertaken. Gradually, as your pupils increasingly demonstrate their ability to take on this responsibility, you may extend the options available to them and, in general, extend their opportunities to practice the tenets of open education.

It is wise to remember that children tend to forget learning experiences that they themselves have not helped to organize. Therefore, provide opportunities for your pupils to construct some of the activities of the centers you establish. An activity-by-activity, center-by-center progression for their implementation is advisable. As your pupils assume greater and greater responsibility in suggesting ideas for and in carrying out the activities of each learning center, you may extend the number and variety of the centers. Figure 7-1 illustrates this progression to the complete decentralization of the classroom.

FIGURE 7-1   Step-by-Step Progression to Decentralizing the Classroom

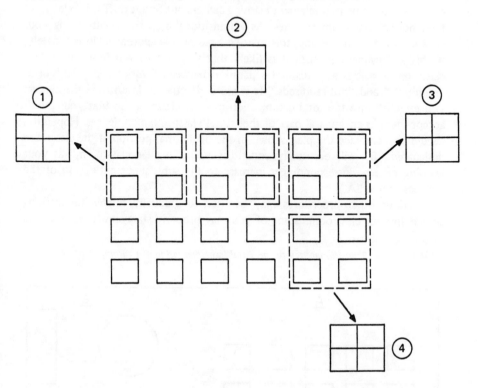

The time spent by your pupils at the initial learning center and in those successively implemented will likely be governed by your expectations as to how each is to be used. You may, for example, find it expedient to first use each strictly as an enrichment center, an approach favored by a good many teachers. If you decide to use this approach as a transitional step to opening up your classroom, it is most important that you differentiate the levels of the work regularly assigned to your pupils so that all have opportunity to make use of and benefit from the centers you establish. That is, you should require less of your slower-learning children than you do of your more capable pupils.

Remember, also, that the "enrichment" approach to the implementation of learning centers is apt to separate the centers from the total fabric of your classroom. Indeed, some teachers use such centers as a "reward" for those pupils who complete their "regular" schoolwork. Consequently, under this arrangement there are pupils who rarely, if ever, get to experience the activities of the centers. It is important, therefore, that you ensure their opportunities to do so by differentiating their daily assignments in accordance with their capabilities.

Figure 7-2 illustrates a transitional step in moving from a conventional classroom to one that utilizes enrichment centers. Note, in Figure 7-2, the clear-cut division between the so-called regular classroom, "A," and the learning centers, "B." This arrangement is a somewhat common practice amongst teachers who take steps to implement learning centers but find it difficult to let go of their normal classroom routines. As a transitional step to decentralizing your classroom for open learning, this may be a reasonable approach. Unfortunately, if this arrangement persists it is likely that your pupils will look upon their classroom activities as a distinct separation between "work" and "fun," or as "requireds" and "not-requireds." It is more effective to intersperse the centers you establish into the total organization of your classroom so that your pupils accept them as an integral part of their total classroom experiences. Hopefully, should you embrace the plan shown in the figure, that portion of the classroom designated "B" will eventually constitute your "regular classroom," as your learning centers correspondingly increase to the subsequent extinction of the area designated "A."

Various other procedures may be used to gradually implement learning centers in your classroom. Some of you may properly start slowly while others

FIGURE 7-2   Transitional Step to the Total Implementation of Learning Centers

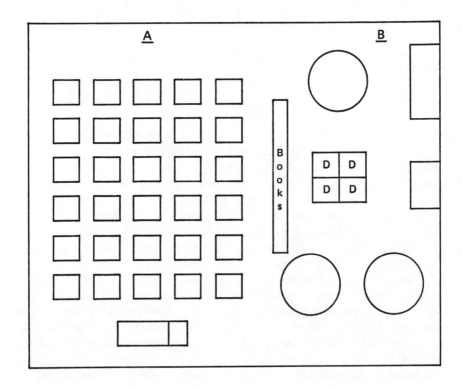

should assume a moderate pace. Whatever your pace and intensity, it is important that you include in your particular approach the ingredients of open learning—first gradually, then more extensively, as previously suggested. You might consider providing opportunities for your pupils to select the particular skills they wish to develop, the topics they choose to explore, the experiments they wish to undertake, and the projects they would like to carry out. Also suggested is that you provide your pupils with the options of choosing whether or not they want to work alone, with a buddy, or in a group. You may extend their open learning experiences further by inviting them to decide on the procedures they wish to follow, the time they want to spend, and the ways in which they want to have their progress evaluated. Whether you start your open learning experiences with one period of time a week, several periods a week, or a period a day in a single subject center or in more than one center, it is necessary that you invite, encourage, and implement as many components of open learning as possible so as to make an effective subsequent total conversion to the open classroom.

TIME ALLOCATION

Other organizational patterns you may select from in gradually implementing your learning centers are those which may be defined as the free activity period, the skills development period, and the interest activity period. The time you allocate for each of these periods may vary to suit your own circumstances and the readiness of your pupils to work at the centers.

The Free Activity Period.   Characterized by the free movement of pupils and the opportunity for them to freely select activities, the implementation of the free activity period is an approach you may find appropriate for introducing learning centers to your pupils. Start slowly if you have any doubts about the consequences of this approach. One hour or so a week may be a reasonable beginning point. So that your pupils feel comfortable, I suggest that you first begin by including in the centers you establish those classroom activities already familiar to them. It may also be advisable that you review the procedures necessary for your pupils to carry out the activities of the centers without your direct supervision. It may even be necessary to "walk" your pupils through the centers to explain what is to be involved and to clarify any questions that may arise. This is particularly important when introducing new activities to your pupils.

Lest management of the free activity period present problems, it is important that the ground rules for the behavior of your pupils be discussed before they use the learning centers. The number of pupils permitted to function at each center, the length of their stay, the learning options available to them, their responsibility to each other and for the materials they are to use and, in general, the behaviors required for good classroom management need to be discussed, clearly understood, and agreed upon. To help your pupils remember the criteria you have established together, you may need to post guidelines at each of the learning centers. Tagging your centers with numbers to indicate the number of pupils who may function at each center, listing the options, and stating directions in written form also serve the purpose of providing opportunity for them to recognize numbers, to read, and to follow directions.

It is important that you make no stipulations about where and how your pupils are to function during the time allocated for free activities, other than those required for the smooth operation of your classroom. In other words, it is important that you encourage your pupils to freely select the learning centers in which they wish to function. At their discretion, for example, they may engage in the games you have made available or in those they bring into the classroom; they can undertake science experiments, construct models, sculpture with clay, paint, clean the aquarium, do workbook exercises, listen to recordings, converse with each other, or read quietly. In the free activity period described here, it is also important that you not center your activities around subject skills to be learned by your pupils such as adding, subtracting, spelling, etc., except as they develop as a direct result of the pupils' interests.

The number of learning centers you utilize during the free activity period will, of course, have direct bearing on the management of your classroom and on the extent of your pupils' response to the centers. Picture, as in Figure 7-3, pupils in a first grade class moving from learning center to learning center during a free activity period. You may find a lesser or a greater number of centers more applicable to your own classroom circumstances. The key factor is that you determine the number needed to both manage and provide the diversity of activities required to capture and hold the interest of all your pupils. In making your transition to the free activity period, you need not remove your desks. Simply cluster them as shown in the figure to create the space you need or place some against the classroom walls. Subsequently, as you include more tables in your centers, it will be necessary to decrease the number of desks. Note also, in Figure 7-3, the use to which you may put your counter tops to create the needed space for your learning centers.

It is interesting to note, as illustrated in Figure 7-3, that pupils are as apt to select formal, on-going activities in the classroom such as letter and composition writing and arithmetic and reading exercises as those of a less formal nature such as puzzle, drawing, and sandbox activities. Too often, too many teachers use the free activity period to implement learning centers strictly on a "fun and game" basis and by so doing communicate to their pupils a separation between learning and enjoyment in their classroom. This approach may lead pupils to view learning centers as having a function quite different from their normal school work. Consequently, this tends to make the transition to decentralizing the classroom difficult. It is suggested, therefore, that you do not create a division between learning and play that, in my opinion, does not have to exist. Do, however, focus your attention on your pupils who learn as they play and who expand their interests as they develop their interpersonal and academic skills.

FIGURE 7-3   *Learning Centers in a Free-Activity Period*

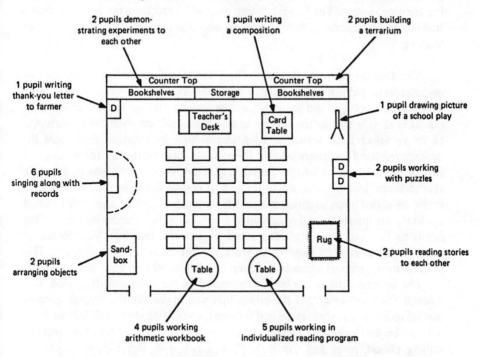

The Skills Development Period.   Another approach you may prefer to use in making the transition to implementing learning centers is one which sets aside a portion of the school day as a skills development period. To implement this approach, it is necessary to formulate group experiences for your pupils that develop skills appropriate to their academic and personal progress. In making this transition, you may begin by first integrating about an hour a day into the total classroom time for your pupils to work together on different aspects of needs common to the group. During this period, for example, one group of pupils may work together on developing a reading skill, another group on writing, still another in the area of computation, and so on. Or, when working on a common subject such as arithmetic, some of your pupils may estimate the weights of objects, others may count them, and the remaining pupils may solve problems by using the objects. There are countless other examples illustrative of the skills development approach that you can implement.

The skills development period is conducted on the principle that no one single skill is taught simultaneously to the whole class. It differs from the free activity period in that the pupils are directed to the activities appropriate to their needs, whereas in the free activity approach, the pupils are encouraged to determine their own needs and to select the activities they feel best meet them. The skills development process is familiar to many of you who have long initiated and practiced group work in your classrooms. If this is the case, you are in a good position to make the transition from your present practices to implementing learning centers. The biggest change you will need to make is not in decentralizing your classroom, but in putting into practice the ingredients of open learning.

   The Interest Activity Period.   The interest activity period is still another organizational pattern you can use to gradually implement your learning centers. This period combines and extends the free activity and skills development periods. It is closely tied to the former in that the pupils are given the opportunity to freely select their activities. It differs in that its activities arise from the pupils' first-hand experiences and from things that matter to them, and not strictly on the basis of what materials and activities of the classroom are available to them. In this approach to the partial conversion of your classroom, you would be called upon to solicit and search for ideas, materials, and activities that are likely to interest and involve your pupils. In other words, you go to the pupils to find out their preferences and suggestions, and then you encourage them to bring in their hobbies to work on, the books they enjoy, etc. This process, then, serves as a transitional step to open learning in your classroom.
   The interest activity period is also related to the skills activity period. It is through the involvement of the pupils that you undertake the formal teaching needed to carry out their expressed interests, correlating their activities with the skills to be developed. To visualize this correlation in the context of the interest activity period, recall in Chapter 1, Figures 1-1, 1-4, and 1-8, in Chapter 3, Figures 3-2, 3-3, and 3-11, and Figure 4-16 in Chapter 4, all of which are illustrative of the development of the pupils' interests. Note that the development of the pupils' skills is very much a part of the pursuit of their interests.

NUMBER OF PUPILS

Not all your pupils may be able to function well in the learning centers you implement. If you find this situation to be the case, it may be pertinent to first identify those pupils who can work well without your direct supervision. Invite them to participate in the activities of the centers while you work with the members of the class who need your direct attention. Start with one group and perhaps with one center. Gradually, as more of your pupils exhibit the interest and behavior necessary to function independently, you may increase the number of pupils to work in the centers, adding to the variety of the centers as you do so.
   Starting with one group of pupils in one center has other important advantages. Chapter 4 illustrated techniques for individualizing and personalizing the mathematical and reading experiences of children. You may wish to initiate the implementation of these techniques with a small nucleus of your pupils. This is to say, you may find it appropriate to pretest a group of pupils rather than the total class to find out where they place on a mathematical continuum. You can then proceed to personalize their learning experiences in a mathematics center

on the basis of the differentiated test results. Similarly, in the area of reading it may be more feasible and manageable to open up reading experiences for your pupils by starting with one group of selected independent readers who can function at a reading center without your direct supervision. Subsequently, as more of your pupils indicate their readiness to function independently, they may be redirected to the reading center.

In utilizing this transitional step to the total conversion of your classroom to open learning, I would not hesitate to integrate formal with informal learning experiences. The extent to which you emphasize each will, understandably, rest on the readiness and preference of your pupils for formal and informal education.

IMPLEMENTING LEARNING CENTERS MODERATELY

Perhaps you are now ready to move from a gradual approach in implementing your learning centers to one which involves a larger block of time for this purpose. Try a "Monday Special"! Or, for that matter, use any other day as a start to converting your pupils' classroom experiences to open learning. You may prefer to start with a half-day a week and subsequently move up to an entire day a week devoted completely to pupil experiences in learning centers. Implement as many centers as are necessary to provide the activities that serve the differentiated needs and interests of your pupils. You may choose to implement them on a totally free-choice basis, inviting your pupils to select and make use of any of the centers they wish throughout the day, or you may prefer to require that they select and complete the work of designated learning centers, as well as choosing work in optional centers available to them. There are, naturally, advantages and disadvantages to both approaches. I suggest you try both to assess and learn from the results of each.

THE ONE-DAY-A-WEEK APPROACH

An increasing number of teachers are finding that the moderate approach of setting aside one day a week for pupil activities in learning centers is rewarding to pupils. Among these is Mrs. Phyllis Gleyre, an experienced third grade teacher who, with the help of her student teacher, Barbara Huff, used each Friday for this purpose. She describes her "Friday Special" as follows:

> Never before have I had the opportunity to give so much individual attention . . . This is probably due to the fact that a good part of the class just literally "takes off" on centers and works independently, reading instructions, completing tasks, and checking work with a key . . . Perhaps the most surprising thing to me about this enterprise has been the consistent quality and quantity of the work done . . . Not only are my slower children producing more work and better work, but abler children have enough of a variety of challenges to keep them productive all day long. (Last Friday one boy completed three requirements and eleven options!)[1]

To help you visualize the establishment of learning centers on the basis of devoting one day a week for this purpose, one of Mrs. Gleyre's "Friday Specials" will be described. Imagine, if you will, a class-made tepee, some desks, tables, appliance cartons, the windowsill, the coat rack, and the floor being put to use as learning centers. The following activities are listed as they were presented to the pupils at each of the centers making up the "Friday Special."

Reading Center

Choose a book to read in the tepee for fifteen minutes.

Read your favorite story to the big stuffed dog, Sparky.

Listen to the story tape in the pueblo.

Use construction paper to make a book for our bookshelf.

Arithmetic Center

Use the electric board to study your facts.

Do problems 1–8, page 51 in the textbook. (Required)

With a friend, roll the blocks to add, subtract, or multiply the number combinations that turn up.

Use the timer to see how fast you can recite multiplication facts.

Take one of the tests played on the record player.

Play "Concentration," "Dominoes," or "Flip-Flops" with a friend.

Language Arts Center

Do page 63 in the text or page 49 in the workbook. (Required)

Select one of the ideas from the "creativity list" to write about. (Required)

Read the first part of the story in *Jack and Jill.* Write the ending.

Select one picture to write about.

Choose one of the thought-provoking questions to answer.

Complete one of the sentence starters.

Use the electric board to match synonyms and antonyms.

Play "Word Lotto," "Sentence Builders," etc., with a friend.

String word cards on the clothesline to make a sentence.

Science Center

Select an experiment to do from the experiment box.

Do page 32 in the science workbook. (Required)

Answer any of the questions attached to the field trip experiences.

Use the magnet to see which of the objects on the table it can attract.

Choose a friend to work with you on one of the science projects listed.

Art Center

Use any of the materials (crayons, clay, paints) to color, sculpture, or paint something of interest to you.

Spelling Center

Choose a partner to play spelling checkers with.

Fish for wordcards with the magnet pole.

Complete a crossword puzzle.

Unscramble words to construct new ones.

Social Studies Center

Locate and label the names of Indian tribes on an outline map of the United States.

Research information on any of the tribes you locate.

Decode the pictographs on any one of the activity sheets.

Reconstruct the pottery fragments to form a vase.

Those of you who are experienced teachers will note that the activities listed in each of the centers are essentially the same as those you use in your classrooms. Clearly, many of the materials you use are applicable for inclusion in learning centers. Remember, however, that the availability of materials in the centers you implement does not guarantee that your pupils will use or know how to use them. Observe carefully which centers your pupils select and how well they use the materials in them. Suppose you find very few of your children going to the social studies center you have implemented. Why? Are they bogged down by excessive writing to be done or with repetitive labeling of maps? Do they find too few options available to them? What if your pupils turn away from the reading center. Why? Is it because you require a book report each time they select a book to read? Is your selection of books for the center such that it does not meet the diverse reading interests of your pupils? Or are your youngsters simply confused by too wide a collection of books to choose from? Clearly, the kinds of activities you include in your centers and the amount of the work required to carry them out will shape their effectiveness.

The one-day-a-week approach to opening up your classroom provides you with the opportunity to combine and extend the components of the free activity, skills development, and interest activity periods. The emphasis you place on each of these may be determined by the needs of your pupils. You can easily add new activities to your learning centers during the week if your pupils evidence skills in need of further development or demonstrate additional interests.

The effectiveness of this moderate approach to the implementation of learning centers in an open classroom environment is clearly expressed by Mrs. Gleyre:

> I feel the open classroom technique has a great deal of merit and is one answer to many problems in public education. Now that I've seen what can be done, I doubt that I'll ever have a classroom without some evidence of learning centers. When my slowest child gleefully declares he's finished all his requirements and has made three "books" for our "bookshelf" for the first time this year; and my ablest child pleads for just ten minutes more to go to the library to finish his eleventh option, I think if these two have utilized their time this well and feel so completely happy about the whole thing, hopefully most of the twenty-three in between have shared a similar experience. We can call it a good day on the "Friday Special."[2]

There are, I feel, other important advantages of this transitional step to the complete decentralization of the classroom. For example, pupils who are reluctant to do their regular daily work are often "turned on" enough to do so in the freer atmosphere of the one-day "special." Moreover, some go so far as to carry over the experiences undertaken in the learning centers to their regular school program. To encourage this further, you could maintain as many centers as possible for your pupils' use on days other than the ones set aside for open learning. By so doing, you will make the subsequent transition to the total decentralization of your classroom less difficult. To make this transition, move to the point where your pupils spend as much time in learning center activities as they do in their regular school work.

EXTENDING THE TRANSITION
TO DAILY ACTIVITIES

Once your pupils demonstrate their ability to function well in learning centers on the one day you set aside for this purpose, you may proceed to extend this period of time. It is advisable to build this process gradually, moving from one day, to two days, and on through the week. I find that a compromise between formal and informal learning experiences often makes this transition palpable to both teachers and pupils. This may take two forms: (1) integrating required activities with optional activities, or (2) dividing the school day into formal and informal blocks of time. You may, for example, devote your mornings entirely to informal work in learning centers and your afternoons to carrying out the formalized classroom activities to which your pupils have been accustomed. Figure 7-4 is representative of a classroom organized on this basis.[3]

You will note in Figure 7-4, sixteen learning centers, all functioning simultaneously. Visualize about twenty-five pupils moving from center to center during the mornings set aside for this purpose. Witness, also, the integration of so-called formal activities with those of a less formal nature. The learning centers illustrated are actually representative of those utilized in Mrs. Sparger's third grade classroom. The directions to pupils found at each center have been modified for brevity. The number of centers typically vary from morning to morning, ranging from fifteen to twenty-five.

In implementing this moderate plan of establishing learning centers, it is necessary to institute at least the minimum number of centers required to sustain the interest and productivity of your pupils during each morning of the week. The kinds and number of centers you establish are therefore important if their interest is to be maintained. The appropriate number of centers would be determined by the breadth of interests and the diversity of needs of your pupils from morning to morning. The proportion of formal and informal activities in the centers would be determined similarly.

To carry out the formalized activities of your afternoon program, you may

FIGURE 7-4   Representative Learning Centers in a Third Grade Classroom

Reading Center

1. Select a book.
2. Draw a picture of what you read.
3. Give your picture a title.

Experiment Center

1. Use the wire, bulb, dry cell, and switch.
2. Write what you did and what happened.

Jelly Bean Center

1. Guess the number of jelly beans in the jar.
2. Write the number and your initials on a paper slip and put it in the tin can.

Discovery Center

1. Feel the things in the box.
2. Write a sentence about each of the things you feel.

Play-A-Tune Center

1. Pick a tune from the music box.
2. Play it on the xylophone.
3. Can you create a tune of your own?

Spelling Center

1. Choose a partner to play spelling checkers with.
2. Pick words from those listed.
3. Challenge each other with words from the list.
4. Move your checkers each time you spell a word correctly.
5. First one across wins.

Taste Center

1. Use a clean toothpick to taste each solution.
2. Check off your choices on the activity sheet.

Listening Center

1. Select a record to listen to.
2. Be sure to put the record back in the proper slot when through.

Arithmetic Center

1. Construct and do ten addition examples.
2. Five must be made up of two-column examples.
3. When through, place your work in your folder.

Olfactory Center

1. Smell the solution in each bottle.
2. Check the appropriate answer on the activity sheet.
3. Show me what you've checked.

Magnet Center

1. Which of the objects on the desk does the magnet pick?
2. Check the results on the "Yes-No" sheet.

Store Center

1. "Sell" any of the items to a friend.
2. Make certain you both exchange the proper amount of the play money.
3. See me if there is a question.

Refraction Center

1. Hold the prism up to the light.
2. What do you see?
3. Make a list.

Unscramble Center

1. How many words can you make?
2. Unscramble and write correctly the following:
   nridk _____
   oeng _____
   etc.

Timmy Time Center

1. Move the hands of the clock to:
   1:15
   2:30
   etc.
2. Have a friend check your accuracy.

Vocabulary Center

1. With a friend, practice reading the words in the vocabulary box.
2. Look up the words you don't know in the dictionary.
3. Write those that interest you in your vocabulary book.

need to make some adjustments. Inasmuch as your classroom is totally decentralized each morning, you may need to shift some of your learning centers, combine others, and clear them of materials so that the space they take up can be used for other purposes in the afternoons. Thus, in planning your centers, it is necessary that you consider the necessary procedures for making this transition as smooth as possible.

THE TOTAL IMPLEMENTATION
OF LEARNING CENTERS

Up to this point, I have advocated a step-by-step, gradualistic approach to the complete decentralization of your classroom. The rate with which you implement your learning centers will naturally vary with each of you. For those of you who are ready to totally implement learning centers in your classroom, one of your most difficult tasks will be to provide the materials necessary to meet the wide range of academic and personal needs of your pupils. In the preceding chapters, ideas and sources of materials useful in helping you get underway were presented. Clearly, adequately equipping the learning centers you plan to establish is a necessary first step.

EQUIPPING YOUR LEARNING CENTERS

Those of you who are experienced teachers will find that some of the materials listed under the various subject centers are quite familiar. Again, this illustrates the point that a good many of you already have the materials necessary to make the transition to the learning-centered classroom. The student and beginning teacher will find the materials listed useful in planning for the implementation of learning centers. Keep in mind, however, that they are merely representative and by no means comprehensive.

   The Arts and Crafts Center.   As is true in other subject centers, you may equip this center with as few or as many materials as needed to meet the diverse needs and interests of your pupils while, at the same time, maintaining the management of the center. Among the materials you may select from in equipping your centers are those that invite your pupils to cut and paste, construct, sew and knit, weave, sculpture, paint, draw, and letter, as well as those materials appropriate to the development of art appreciation, such as art prints, graphics, books, and records. A partial list follows:

easels	pipe cleaners
paints	cotton
brushes	beads
paper	string
water	cellophane
crayons	leather
painting shirts	buttons
newspaper	thread
paper towels	yarn
colored chalk	thimbles
sponges	needles
salvage materials	pins
cardboard rolls	pin cushions

clay
soap
scrap wood
glue
nails
hammer
saw
screwdriver
carving tools
Lincoln logs
play tiles
Tinker toy sets
toothpicks
construction paper
paper bags
oak tag
paste
masking tape
cardboard
felt scraps

scissors
cloth scraps
foil
wallpaper samples
Q-tips
pine cones
art prints
art objects
books of crafts
books about artists
record player
music records
ear phones
printing materials
stencils
old magazines
old jewelry
boxes
driftwood

The Mathematics Center.   Ranging from materials useful for developing skills of linear movement and containers appropriate for measuring liquid, to books depicting the history of numbers or containing problems that pupils may work for themselves, you have much to choose from in equipping your arithmetic center. Consider equipment such as:

place value charts
Cuisenaire rods
tally counter
number readiness posters
magnetic numerals
beaded number cards
one hundred chart
geo-boards
geo-sticks
geo-blocks
geo-strips
tangrams
number board
egg cartons
measuring cups & spoons
abacus
felt bound & cut-outs
pint, quart, gallon cartons
scales
rulers, yardsticks, tape measures
cardboard clocks
Dienes blocks
Napiers, rods
activity sheets

popsicle sticks
pebbles
beans
bottle caps
pegboards & pegs
shells
buttons
acorns
golf tees
paper plates
washers
assorted jars
spools
play money
cash register
counting cubes
Chinese checkers
dominoes
Lotto & Bingo games
checkers
chess
monopoly game
playing cards
attribute games

workbooks & textbooks	calendar
magic squares	dice
numeration charts	

The Social Studies Center.   In Chapter 4, a wide variety of materials were presented that you may find useful for inclusion in your social studies center. Also useful are:

globes & maps	filmstrips & viewers
artifacts	dioramas
tour guides	electric board
train & bus schedules	simulation games
airplane timetables	charts & graphs
atlas	information & study banks
coin & stamp collections	pamphlets
dolls & toys	cartoons
travel folders	illustrations
compass	exhibits
salt & flour	slides
costumes	posters
pictures	encyclopedias
study prints	bibliographies
records & tapes	reference books
newspapers	historical documents
library books	catalogues
handbooks	

The Language Arts Center.   You may prefer to subdivide this center into reading, writing, spelling, and penmanship centers. Otherwise, materials appropriate to this center may include:

dictionaries	pegboard for displaying stories
textbooks & workbooks	starter sentences
library books	postcards
reading laboratories	stationery
plastic or wooden letters	transparencies for writing
book jackets	puppet theater & puppets
typewriters	tape recorder & headphones
rocking chair	idea cards
rug & pillows	newspapers
plastic page protectors	magazines
sight vocabulary games	letter board
picture file	self-correcting worksheets
picture sound cards	telegram forms
picture vowel cards	crossword puzzles
word cards	phonics games
reading games	

The Science Center.   Constructing a center around science activities should not pose too many problems to you as it lends itself to materials that are, in most instances, easily collected. Your pupils can contribute numerous items here. Think of those found in nature alone such as rocks, shells, bark, insects, soils, leaves, plants, feathers, and nests. Use what may be brought in from your pupils' homes: straws, plastic tubing, cornstarch, vinegar, oil, salt, sugar, food coloring, paper cups, and all kinds of food, containers, and utensils. All of the multisensory objects to smell, touch, listen to, describe, experiment with, and classify are too numerous to list. Consider, however, the materials available from your own school. Perhaps you are fortunate enough to select from the following:

balloons	pond water
sandpaper	mealworms
corks	seeds for planting
clock	earthworms
tire pump	mosquitoes
auto jack	assorted animals
microscopes	fish
measuring devices	aquarium
litmus paper	terrarium
stethoscope	printed materials
mirrors	study guides
prisms	picture file
geo-blocks	iron filings
electric bells	old motors
pulleys	books
magnifying glasses	tools
magnets	egg beater
thermometers	can & bottle openers
pendulums	strainer
batteries & bulbs	scissors
electrical equipment	test tubes
compass	alcohol lamps
optics	tuning fork
scales	simple machines
models	dissecting kit
wind-up toys	wheels & gears
water & sand trays	gyroscope
candles	beakers
weights	charts
incubator	

Additionally, commercial enterprises, such as the ESS Science Units, Webster Division, McGraw-Hill Book Company, Manchester, Missouri 63011, are good sources for materials you'll find useful for inclusion in your science center.

In equipping these and other centers you plan to implement, you will need to obtain space for storage of materials not in use. If sufficient commercial furniture is not available to you for this purpose, you may need to make your own. Earlier, I cited the use of deep dish pans, vegetable bins, ice-cream buckets, and various kinds of boxes for storage. Consider, also, such items as shoe holders for pocket storage of odds and ends in the form of paper clips, rubber bands, pencils, and rulers; upside down saw horses for holding large sheets of poster board, oak tag, construction paper, art prints, and flat maps; wastebaskets for the storage of paper rolls and curtain blinds; manila folders in which to place directions for games, puzzles, and experiments; egg boxes for storing buttons, pins, sequins, soil samples, and minerals; and refrigerator boxes for the display of pupils' work and announcements.

The amount and kinds of materials you make available in your learning centers, in addition to the interest they arouse, may play a significant role in the management of your classroom. You can assume that the greater the variety of materials you utilize, the greater is the likelihood that something will attract your pupils. Also, the greater the availability of the materials to your pupils, the less likely will conflicts arise among them. In the event that conflicts do arise, however, it may be necessary to remove the contested materials from your centers. Keep in mind, moreover, that too many materials in any one center may make the selection of appropriate activities difficult for some pupils and may discourage others who seek fresh stimuli from day to day.

Subsequently, you can expect the physical appearance of your classroom to change as a result of your pupils' activities in the centers. The experiments they conduct, the edifices they construct, the exhibits they create, the dioramas they build, and the items they bring in, as well as the art they express and the poetry and prose they write, will all have bearing on the kinds and amount of materials you select for inclusion in your centers. That is, your learning centers will need to expand and change as the needs and interests of your pupils grow and change. To carry out this expansion and change, two approaches are presented, either one of which you may adapt to fit your own classroom situation.

THE SINGLE-SUBJECT APPROACH

Some of you perhaps now teach along departmentalized lines in your class-rooms, your school day being segmented into a reading period, an arithmetic period, a spelling period, and so on. Others of you who are about to go into teaching may also choose to organize your classroom similarly. Under this arrangement, you will find the use of learning centers most appropriate in diversifying the activities of your pupils. Figure 7-5 is representative of this diversification in the area of reading, although it may be used as the format for other subject centers as well. For example, you may establish arithmetic centers to capitalize on the various learning styles and preferences of your pupils. For instance, as indicated in Figure 7-5, some pupils function best with books, others prefer to work with games, some enjoy exercises on the blackboard, and still others learn best through manipulative experiences such as those that involve the use of puzzles, blocks, flannelgraph cut-outs, clay, erector sets, and assorted tools. This figure is an actual representation of a primary-grades class-room in which the activities of an arithmetic period are decentralized in the form of learning centers. It also indicates that the pupils working in the various centers may be functioning at different levels of arithmetic competency, as well as in the areas of their preference. It is appropriate that you either direct them to those centers which best develop their needs, or give them the opportunity to select those centers which they personally feel best meets their needs.

FIGURE 7-5   *Diversification of Arithmetic Experiences in Learning Centers*

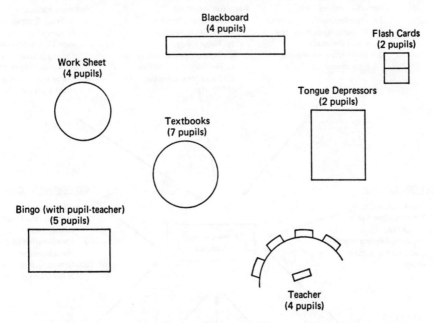

The implementation of learning centers along single-subject lines can be illustrated further. The experiences of one of my student teachers who taught in a departmentalized seventh grade social studies class are presented in Figure 7-6.[4] Figure 7-6 shows a theme-centered classroom environment focusing on the study of Mexico.

In undertaking the single-subject approach to the decentralization of your classroom, you need to consider the disadvantages along with the obvious advan-tages of this approach. Clearly, if you teach in a departmentalized school where you are responsible for teaching only one subject to successive classes of pupils, the approach described permits you to concentrate your time and energy in such a way that diversified and enriching kinds of learning centers can be imple-mented successfully. On the other hand, if you are held responsible for teaching all subjects in your classroom, this approach makes it very difficult for you to move from subject to subject without replacing the materials in centers you have established in one subject with those appropriate to the subjects to be taught in successive time periods. Consequently, if you do not teach in a school organized along departmental lines, a more suitable approach for the implementation of learning centers is that which is organized around the simultaneous teaching of multiple subjects.

FIGURE 7-6   *Representative Learning Centers of a Theme-Centered Classroom*

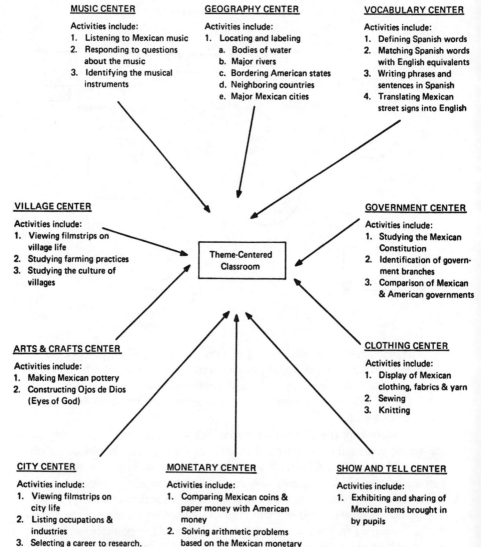

MUSIC CENTER

Activities include:
1. Listening to Mexican music
2. Responding to questions about the music
3. Identifying the musical instruments

GEOGRAPHY CENTER

Activities include:
1. Locating and labeling
   a. Bodies of water
   b. Major rivers
   c. Bordering American states
   d. Neighboring countries
   e. Major Mexican cities

VOCABULARY CENTER

Activities include:
1. Defining Spanish words
2. Matching Spanish words with English equivalents
3. Writing phrases and sentences in Spanish
4. Translating Mexican street signs into English

VILLAGE CENTER

Activities include:
1. Viewing filmstrips on village life
2. Studying farming practices
3. Studying the culture of villages

Theme-Centered Classroom

GOVERNMENT CENTER

Activities include:
1. Studying the Mexican Constitution
2. Identification of government branches
3. Comparison of Mexican & American governments

ARTS & CRAFTS CENTER

Activities include:
1. Making Mexican pottery
2. Constructing Ojos de Dios (Eyes of God)

CLOTHING CENTER

Activities include:
1. Display of Mexican clothing, fabrics & yarn
2. Sewing
3. Knitting

CITY CENTER

Activities include:
1. Viewing filmstrips on city life
2. Listing occupations & industries
3. Selecting a career to research.
4. Studying the architecture of cities

MONETARY CENTER

Activities include:
1. Comparing Mexican coins & paper money with American money
2. Solving arithmetic problems based on the Mexican monetary system

SHOW AND TELL CENTER

Activities include:
1. Exhibiting and sharing of Mexican items brought in by pupils

THE MULTIPLE-SUBJECT APPROACH

Many teachers are, of course, familiar with simultaneously teaching multiple subjects in heterogeneous classroom settings. It has been illustrated, moreover, how this practice is applicable to the establishment of learning centers in such classrooms. Additionally, a gradualistic approach to the total implementation of learning centers that lend themselves to this approach has been advocated. Assume, then, that you now wish to decentralize your classroom for this purpose. You will need to consider: (1) the objectives to be attained by your pupils, (2) the placement of your pupils in learning centers relevant to their objectives, and (3) the record-keeping necessary to keep track of their progress.

Objectives.   As previously pointed out in the first chapter of this book, the well-documented theory that children actually learn what they wish to learn is the very heart of the learning-centered classroom. Ideally, the skills and knowledge your pupils achieve should evolve out of their interests. In implementing your learning centers, it is important that you encourage your pupils to develop their own goals. To accomplish this, you will need to spend considerable time planning with your pupils—first with the total class and subsequently with groups of pupils and with individual pupils.

Translating the values your pupils hold along with your own into specific educational objectives is clearly a necessary first step. How essential, then, is the establishment of behavioral objectives and performance criteria for each of the learning centers you implement? In an open environment, it may be difficult to pin down precisely *what* is to be demonstrated by your pupils and *when.* I feel, therefore, that process and expressive objectives are more intrinsic to your classroom's operation inasmuch as they are predicated on the assumption that pupils' behavior constantly changes. In fact, the use of instructional or behavioral objectives is typically avoided by most open education advocates as is indicated in the following statement:

> Expressive objectives differ considerably from instructional objectives. An expressive objective does not specify the behavior the student is to acquire after having engaged in one or more learning activities. An expressive objective describes an educational encounter: it identifies a situation in which children are to work, a problem with which they are to cope, a task they are to engage in—but it does not specify what from that encounter, situation, problem, or task they are to learn. An expressive objective provides both the teacher and the student with an invitation to explore, defer or focus on issues that are of peculiar interest or import to the inquirer. An expressive objective is evocative rather than prescriptive.[5]

Despite my belief that process and expressive objectives undergird the operation of the learning-centered classroom, I do not rule out the importance of behavioral objectives. I feel it is important to *prescribe* as well as to *invite* learning experiences for your pupils when necessary to develop the scope of their interests. The two processes are compatible. Clearly, the nature and scope of the learning centers you implement will be determined by the objectives and criteria set forth by both you *and* your pupils. Must you, then, reduce all conjunctively planned learning experiences to written statements expressed as behavioral objectives at each of your learning centers? Such a procedure is unrealistic and unnecessary. What is important, rather, is that you know how to communicate objectives to your pupils so that they understand the purpose and usefulness of the various experiences in each center. This communication may take either a written or a verbal form, depending on the particular learning center in question. Moving from teacher-stated instructional objectives, such as those found in curriculum guides, manuals of instruction, and commercial monographs, to writing directions that children can clearly understand is a real art. Figure 7-7 illustrates how this can be done.[6]

FIGURE 7-7   *Representative Teacher-Stated Instructional Objectives Transcribed to Directions for Pupils in Learning Centers*

MOVE FROM TEACHER OBJECTIVES . . .	TO PUPIL OBJECTIVES . . .
1. Given a familiar word of multiple functions (parts of speech), the pupil will be able to use the two or three functions of a word in sentences.	1. The words on the activity sheet have more than one meaning. Select any five of the ten words listed. Write two sentences for each word. Show a different meaning for the words in each of the sentences.
2. Given a suitable passage to read that contains a character's physical description, the pupil will be able to draw a picture of that character.	2. Read the poem on page 45 of When We Were Very Young, and draw a picture of the character described.
3. Given a set of pictures, the pupil will be able to state the name of a familiar character from a story associated with each illustration.	3. Match the appropriate name card with each of the pictures you select. Show me your results when you are finished.
4. Given a group of letters, some of which are dissimilar in size or design, the pupil will be able to identify those which are the same.	4. How well do you know the letters of the alphabet? Match those you know by drawing lines from those in Column A with those that look the same in Column B. (Note to the teacher: this exercise is to be explained verbally to pupils who elect or are directed to this activity.)

In my opinion, writing detailed plans in a planbook and duplicating them to serve as directions for pupils at the learning centers places an undue burden on you. Hopefully, you'll gain the support of your principal in accepting your objectives for each center. Your planbook may then be used to record the general objectives you have in mind for your pupils' learning, the references essential to carrying out these objectives, and your personal observations of their progress. Following the establishment of your learning centers and the directions necessary for them to function effectively, your next step is to consider your procedures for moving your pupils to them.

The Movement of Pupils.   Moving your pupils to learning centers may take several forms. To begin with, it is very important and necessary that you discuss the plan of action with your class. Present and explain each center and invite questions from your pupils concerning their activities. Go over the ground rules for the pupils' movement, their responsibilities, and what is expected of them in general. Clarify your management objectives. If you anticipate problems of movement and/or lack of pupil interest in the work of the centers, present and discuss these with the pupils prior to their possible occurrence.

Throughout your planning with your pupils, it is necessary that you gear your thinking to their specific needs as well as to their interests. To what parts of the curriculum should all of your pupils be exposed? Where might they branch off? Which of your pupils are in a position to work independently of you during the day? For how long? Which will require your continuing attention? Knowing the objectives of each of the centers you have instituted, the materials of which they are composed, and the tentative time schedule of each will, of course, enable you to respond to these questions.

The method of pupil movement to the learning centers you institute is tied closely to your personal philosophy of education. For example, if you believe that no new concepts can be taught through a center, it is likely that you will view your learning centers strictly as a follow-up to introductory lessons and will assign your pupils on this basis. If you feel that each child must go to all the centers you have established, this too will affect the kind and extent of movement that will take place in your classroom. If you believe that all your pupils must complete assigned work before they can move to the learning centers, this also influences the amount of the movement required of your pupils. Among the procedures you may wish to consider for the movement of your pupils to learning centers are (a) verbal directions, (b) posting of a schedule, (c) distributing personal folders in which the centers are listed, (d) using sign-up sheets, and (e) the contract system. Any one of these may work well for you. I suggest you experiment until you find the procedure(s) that best fits your situation.

Some of you may find that your daily planning schedule sessions are such that announcing, presenting, and explaining the learning centers implemented is adequate for the smooth movement of your pupils to them. Others of you may prefer to combine this approach with posting the learning centers as reminders to your pupils of what is available to them. Should you have reason to introduce a new center or require that the activities of certain of your centers be undertaken, a simple expedient would be to place an asterisk before each; for example, *reading center, listening center, science center, *arithmetic center, social studies center, etc. In utilizing this particular approach, you can increase flexibility by encouraging your pupils to make use of any center they wish in the order they wish, the only requirement being that they all complete the activities of the reading and arithmetic centers by the end of the day or days established for this purpose.

Perhaps you will prefer to make the movement of your pupils to learning centers a bit more personal. An effective approach would be to compile a folder for each of your pupils. Place in the folder a list of the learning centers available for their use. In conference with your pupils, check off those centers each selects to work in. One technique is to have each pupil draw an "o" before each center selected and place an "x" inside the "o" when the activity or activities of the selected centers have been completed. If paper work is involved, see to it that your pupils place their completed work in their personal folders for your evaluation.

An alternative to the conference approach would be to write personal notes to your pupils and place them into their folders for them to act on. The following is an example of such a note.

Dear Betty Jo,

In looking at the work you put into your folder yesterday, I found _____ _____. Go to the arithmetic center today. Select any seven to ten examples of those found on Activity Sheet No. 1. This will help you learn how to add _____ better. When through, put your results into your folder. Or, if I'm free, show me your results.

—Mr. Thomas

A variation of this approach is to "mail" a letter or postcard in a pupil-constructed post office. In this letter give your pupils directions to learning centers appropriate to their needs. For example:

"For your interest please read _____."

"Study pages _____ in _____."

"See the filmstrip on _____."

"Speak with _____."

"Listen to the tape by _____."

"Do exercises _____ on pages _____ of _____."

"Your _____ skill needs attention. Practice this with _____ in the _____ center."

Note-writing may be time consuming if it can't be held to a few simple sentences. Consequently, if you find this method of involving your pupils in learning centers difficult, it is best to turn to a less demanding approach.

Some teachers prefer to use an approach that invites pupils to sign up for the centers of their choice each day. Each pupil determines his own daily schedule by filling in an index card as shown in Figure 7-8.

Although this approach is meritorious for the opportunity it gives to pupils to select their own experiences, it also has some shortcomings. The paper work alone may be a prohibitive factor. Considerable time is required to tabulate the

FIGURE 7-8   Illustration of Pupil-Selected Learning Centers

NORA		5/20/74
LEARNING CENTER	ACTIVITY	PERIOD
Arts and Crafts	Sculpturing	6
Typing	type a story	2
Mathematics		
Drama	Show and tell	5
Social Studies		
Conference	talk about my work	4
Listening		
Science	Experiment with magnet	3
Language Arts	write a story	1
Hobby		
Games		

choices made by pupils because of the conflicts likely to arise—for instance, when excessive numbers of pupils opt for the same centers in the same time slots and when their work is completed before the designated periods end. Segmenting the day into periods of time for the use of learning centers often inhibits pupils from devoting the time needed to pursue a task or sustain an interest. *Time* rather than the pupils' *objectives* is the governing factor. Additionally, despite the openness ascribed to pupils choosing their own centers of activities, you will most likely also find it necessary to prescribe learning experiences beneficial to their academic progress and personal growth.

A more effective procedure for involving your pupils in learning centers is one which allows for input by both you and your pupils. This may involve frequent conferencing. To lessen the pressure on your time that this may incur, you should plan with your pupils on a long-range rather than on a short-range basis. For example, you may try planning broadly on a weekly basis, thus saving both the time and the paper work necessitated by more frequent conferences. Figure 7-9 is representative of such a plan. Note in the figure the provision for the pupil to select certain experiences and for the teacher to prescribe others.

Keep in mind as you look at Figure 7-9 that it represents just one pupil's plan for a week's program. Under this arrangement, the programs of pupils differ from pupil to pupil. Conceivably, some plans would consist almost entirely of pupil-selected activities in the various learning centers; others would consist largely of activities you initiate as the need for them becomes apparent. In most instances, the plans of your pupils will more than likely reflect a balance between pupil-selected centers and those prescribed by you.

Observe in Figure 7-9 the kinds of learning centers selected by Johnny. Presumably, his selection is a result of his personal interests, a factor which is recognized by his teacher. You may assume, furthermore, that Johnny's reading needs considerable attention, as is evidenced by the daily schedule of activities in this area prescribed by the teacher. Less emphasis is given to his need to undergo mathematics experiences, since only two periods are established for this purpose.

Note also the broken lines in the figure. This suggests that the purposes and activities of the learning centers, rather than time, determines the pupil's program. This means that if you should adopt this approach, the work of the various centers would not be segmented into periods of time. It is preferable that your pupils devote as much time as is necessary to achieve their objectives. You can expect, therefore, that the agreed-upon plan of each of your pupils may not be realized as indicated. Consequently, further conferencing and revision of the plan may be needed.

An important question is when you can find the time to confer with each pupil. Clearly, this is still another advantage of the learning-centered classroom. The fact that you have completely decentralized the classroom and prepared your pupils to work independently in the learning centers you have established provides you with the time needed for conferences, inasmuch as you need not be directly involved with the activities of the centers. As is the case with the

FIGURE 7-9   Teacher-Pupil Planned Sequence of Activities in Selected Learning Centers

| Name _Johnny_ | | Week of _____ | | |

Monday	Tuesday	Wednesday	Thursday	Friday
Science Center (Pupil-selected experiments)	Science Center (Pupil-selected experiments)	Science Center (Pupil-selected experiments)	Arts & Crafts Center (Pupil-selected activity)	Arts & Crafts Center (Pupil-selected activity)
Reading Center (Teacher-determined activities)	Reading Center (Teacher-determined activities)	Reading Center (Teacher-determined activities)	Reading Center (Teacher-determined activities)	Reading Center (Teacher-determined activities)
Games Center (Pupil-selected)	Games Center (Pupil-selected)	Creative writing Center (Pupil-selected activity)	Music Center (Pupil-selected activity)	Music Center (Pupil-selected activity)
Social Studies Center (Pupil-initiated project)	Library Research (Pupil-initiated)	Social Studies Center (Pupil-initiated project)	Library Research (Pupil-initiated)	Social Studies Center (Pupil-initiated project)
Mathematics (Teacher-determined activity)	Mathematics (Teacher-determined activity)	Hobby Center (Pupil-selected)	Conference Center (Pupil-initiated progress report to teacher)	Social Studies (Pupil-initiated project)

previous figure, Figure 7-9 also entails the tabulating and sorting of the number of pupils to determine their distribution to the various learning centers.

Despite the paper work involved, this approach to pupil movement in the classroom has its advantages. As well as allowing for both teacher and pupil input, it gives direction to the scope and sequence of the activities to be undertaken by your pupils. In effect, it constitutes their plan of action and enables you to account for their course of learning. It is a contract for the learning to take place, a subject which is treated more extensively in the next chapter.

It is my belief that the simplest, and probably the most effective, approach to involving your pupils is verbal communication. This may be the result of a teacher-pupil class planning session or of a personal conference with each of your pupils. I favor this approach because it reduces the quantity of paper work of the other approaches. Knowing your pupils as you do, a few simple techniques for identifying which of your pupils is doing what and where are sufficient. Let us now turn to these.

Record-keeping. A chief criticism of the open classroom is that it entails extensive record-keeping because of the personalized learning practiced and the necessity to account for this learning. Record-keeping is a very important factor to the success of the open classroom; nevertheless, in accounting for the personal progress of your pupils, the problem of excessive paper work may indeed be a reality. It is necessary, therefore, that you devise procedures to hold your record-keeping down to a minimum. Simple checklists, a number of which were presented in Chapter 4, may be constructed for this purpose. Figure 7–10 is a checklist which shows the learning centers used by various pupils on a given day.

Such a checklist will give you a quick picture of the extent to which your centers are being used and thus provide you with direction for modifying or eliminating those not in use. It also will provide you with information on the

FIGURE 7–10   *Checklist Useful in Identifying the Extent of Pupil Participation in Learning Centers*

DIRECTIONS: Draw a circle alongside your name under the learning centers you have selected to work in. Place an X in each circle when you have completed the work of that center.	LEARNING CENTERS											
	Language Arts	Experiments	Games	Typing	Spelling	Mathematics	Listening	Social Studies	Arts & Crafts	Conference	Ecology	Etc.
Johnny B.												
Susan												
Martha												
Johnny M.												
Tom												
Gloria												
David												
Pat												
Eddie												
Etc.												

personal preferences of your pupils, an important factor which you may subsequently put to use in implementing new learning centers. You will also find a checklist, such as that shown in Figure 7-11, useful in obtaining information on which activities in a particular learning center are being selected by your pupils. A simple expedient is to place a checklist at each of the learning centers you implement. A more extensive form of record-keeping which you may also find useful is shown in Figure 7-12.

FIGURE 7-11   Checklist Useful in Keeping a Record of Activities Initiated and Completed by Pupils in a Learning Center

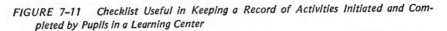

Name					
				Date	

_____Center

Place a circle alongside your name under the activity you have chosen to do, or to which you have been directed. Place an X in the circle when you have completed the activity.

Name	Activity 1	Activity 2	Activity 3	Activity 4	Activity 5
Elvira					
Judy					
Bill					
Jan					
Jimmy					
Jesús					
Keith					
Etc.					

A checklist like this can be used by each of your pupils for self-assessment and by you for evaluating their progress. Note, also, the built-in provision for both your input and that of your pupils; for instance, the opportunity for you to require needed work in designated activities and for your pupils to select activities of their own choosing. You can use 5" X 8" index cards to record the necessary information as shown in the figure. Or, if you prefer, a notebook or

FIGURE 7-12   Illustrative Record-Keeping Instrument Useful in Accounting for Pupil Progress

Name_____
Directions: When you have completed the work of the centers to which you have been directed or have selected, place this record in your personal folder for me to look at. Also, when you see me free, show me what you have done.

Learning Center	You need to do	Choose any activity you wish	Date Started	Date Completed	Self-Assessment of my Work
1. Social Studies Activity No. 1 Activity No. 2 Activity No. 3 Activity No. 4					I had trouble finding information on . . . .
2. Science Center Experiment 1 Experiment 2 Experiment 3					I discovered that . . . .
3. Etc.					

personal folder may be used to record all the learning centers and activities in which your pupils participate.

Do away with as much paper work as is possible in recording the activities of your pupils. Figure 7-13 illustrates one method for doing this. You'll find it an expedient device for knowing where your pupils are functioning at a given moment. As shown in the figure, a pegboard, strips of tape, discs, and hooks are used to list learning centers and to identify which pupils are working where. When directed to, or selecting a center, pupils merely hang their name discs on the hooks alongside the appropriate center. To indicate the number of pupils who are to work in the various centers, simply place the prescribed number of hooks alongside each center as illustrated in the figure. Observe, for example, that the mathematics center has five hooks, indicating that up to five children may work in this center at one time, three may work in the language arts center, and as many as six pupils in the science center.

In addition to its usefulness for record-keeping purposes, this pegboard device facilitates the smooth movement of pupils from learning center to learning center. Your pupils may at a glance quickly identify those centers which are filled to capacity and those which are available to them. On completion of their work at a center, all they need to do is remove their name discs from the hooks and move on to open slots in other centers either of their own choosing or to which they have been directed by you. Furthermore, under this arrangement, no recording of time is necessary. You merely look at your watch or the room clock and the pegboard to find out which of your pupils is doing what, where, and when.

FIGURE 7-13   *Pegboard Device Useful in Identifying Pupils in Learning Centers*

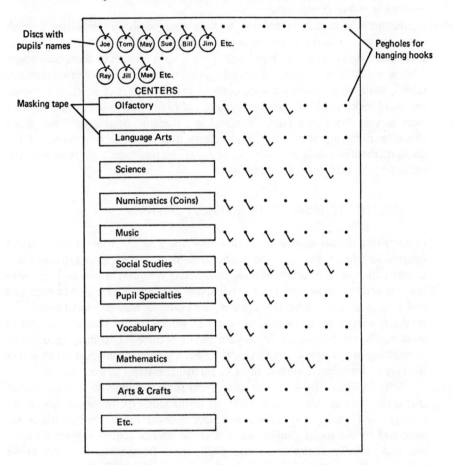

There are, of course, countless other forms of record-keeping that may be utilized, some of which are being used by those of you who are experienced teachers. These range from anecdotal records to the comprehensive materials placed in personal files and cumulative folders. You can devise charts, graphs, contracts, checklists, and personal accounts which include brief descriptions of the activities undertaken by your pupils, the projects they have initiated and completed, the vocabulary they have learned, the skills they have developed and those to be learned, the reading they have done, and the experiments in progress. You can also include other important observations such as the friends they choose to work with, the extent of their enthusiasm for learning, their ability to initiate programs of study, and so on.

To keep records of your pupils' progress in manageable proportions, it is necessary that you give them much of the responsibility for record-keeping. Moreover, do not concern yourself with recording everything that your pupils do every day. Your long-range perspective of your pupils' progress is more reasonable and of greater value.

Is there, in fact, a better way to note your pupils' progress than through observing their actual performances and accomplishments? What could be better than your observation of how well your pupils construct dioramas, shape models, make films, create and record musical pieces, solve problems, dramatize stories, write plays, paint pictures, conduct experiments, put on fashion shows, and build rockets? Clearly, your observation of each of these activities will reveal more to you about your pupils' personal and academic development than will a check, a numeral, or a letter grade ascribed to their performances. In my opinion, these symbols are used too often as the sole means for recording and evaluating the performances of pupils.

MAKING THE TRANSITION TO INTEREST CENTERS

In discussing various approaches to decentralizing your classroom, I have thus far focused largely on the implementation of subject centers as an expedient and comfortable means of accomplishing this. I have encouraged you to begin with learning centers whose subjects, materials, and processes are familiar to both you and your pupils. A mathematics center, for example, may be constituted of the textbook already in use, a spelling center of workbooks or exercises familiar to your pupils, etc. Subsequently, as your pupils become increasingly accustomed to working in the subject centers established, a greater diversification of activities may be introduced, such as those of particular interest to your pupils.

Note in Figure 7-14 the transition from subject centers to interest centers that takes place as pupils express interest in the study of inventions, pollution, ecology, and medicine—interests that have evolved out of the activities experienced in the social studies center and the science center. Subject divisions blur and virtually disappear as your pupils move from center to center in the pursuit of their interests. It is likely that even greater flexibility may be built into your learning-centered classroom as the interests of your pupils are integrated into the other centers you have established (such as the language arts center, the mathematics center, and others). Consequently, you may expect that, although your pupils may be developing skills and deriving concepts associated with the study of social studies, science, language arts, and other subjects, they will be doing so in the pursuit of their specific interests such as inventions, pollution, ecology, and medicine. In the process of this pursuit, centers based on interests such as these will increasingly be established, thus changing the format and shape of your classroom from a subject-centered to an interest-centered environment. That is, your learning centers will evolve out of your pupils' interests as the invention center, pollution center, ecology center, and medicine center evolved out of the science and social studies centers.

No matter what the approach you utilize in implementing your learning centers—gradual, moderate, or total—or whether your centers have a subject emphasis or interest emphasis, the question often arises whether or not pupils, once they have selected a learning center in which to work, should be required to complete the activities of that center. As the teacher, you are in the best position to make the appropriate decision. Certainly, your pupils learning to accept their choice of learning centers is an important step for them in assuming the responsibility associated with freedom. Given the option of choosing any center they wish, what if they make a poor choice? Should you hold them to such a choice, or should you permit them to select another center in which to work? Do not pupils have the right to change their minds? Indeed, these are difficult questions to answer.

FIGURE 7-14   *Transition from Subject Centers to Interest Centers*

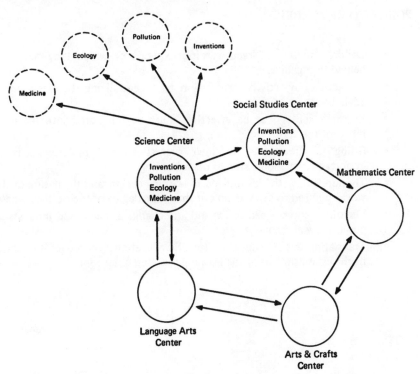

Some teachers take the position that once pupils have committed themselves to a learning center, they must accept the responsibility of their choice, even though it may be a poor one. The assumption underlying this position is that when faced with subsequent opportunities to choose, pupils will think more carefully and wisely before deciding. Also, they maintain, if pupils are permitted to flit from learning center to learning center without completing its activities, they will accomplish little towards advancing their academic and personal growth. Other teachers assume the position that holding pupils to choices they make is undemocratic. In my opinion, there is merit to both points of view. I feel that pupils should be given the opportunity to move from center to center to help them decide on their courses of learning. However, once they make these decisions, as well as those agreed upon in conference with you, it is important that they follow through on them. I do not mean to suggest here that you must necessarily hold your pupils to the centers they select or those to which you direct them. This decision would depend on the nature of the centers. For example, should a poem be "completed," an experiment "proved," or a game "won or lost" *before* pupils are allowed to move on to other centers of interest or need? These are some of the decisions you will have to make in getting your learning-centered classroom underway.

POINTS TO REMEMBER

- Children tend to forget learning experiences which they have not helped to organize.
- An activity-by-activity progression to decentralizing the classroom is advisable.
- Learning centers, to be effective, must be integrated into the total fabric of the classroom.
- Going to the pupils for their suggestions and preferences is an important transitional step to open learning.
- The kinds of activities utilized in learning centers and the nature of the work required to carry them out shape the degree of their effectiveness.
- Learning centers need to expand and change as needs and interests of pupils grow and change.
- Translating pupils' values into specific educational objectives is essential to the establishment of the learning-centered classroom.

NOTES

1. Phyllis Gleyre, "My Experience with the Open Classroom," unpublished paper, University Hills School, Las Cruces, New Mexico, 1972, p. 1.
2. *Ibid.*, p. 5.
3. Adopted and modified from Roberta Sparger's third grade classroom, Fairacres School, Las Cruces, New Mexico, 1972.
4. Adopted and modified from the experiences of Tom Bolles, a student teacher, Gadsden Junior High School, Anthony, New Mexico, 1972.

5. E. Eisher, "Instructional and Expressive Educational Objectives: Their Formulation and Use in Curriculum." In *AERA Monogram Series on Curriculum Evaluation: Vol. 3, Instructional Objectives* (Chicago: Rand McNally, 1969), pp. 15–16 as quoted by Bussis and Chittenden, 1970.

6. Adopted in part and modified from *Language Arts: Comprehension Skills, Grades K–12*, rev. ed., Instructional Objectives Exchange, Box 24095, Los Angeles, Calif. 90024, pp. 21, 49, 60.

Larry—

I don't lick girls any more. Do you?

— Steve

(Age 12)

eight

Evaluating the Effectiveness
of Open Learning
in the Classroom

"Evaluation ... should shape without limiting, point without directing, probe without destroying, mould without molding, motivate without mutilating."
—Leonard Douglas, New Mexico State University, April 3, 1968.

Why do so many pupils respond negatively to the evaluation of their academic work? Possibly the work itself is the reason. Too often, teachers use only the curriculum guides and the texts provided them because they find it expedient to do so. Unfortunately, this often limits the pupils' learning experiences to what the teachers are able to process and evaluate. If you follow this course, it will be exceedingly difficult for you to conduct your classroom in terms of open learning experiences and even more difficult to evaluate the effectiveness of those experiences.

Clearly, in order to open up your classroom, new roles will be required of both you and your pupils. These, in turn, will require a new means of evaluation. Although traditional methods of evaluation may be useful in assessing content areas of your curriculum, the challenge you face is to seek methods for effectively evaluating both your new behaviors and those of your pupils. Prerequisite to this evaluation is your assessment of your total classroom environment and the learning centers of which it is composed.

ASSESSMENT OF CLASSROOM READINESS
FOR OPEN LEARNING

It is generally agreed that there are two central purposes for evaluating the effectiveness of learning in a classroom: (1) its usefulness to pupils and (2) its usefulness to the teacher in helping the pupils. The open classroom is no exception. In the first chapter, the point was made that it is difficult to define the open classroom in precise, absolute terms. Consequently, you may assume that it is also difficult to evaluate the open learning experiences that take place in your classroom. Although it is difficult, it is not impossible. In fact, the open classroom, because it is a relatively new approach to the teaching of children, will provide you with considerable and interesting opportunities to learn more about *how* your pupils learn and what they *feel* about their learning. In assessing your classroom, a first step would be to examine its dimensions and the characteristics of its dimensions.

It is important in evaluating the dimensions and characteristics of your classroom that you use the results of your assessment as guidelines for making the transition to open education practices. How, then, might you make this assessment? Clearly, the initial step in any process of evaluation is the establishment of criteria by which your assessment can be made. Pertinent criteria for opening up your classroom have been presented. Hopefully you will find these criteria useful in making your assessment of: (1) the extent to which you have prepared your environment for open learning and (2) the nature of the operational practices in your classroom. To discover these, you will need to evaluate each of your learning centers and your total classroom.

EVALUATING THE LEARNING CENTER

My thesis has been that learning centers are not goals in themselves, but are the means by which your pupils may achieve better educational experiences. It is important, therefore, that you evaluate the effectiveness of these means—first, by assessing *each* of the learning centers you implement and second, by assessing the function of your learning centers in your total classroom environment. Figure 3–11 presents one means by which you can evaluate each learning center. To assess each of your learning centers, prior to and after its use by your pupils, turn to the criteria shown in that figure for your points of referral. Or, if you prefer, establish a series of questions to help you evaluate each of the centers you implement. Consider the following:

1. Is the learning center constructed so that your pupils are attracted to it?
2. Do the activities of the center invite and encourage participation by your pupils?

3. Is the purpose of the center clearly expressed to your pupils so that they recognize it as being of value to them?

4. Does the learning center provide for sufficient working space?

5. Are the directions for pupil activity at the center clear enough for your pupils to understand and follow?

6. Is the center stocked with easily accessible materials stored in clearly designated places?

7. Where appropriate, are self-correcting keys placed at the center for pupil self-checking and assessment?

8. Is the center constructed so that it leads your pupils to increase the number and variety of their interests?

9. Does the center, where appropriate, encourage your pupils to deal with their own interests or needs through inquiry, study, thought, and application?

10. Does the learning center invite your pupils to create their own responses, organize their own materials, and share in the management of their learning experiences?

EVALUATING THE DIMENSIONS OF THE CLASSROOM

To evaluate the total dimensions of your classroom, you will need to utilize existing referral points or devise your own by which you can make your assessment. Figure 6–3 illustrates some very important dimensions and characteristics by which you can judge whether or not your classroom environment is prepared for the implementation of your learning centers. If you can answer "yes" to each of the criteria shown in the figure, you have prepared your classroom well. Similarly, you can use the dimensions and characteristics outlined in Figure 1–2 to assess the readiness of your classroom for open learning experiences. Where do your practices stand in terms of each of the characteristics shown in the figure? To what extent? Perhaps you can create your own instrument to make this assessment. You may find it useful to first establish a series of questions as guidelines for this purpose. Ask yourself:

1. Who is to determine the objectives to be achieved in your classroom? You? Your pupils? Both you and your pupils?

2. To what extent will you select the content of your classroom curriculum from your curriculum guide? From your pupils' needs and interests? From both sources?

3. To what extent do you plan to decentralize your classroom environment for maximum learning by your pupils?

4. To what extent do you plan to diversify the learning experiences of your pupils to meet their varied needs and interests?

5. How will you find out what your pupils are interested in and what they will need to do to meet their interests?

6. To what extent do you plan to involve your pupils in the planning, organization, and implementation of your classroom activities?
7. To what extent do you plan to have the activities of your learning centers allow for the differences in the rate of work and progress of your pupils?
8. To what extent will the interaction between you and your pupils and among your pupils be the result of their input? Your input?

You may find Figure 8-1 useful in extending the degree of your total classroom evaluation. I include it here to help you summarize the dimensions and characteristics of the open classroom, particularly with reference to its operational procedures. Study Figure 8-1 carefully. Note its diagnostic and evaluation components. Observe the important references it makes regarding your need to: (1) assess your pupils' prior progress and readiness to engage in the activities of the learning centers you establish and (2) assess the effectiveness of your pupils' experiences in the learning centers. This assessment is necessary, for the results of your evaluation will likely determine the number and kinds of learning centers you establish and the approaches you take towards their implementation.

Your evaluation of the effectiveness of the learning that takes place in your classroom and in each of the learning centers of which it is composed must, of course, be based on the extent to which the interests and needs of your pupils are being met. Perhaps your most important task in making the transition to open education practices in your classroom will be to find out what your pupils are interested in, want to accomplish, need to accomplish, think about, understand, feel, and enjoy. School records and various standardized survey instruments may provide you with some pertinent information. More likely, however, you will need to devise your own procedures for making these judgments.

ASSESSMENT OF PUPILS' NEEDS, INTERESTS, AND PERFORMANCE

As you open up your classroom, you will probably find that your relationships with your pupils and the relationships between your pupils will have more impact on the effectiveness of the learning taking place in your classroom than will a particular philosophy or approach to teaching and learning. Thus, in making your assessment of your pupils' needs, interests, and performance in your classroom, it is important that you start with their experiences. The more you know about your pupils, the more information you will gain that you need to establish effective learning experiences in your learning centers. Some of the

FIGURE 8-1   *Major Components of an Instructional System Unique to the Open Classroom*

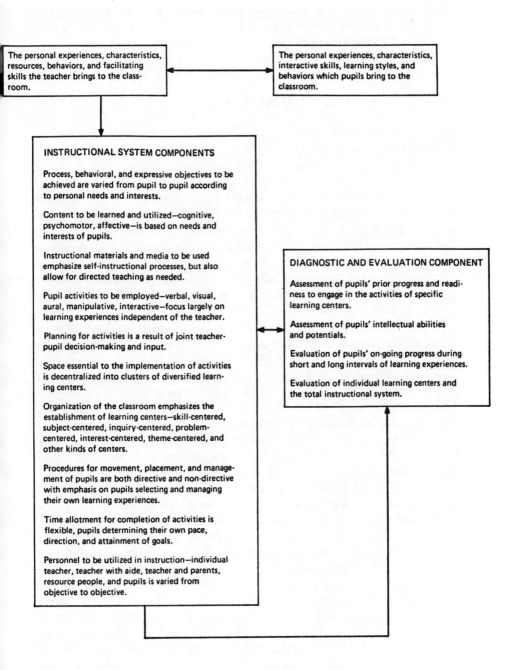

The personal experiences, characteristics, resources, behaviors, and facilitating skills the teacher brings to the classroom.

The personal experiences, characteristics, interactive skills, learning styles, and behaviors which pupils bring to the classroom.

INSTRUCTIONAL SYSTEM COMPONENTS

Process, behavioral, and expressive objectives to be achieved are varied from pupil to pupil according to personal needs and interests.

Content to be learned and utilized—cognitive, psychomotor, affective—is based on needs and interests of pupils.

Instructional materials and media to be used emphasize self-instructional processes, but also allow for directed teaching as needed.

Pupil activities to be employed—verbal, visual, aural, manipulative, interactive—focus largely on learning experiences independent of the teacher.

Planning for activities is a result of joint teacher-pupil decision-making and input.

Space essential to the implementation of activities is decentralized into clusters of diversified learning centers.

Organization of the classroom emphasizes the establishment of learning centers—skill-centered, subject-centered, inquiry-centered, problem-centered, interest-centered, theme-centered, and other kinds of centers.

Procedures for movement, placement, and management of pupils are both directive and non-directive with emphasis on pupils selecting and managing their own learning experiences.

Time allotment for completion of activities is flexible, pupils determining their own pace, direction, and attainment of goals.

Personnel to be utilized in instruction—individual teacher, teacher with aide, teacher and parents, resource people, and pupils is varied from objective to objective.

DIAGNOSTIC AND EVALUATION COMPONENT

Assessment of pupils' prior progress and readiness to engage in the activities of specific learning centers.

Assessment of pupils' intellectual abilities and potentials.

Evaluation of pupils' on-going progress during short and long intervals of learning experiences.

Evaluation of individual learning centers and the total instructional system.

procedures and instruments you may find useful for evaluation include: teacher-pupil planning, conferencing, pretesting, needs and interest surveys, observations, behavioral notes and anecdotal records, diaries, and contracts. The first three procedures have already been presented and illustrated. Let us now turn, then, to some important uses of needs and interests surveys, observations, behavioral notes, diaries, and contracts.

FINDING PUPILS' NEEDS AND INTERESTS

Central to and underlying your pupils' capacities to perform successfully in your learning-centered classroom are how they feel about themselves, how they view others, what they think about, what they prefer to do, and what they don't like to do. It is very important, therefore, that you find out what your pupils are all about. It is especially important because the feedback you get will help facilitate and guide the learning experiences of your classroom. You can use various self-concept rating instruments and interest surveys for this purpose. Figure 8-2 illustrates one such instrument.[1] In using a survey instrument of this type, you may find that some of your pupils, particularly those in their first year of schooling, are unable to respond fully to it because they are unable to read and write well. Thus, it will be necessary to have them respond orally to each of the statements in the instrument.

Note the use to which you can put the information gained from a self-concept rating instrument such as that shown in the figure. Clearly, it is an important tool for learning your pupils' thoughts. It will reveal what your pupils feel about required reading, homework, report cards, the kinds of arithmetic and science activities they undergo, their academic references, and their personal feelings. In addition to the valuable feedback it may give you about your pupils, it is also useful in providing feedback essential to the pupils themselves. It will help make your pupils' feelings visible to them, especially if you discuss their responses with them. It is, consequently, a valuable means for developing your pupils' understanding of their competence, progress, and potential.

There are, understandably, advantages in creating your own survey tools simply because you are in the best position to determine the kinds of things you'd like to find out about your pupils. Thus, you may prefer to construct your own survey instrument for obtaining information which is necessary to implement appropriate learning experiences for your pupils. Figure 8-3 is representative of a teacher-constructed instrument designed to do this.[2]

The kinds of learning centers you implement in your classroom will, without question, affect each of your pupils differently. Therefore, your centers can provide successful experiences for them only when you consider each pupil as an individual. Perhaps Figures 8-2 and 8-3 will prove useful in helping you do this. Keep in mind that both of these figures are representative of self-evaluation instruments to be completed by pupils. For you to accept the results and to use them to best advantage, it is necessary that you:

1. Respect and believe in your pupils' capacities to evaluate themselves and their learning.
2. Accept somewhat different goals for your pupils than those you may have had in mind for them.
3. Accept your pupils' own sequences of learning experiences and their elimination of certain activities that they can demonstrate they do not need.
4. Accept your pupils' plans, strategies, and approaches for achieving needed skills and knowledge.
5. Accept your pupils' selection of experiences in the pursuit of learning of special interest to them.[3]

FIGURE 8-2   *Self-Concept Rating Instrument for Pupils*

DIRECTIONS: I am going to begin certain sentences for you.
I want you to finish each sentence with the first idea that comes to your mind.

1.   My idea of a good time . . .

2.   When I have to read, I . . .

3.   I wish my parents knew . . .

4.   I can't understand why . . .

5.   I feel bad when . . .

6.   I wish my teacher . . .

7.   I wish my mother . . .

8.   People think I . . .

9.   I like to read about . . .

10. To me, homework . . .

11. I hope I'll never . . .

12. I wish people wouldn't . . .

13. When I take my report card home . . .

14. Most brothers and sisters . . .

15. I'd rather read than . . .

16. I feel proud when . . .

17. When I read arithmetic problems . . .

18. I wish my father . . .

19. I like to read when . . .

20. I would like to be . . .

21. I often worry about . . .

22. Reading science . . .   Name _____

23. I wish someone would help me . . .   Date _____

FIGURE 8–3   Teacher-Constructed Needs Analysis Instrument

DIRECTIONS: Respond to the following statements as accurately as you can. What you have to say will be very important in helping us develop our classroom as interestingly as is possible.

1.   If you could learn anything you wanted in this classroom, what would you choose? (Does not have to be a school subject).

_____

2.   What one thing is <u>most</u> interesting to you? (Does not have to be a school subject).

_____

3.   What is the one thing that bothers you most about your teacher?

_____

4.   What is the one thing about your teacher that you like most?

_____

5.   To help you get ready for adult life, what do you think you really need to learn in this classroom?

_____

6.   Which of the items on the following list should your teacher give you more time for? Write a 1 by the most important, a 2 by the next most important, a 3 by the third most important, etc.

_____   Personal reading time (for any book or reading material)
_____   Science (experiments)
_____   Free activities (things <u>you</u> choose to do)
_____   Math
_____   Art
_____   Music
_____   Talking to other children
_____   Finding out what's happening in the world

7.   Write a + before each of the statements you feel is <u>true</u>, and a 0 before each of the statements you feel is <u>false.</u>

_____   The classroom is as good as it can be.
_____   I have never been afraid in the classroom.
_____   The teacher most always gives me fair grades.
_____   I can't work too well without help.
_____   Sometimes I wonder why I do the work I am expected to do.
_____   I think I could learn all the stuff the teacher gives me if she wouldn't push me so hard.
_____   If I didn't have to go to school I'd never read a book.

FIGURE 8-3—Continued

	I'm really pretty dumb.
	Most of my subjects are fun.
	I'm treated like a kid too much.
	When I learn something, it sticks with me.
	I get attention when I need it.
	The teacher should never blow her cool.
	I only want good grades—bad grades show how dumb I am.
	I need to be alone in a quiet place sometimes.
	It's fun to make the teacher mad, but I wouldn't do it if school were better.
	I need important things to do.
	I can decide what I like and need better than my teacher can.

Inasmuch as the activities of your learning-centered classroom are to be constructed around the behavior of your pupils, it is important that you evaluate their behavior as indicative of their needs and interests. You will find this kind of assessment pertinent to the kinds of learning experiences you need to provide your pupils in the various learning centers you plan to establish. For example, if the results of your evaluation show that certain pupils are reluctant to share their information, opinions, and feelings, it might be appropriate for you to guide them to learning centers where they are invited to do so. If others find it difficult to evaluate their own progress, you could direct them to activities that would provide them with the opportunities that would help to develop this ability. Figure 8-4 illustrates the series of events following the signing of a contract that may be used for these purposes. The subsequent evaluation may be made by you, by your pupils, or by both of you.

ASSESSING PUPILS' PROGRESS TOWARDS FULFILLMENT OF NEEDS AND INTERESTS

Putting the feedback you get from the results of your surveys to work and assessing the progress made by your pupils will likely pose a challenge to you. Contracts, diaries, and observational and anecdotal records may be used to determine pupil progress. A natural transition to assessing their progress may, for example, consist of contractual agreements between you and your pupils and your observation of their performance in the classroom. You may find that a contract may work well for those pupils who find it difficult to pursue their own goals and interests when no time or production demands are placed upon them.

The Contract. An increasing number of teachers are finding it helpful to make use of contractual arrangements with their pupils to evaluate their

FIGURE 8-4   Pupil Self-Evaluation of Behaviors in the Classroom

My Behavior	WAYS I LOOK AT ME!			
	I do this most often	I would like to do this most often	I do not do this well	I would like to do this well
Initiate action				
Seek information and opinions				
Share information, opinions, and feelings				
Lead activities				
Encourage classmates' participation				
Follow class leaders				
Monopolize activities				
Butter up classmates				
Seek recognition and rewards				
Fight for rights				
Withdraw from competition				
Horse around				
Seek sympathy				
Evaluate self-progress				

progress. The ideal learning contract invites *both* pupil and teacher input. This input will vary with each of your pupils. For some pupils, the commitment recorded on the contract might consist almost entirely of the pupils' own input; for other pupils, you would take the major responsibility for the decisions to be made. Ideally, the ultimate agreement would be based on the interests expressed by your pupils and on what they need to do to achieve their goals. Thus, the nature of each contract would vary from pupil to pupil and from objective to objective. Figure 8-5 illustrates one such approach.

FIGURE 8-5   Sequential Development of a Contract

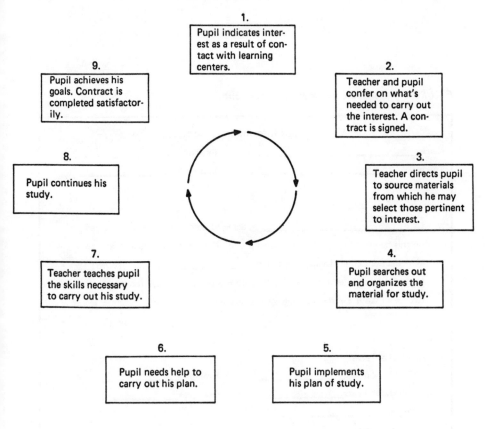

Each contract between you and your pupils must be a natural outcome of the conferences you hold with them. You will find that while some of your pupils will be capable of writing their own contracts, others will likely have difficulty formulating their ideas and setting forth their terms. Contracts may be either very simple or very complex. They may take the pattern of handwritten statements by your pupils: for example, "I will complete my social studies project on the Navajo Indians by _____ (date)," or "I agree to finish at least ten examples from each of the assigned pages of my arithmetic book by the end of the week." A more formal contract might take the form shown in Figure 8-6.

FIGURE 8-6   *Representative Mathematics Contract*

Mathematics Intermediate Contract

Name_____   Beginning Date_____

Teacher _____   Ending Date _____

I, _____, agree to complete the work recorded

on this contract by the date stipulated above. If I need any help at the

Mathematics Center, I will ask a friend or _____ (the teacher)

for it. If I continue to have difficulty with my work, I will ask for a con-

ference to see if a different contract is indicated.

Contracted Work

    Textbook pages_____   Examples_____

    Workbook pages_____   Examples_____

    Project_____

                                Signed_____
                                        Pupil's Signature

                                        _____

                                        Teacher's Signature

Even primary schoolchildren may enjoy some forms of contractual arrangement for their learning experiences. The agreed-upon plan need not be complex. Look at the reading contract illustrated in Figure 8-7, for example.

FIGURE 8-7   Sample Reading Contract

Primary Reading Contract

Name _____   Date _____

1. I will listen to _____ recorded stories at the Listening Center.
2. I will read _____ of the stories I listened to at the Reading Center.
3. I will learn _____ new words from the vocabulary cards that match the _____ stories I have read.
4. I will tell a story that I have made up in the Story Center.

Signed _____
Pupil's Signature

_____
Teacher's Signature

Another version of a learning contract suitable for primary school pupils may be similar to the arrangement shown in Figure 8-8. As is apparent, it involves multiple experiences with arithmetic, science, and reading, the specificities of which are recorded in the appropriate spaces for the pupil's attention.

FIGURE 8-8   Multiple-Purpose Learning Contract

Primary Learning Contract

Name_____   Grade_____

I agree to do the following work this week, March 23 to March 27.

Signature_____
Pupil's Name

_____
Teacher's Name

Numbers	Sounds	Senses	Reading

Those of you who plan to or are presently teaching in the upper grades may find the form shown in Figure 8-9 more suitable for your purposes. It is subject-centered and, as is the case with other kinds of contracts, should be the result of your mutual agreement with a pupil on what needs to be accomplished. The contract shown in Figure 8-9 differs from those previously illustrated in that it brings the pupil's parent(s) into the contractual agreement.

FIGURE 8–9   *Multiple-Subject Learning Contract*

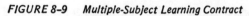

Individual Learning Contract

I, _____ hereby do contract with myself to satisfactorily

complete the following tasks as agreed upon by _____

(the teacher) and me by the dates recorded after each task to be done.

Subject	Task to be accomplished	Date to be completed
Reading	1. 2. 3. Etc.	
Arithmetic	1. 2. 3. Etc.	
Social Studies	1. 2. 3. Etc.	
Language Arts	1. 2. 3. Etc.	
Science	1. 2. 3. Etc.	
Special Projects	1. 2. 3. Etc.	

_____
Pupil's Signature

_____
Teacher's Signature

_____   _____
Date of Agreement   Parent's Signature

The contract format that I prefer is one in which the pupils are encouraged to pursue their own interests while at the same time utilizing the different options available to them. Figure 8-10 illustrates this arrangement. In working out your agreement with an individual pupil, it is important that you encourage him to respond as openly as he can to the things he'd like to do to fulfill his goals.

FIGURE 8-10   *Personal Interest Contract*

Intermediate Interest Contract

Name_____   Date_____

1.   I,_____, am interested in researching the topic
     of_____ . To fulfill this interest, I
     will spend a minimum of _____ hours in the appropriate
     learning center and in the school multi-resources center each day
     searching out materials I need, reading, and taking notes on the subject
     of my interest.

2.   Additionally, I will do_____of the following projects, as agreed upon
     in my conference.
     a.   Prepare a chart which helps explain my research findings.
     b.   Construct and demonstrate a model, diorama or exhibit
          related to my interest.
     c.   Compile a scrapbook of materials accumulated as a result
          of my research.
     d.   Write a report on the topic of my research.
     e.   Prepare and make a talk about what I find out.
     f.   Invite a guest speaker to talk, if appropriate, about the
          importance of my interest.
     g.   Record a tape on my research and place it in the Listening
          Center for others to listen to.

                              Signed _____
                                     Pupil's Name

                                     _____
                                     Teacher's Name

Some of you may be interested in utilizing a contract in which your pupils are given the option of determining their own grades and the activities they will do to achieve the grades. Figure 8-11 is representative of this form of contract.

FIGURE 8-11   Grade Contract

Grade Contract

Name _____   Date _____

I, _____ , wish to earn a grade of _____

in_____ (the subject or topic). To earn this grade, I agree to do the

following things:

1.   Complete the assigned written work agreed upon in conference with
      my teacher, to be undertaken at the _____ Center.

2.   Read a minimum of _____ books which are related to my
      assignment.

3.   Learn the meaning of _____ new words taken from
      my readings and demonstrate my understanding of the words by
      using each correctly in sentences that I write.

4.   Take and successfully pass, as determined by my teacher, a written
      examination on my assignment.

5.   Complete a project of my choice for use in the _____ Center.

Signed _____
                              Pupil's signature

_____
Teacher's signature

Contractual agreements are not necessarily good for all pupils. Although contracts are used successfully by an increasing number of teachers, you may discover that they become dull and monotonous mechanisms for accomplishing specified learning experiences. This is most likely to occur when they are used excessively and are exclusively oriented to be used with textbooks, with little or no input allowed by pupils. Only you, with your unique set of circumstances, can determine the effect of the contract system as a vehicle for assessing the progress of your pupils.

If you feel that contracting is an approach that works well for some of your pupils, then by all means use it. I suggest, however, that you break up the repetitive experiences that contracts call for by including options for your pupils that extend and enrich their learning. Utilize projects at every opportunity. For example, in a mathematics contract pertaining to a study of measurement, a related activity might invite your pupils to measure objects and places other than those presented in the textbook. Your classroom itself might be measured, drawn to scale, and the results compared with the plan of the classroom drawn by the school's architect. In conjunction with their focus on measurement, a project some of your pupils are apt to find interesting is the study of the historical development of measurement. A great number of rather intriguing materials are available on this subject from various business and industrial corporations, usually without charge.

It is important that you do not construe the contract as inflexible with respect to time and scope. It must be designed to provide both you and your pupils with a perspective on what is to be achieved and should indicate the direction that should be taken to achieve these goals. The contract may range from a very simple commitment by your pupils, such as promising to learn to spell a few words, to a more extended commitment which may involve a period of several weeks, such as completing a long-range experiment in science or a special project in the social studies.

It is also important that you do not penalize your pupils if they do not complete the stipulated terms of the contracts. Rather than assigning a poor grade to an incompleted contract or one not done well, for example, you should rewrite the contract to meet more nearly the intellectual capacities and abilities of your pupils so that they are provided with both a challenge and the probability of success.

In assessing the contractual performance of your pupils, you may find the use of pupil diaries helpful. The effectiveness of diaries in disseminating information to you concerning your pupils' progress would, of course, be determined by the pupils' ability to express themselves in this form.

The Pupil Diary.   The use of a pupil diary as an instrument for evaluating pupil performance is being used successfully by some teachers. Diaries, if skillfully evaluated by you, may provide you with information about your pupils that may not otherwise be revealed to you. That is, your pupils' innermost thoughts may be brought to the surface where you can examine and study them. Note the following entry, for example, in which a pupil discusses his work at a learning center and his personal relationship with another pupil:

> . . . . It is comeing along fine. But has gotten to the point where I can hardly finsh my work. I have not better stick with G_____ any more. He does not finsh his work then he does not let me do my work. I think if G_____ leves me alone I might finsh work.

Obviously, such an entry in a diary provides the teacher with information about the relationship between G_____ and the writer of the entry. Should the teacher talk with both pupils concerning their relationship, or should they be encouraged to work things out for themselves? The diary entry also suggests that the pupil is having some difficulty with spelling and written expression. Should the pupil be given formal instruction in spelling and language skills at this time? Clearly, the diary entry provides the teacher with information about the pupil and suggests directions that possibly need to be taken with respect to his academic and personal progress.

A further entry in the same pupil's diary reveals:

> My partner is a lazy guy and he slows me down then I can't do my my work and thats what I hate.

Without question, the entry points out the writer's relationship with G_____ is worsening. If you were called upon to evaluate this situation, what would you do?

As is the case with the contract approach to teaching, the use of diaries for purposes of evaluation is not necessarily appropriate for all pupils. This ought to be an option that the pupils themselves select or reject. Some of your pupils may enjoy writing diaries; others may find it a chore. Still others may not yet have developed the written skills necessary to express their thoughts. There is also the danger that recording entries in a diary may discourage certain pupils from other forms of written expression. If not handled carefully, diary writing will, in fact, lose the interest of the pupils. It is difficult for a good many children and, when done routinely and in excess, such as on a day-to-day basis, it tends to result in dull, repetitive, meaningless entries. In using the diary as an instrument for evaluating your pupils' thoughts and academic progress, it is important to note that diaries are their intimate and personal expressions. You must, therefore, reach a mutual understanding that their diary entries are to be shared only between you and them and are not to be revealed to others without their permission.

In my opinion, the most effective means you have at your disposal for evaluating your pupils' progress toward the fulfillment of their needs and interests, other than by personal conferences with them, is by observing their behavior and performance in your classroom. The section that follows is designed to acquaint you with some procedures you may wish to consider for this purpose.

Observation of Pupil Behavior.   Observing your pupils' behavior in the classroom is one of the best single means you can use to assess your pupils' progress, simply because it is an ongoing evaluation that you need to make to personalize your pupils' learning experiences. It is, of course, difficult to evaluate your pupils' growth unless you establish some criteria or objectives against which their growth can be measured. Instruments based strictly on norms are not the answer because they reveal very little about the specifics of the growth processes that are experienced by pupils in the learning-centered classroom. Nor are grades the answer for an effective evaluation of your pupils' progress. Nor do standardized tools or grades tell much about what your pupils have experienced beyond the superficial achievements such as an answer derived in arithmetic, a word spelled, or a level reached in reading. Neither approach will measure your pupils' new and important behaviors as they satisfy their needs and interests through open learning experiences.

Inasmuch as the needs and interests of your pupils cannot be judged as either "excellent or poor," "good or bad," or "A or F," you must come to the decision that grades are inappropriate for evaluating the behavior and performance of your pupils. In fact, grades are merely symbols, and you must not consider them as a just measure of pupil progress. Because the open, learning-centered classroom is largely process-oriented, it is important that you identify and evaluate many processes rather than restricting yourself to those you personally like and feel at ease with and which will present the fewest problems to you. Clearly, old methods of evaluation intended strictly as an assessment of knowledge of content are not appropriate to the new roles and behaviors of the open classroom. You will need to find more pertinent ways, for example, to assess your pupils' adjustment and adaptation to change, their receptiveness to different points of view, their ability to think and work independently, their capacity for leadership, and their ability to make their own judgments, as well as other processes that are involved in open learning experiences.

Among these very important processes is decision-making by your pupils. In assessing their ability to make decisions essential to the operation of your classroom, you must first consider three basic questions:

1. What kinds of decisions do your pupils have the right to make?
2. What kinds of decisions do your pupils have the competence to make?
3. What kinds of decisions do your pupils have the responsibility to make?

It is important that you study your responses to these questions before you determine the extent to which your pupils should make decisions.

Integral to the processes of the open classroom are those that invite your pupils to exercise initiative, originality, and creativity. The challenge, then, is to develop the procedures for evaluating the degree to which your pupils exercise these in your classroom. Can your pupils' initiative, originality, inventiveness, perseverance, resourcefulness, industriousness, enthusiasm, motivation, and other important behavioral characteristics underlying open learning be evaluated? I feel they can and need to be evaluated by you since they lie at the very heart of open educational practices in the learning-centered classroom. You can use each of these important components as referral points for evaluating your pupils' progress and growth.

Unfortunately, very little is presently available to help you evaluate the open learning experiences to be undertaken by your pupils. Although there are standardized observational scales that are available, they are not generally used to assess the behavior unique to the open classroom. Consequently, you will need to devise your own instruments of observation. To establish the necessary criteria for this purpose, recall the behavioral characteristics of the preceding paragraph and those listed on page 9 of the first chapter. Included in these ingredients are pertinent criteria which you may use to assess your pupils' abilities to work independently and creatively in your classroom, to interact with each other, and to self-select, self-pace, self-manage, and self-evaluate their learning experiences.

To formally assess the creative expression of your pupils, for example, you must first identify the behavioral characteristics that constitute this expression[4] and then develop a format for evaluating the extent to which the characteristics are expressed by each of your pupils. Figure 8-12 is representative of one such format.

In evaluating the extent of your pupils' creative expression, you will need to utilize a rating scale. Figure 8-12 illustrates one kind of scale you can use. To put the scale in the figure to work, simply place an "X" in the appropriate column alongside the behavioral characteristics to be assessed according to the scale of values found at the head of each column. This assessment will thus provide you with an important insight into the creative expression of each of your pupils. To keep your total class in perspective, a necessary next step would be to construct a class profile of this expression, as shown in Figure 8-13.

You may, in recording your assessment of your total class membership, ascribe a numerical value to each of the behavioral characteristics exhibited by your pupils. Should you be called upon to do so, you will thus be able to convert your numerical scores to a statistical interpretation of what they represent, for example, as in finding the frequency of distribution in your class. This, in turn, will provide you with a picture of your class in creative action.

Note, in Figure 8-13, the utility to which you may put the behavioral characteristics observed. For example, as indicated in the figure, Dan almost never asks questions and presumably shows very little resourcefulness in his approach to work. Alice, on the other hand, persistently inquires and displays much resourcefulness, in the process of which she initiates and produces new

FIGURE 8-12   Criteria for Observing Pupils' Creative Behavioral Characteristics

	4 Almost always	3 Much of the time	2 Some of the time	1 Almost never
Pupil _____ Period Beginning _____ Ending_____ Behavior Characteristics				
1. Employs unique, novel approaches to experimentation.				
2. Looks for fresh patterns and arrangements in designing and building things.				
3. Self-initiates and produces new hypotheses, new ideas, new solutions, new experiences.				
4. Enjoys working independently of peers.				
5. Searches out questions, as well as solutions to problems.				
6. Speculates and imagines about phenomena of all kinds.				
7. Invents imaginatively and with originality new words, new formulas, new codes, new things and gadgets.				
8. Displays resourcefulness and flexibility. Brings to bear the unusual, the unexpected.				
9. Thinks and responds divergently. Moves and performs in different directions, away from established norms and standards.				
10. Develops own novel plans and strategies for solving problems.				
11. Projects own interpretation of issues and events, producing different ways for doing things.				
12. Displays extensive curiosity, persistently and constantly asking questions.				
13. Expresses self freely and spontaneously without inhibition.				
14. Absorbs self deeply and persistently in ideas, not concerned with time.				
15. Retrieves information and builds associations necessary to produce efficiently.				
16. Shows willingness to take a chance, to venture into the unknown.				
17. Integrates complex experiences into simpler arrangements; develops satisfying order from disorder.				
18. Shows humor, playfulness, lack of rigidity, and relaxation in the performance of work.				

ideas and experiences. Ostensibly, if Dan and Alice were in your class, you would need to approach each differently and provide each with considerably different learning experiences in the learning centers you establish. The same would be true of the rest of your pupils. Different behaviors would reflect different needs and would, without question, require different experiences.

Your assessment in this manner will reveal much to you about the extent of the creativity, or lack of it, of your children. Given this information, then, you

FIGURE 8-13   Class Profile of Pupils' Creative Expression

	Employs unique, novel approaches to experimentation	Looks for fresh patterns and arrangements in designing and building things	Self-initiates and produces new hypotheses, new ideas, new solutions, new experiences	Enjoys working independently of peers	Searches out questions as well as solutions to problems	Speculates and imagines about phenomena of all kinds	Invents imaginatively and with originality new words, new formulas, new codes, new things and gadgets	Displays resourcefulness and flexibility. Brings to bear the unusual, the unexpected	Thinks and responds divergently moves and performs in different directions, away from established norms and standards	Develops own novel plans and strategies for solving problems	Projects own interpretation of issues and events, producing different ways for doing things	Etc.
Alice			4		4			4				
Billy												
Clara												
Dan			1					1				
Eddie												
Freda												
Etc.												

SCALE

4 - Almost always
3 - Much of the time
2 - Some of the time
1 - Almost never

can take the appropriate steps to establish experiences in your learning centers that will provide pupils who have not exhibited creative behavior with the opportunities to creatively express themselves and that will extend the creative expression of those pupils who have already made progress in this direction. A careful, item-by-item analysis of the behavior you observe and record will subsequently lead you to more creative teaching.

Remember, the evaluation procedures shown in Figures 8-12 and 8-13 are representative. In constructing your own evaluation instruments, I suggest that you modify their criteria to suit the creative characteristics unique to your own pupils and to the classroom situation in general.

You can even assess the degree of imagination shown by your pupils in creatively expressing their ideas. Indeed, those of you who are experienced teachers are already informally testing your pupils' imagination by encouraging classroom activities that are designed to put it to work. However, informal evaluation, as important as it is, is often not communicated to school administrators and parents and to others who may hold you accountable for the progress of your pupils. An important step, therefore, is to formalize your assessment so that this progress becomes a matter of record. Even more important is that this will also make your targets for enhancing your pupils' learning experiences more apparent to you.

There are unique and fascinating approaches to the formalized assessment of children's imaginations. In constructing and validating the Minnesota Tests of Creative Thinking, E. Paul Torrance and his associates developed tests which called upon children to test their imagination by responding to:

"Unusual uses" (of tin cans)

"Consequences" (what would happen if animals could talk)

"Just suppose" (that shadows became real)

"Situations" (handling a friend who likes to kid others but cannot stand to be kidded)

"Common problems" (such as in taking a bath)

"Improvements" (how to make a toy dog more fun to play with)[5]

I'm certain that you can use and expand criteria such as these in building a test which evaluates your pupils' extent of imaginative expression. To evaluate this extent, you will, of course, need to develop a rating scale. You may find the scale shown in Figures 8–12 and 8–13 appropriate for this purpose.

Similarly, in developing and utilizing other instruments for assessing the behaviors and performances of your pupils, you will first need to identify the components you wish to evaluate. How well do your pupils work without your detailed directions? How well do they initiate their activities? Do they follow through on ideas expressed or questions raised? How do they cope with and adjust to new situations and new learnings? Can they explain, demonstrate, or teach an idea or process to each other? Do they dig out key issues and facts important to them? Can they set up experiments and work with materials at learning centers, interact with each other, and assume responsibility for their own behavior? All of these elements are important to the learning-centered classroom and need your careful evaluation if you are to open up your classroom successfully.

You may find it expedient to use index cards for recording pupil behaviors such as those cited in the preceding paragraph. Figure 8–14 illustrates one format for doing this. There are, of course, variations you may prefer to use, such as a rating scale to evaluate the extent of the behavioral characteristics you record.

Checklists, rating scales, and behavioral notes, as valuable as they are as tools for assessing the behavior and performances of your pupils, are not always sufficient for evaluating precisely what they have accomplished in a particular context. Consequently, you may find anecdotal records more useful for this purpose. When well-written, they are especially useful in objectively describing the behavior of your pupils. Much time, of course, is required in compiling anecdotes. In writing your descriptive statements, therefore, it is important that you carefully select the behaviors you record. Be as specific and as concrete as you can and pick out only significant behavior. Use your pupils' own words so that what you record reflects their actual behavior and not your personal interpretation of their behavior. Be sure to include in your anecdotes those that clearly express the results of your pupils' efforts, such as a diorama constructed, a painting completed, a verse written, a model sculptured, or a graph or chart designed.

FIGURE 8-14   *Criteria for Behavioral Notes*

BEHAVIORAL NOTES

Pupil's Name_____   Week Beginning_____

Week Ending_____

I.   Characteristics to build on

Initiates own activities (the pollution project)

Contributes useful ideas (on arrangement of materials in the social

studies center)

Follows through plans (almost always)

Offers positive criticism (helped to solve arithmetic problems)

Displays leadership (on pollution project)

Very inventive (the "Jensenada")

Poetic (note the three poems written in the language arts center)

Etc.

II.   Characteristics which need to be modified

Monopolizes conversation (on pollution project)

Untidy written work (typewriter ??)

Interrupts others at learning centers (conference required)

Etc.

Also include in your records the number and kind of learning centers in which your pupils have participated, the classmates they've worked with, the projects initiated, the reports made, and the work completed. Show precisely where they have exercised leadership, contributed ideas, shared materials, and taken responsible action. Describe their emotional and social behavior as well as their academic performance. Look for the positive components of their behavior and cite the actual incidents that reflect these. It is also important to describe those areas in which your pupils need help. Pin these down as specifically as you can so that you can plan to build into each of your pupils' subsequent learning experiences work in the necessary areas.

There are, certainly, other procedures you may utilize to assess your pupils' progress toward the fulfillment of their personal needs and interests. Those of you who are experienced teachers are ostensibly utilizing standard techniques for evaluating your pupils' academic growth. Those of you who are training to become teachers are most likely studying various standard procedures for evaluation. However, in evaluating open learning experiences in your learning-centered classroom, it is most important that you go beyond standard procedures to more imaginative and valuable forms of evaluation.

Consider, for example, the use of videotapes or photographs of your pupils' activities as media for recording and elucidating the behaviors that occur in your classroom. What do your pupils talk about? Try using a tape recorder to capture the conversations that take place among your pupils. What do your pupils think about? Utilize a graffiti-type notebook in which they may write freely expressed, non-academic kinds of responses of whatever comes into their minds. As often as not, your pupils' expressions will provide you with pertinent data concerning their feelings, needs, interests, and aspirations. You can, consequently, build experiences based on your assessment of such extremely informal but valuable data in the learning centers you establish.

Less imaginative, perhaps, but certainly not traditional are other approaches you may find useful in evaluating your pupils' progress. Try logging their accomplishments. Tape their stories and verse. Put together a book of their paintings. Make the puzzles they invent available. Provide room for exhibits they create. Take these as means for evaluating their performance and growth as well as at face value. Compile individual folders of their work. You will probably find folders in which you place representative samples of your pupils' work, including their artistic and creative expression, very useful in reporting and demonstrating your pupils' progress to school administrators, parents, and to the pupils themselves.

Much, of course, has already been written on procedures for assessing the academic progress of pupils in the various subject areas. I will not, therefore, belabor the conventional techniques utilized in many classrooms for this purpose. Here too, I feel, it is important to go beyond the use of grades to more provocative approaches to evaluation. Try, for example, using notebooks to accumulate your pupils' written expressions, their vocabulary development, and the arithmetic problems they solve. Compositions may be written in a composition book, spelling words in a spelling booklet, etc. In contrast to having work done on isolated sheets of paper, this procedure is valuable because you will be able to view the scope and sequential development of your pupils' performance and thus more accurately assess their progress over a period of time. Equally important, your pupils will be able to see their own progress from composition to composition and exercise to exercise simply by turning the pages of their notebooks. In conference with you, they will be able to see their progress as well as their need to work in certain areas.

In evaluating your pupils' growth in various subjects, it is important that you assess the processes they undergo along with the actual knowledge they learn and the understanding they derive. For example, what are the processes pertinent to scientific study? Figure 8-15 lists some of the criteria involved. Where do your pupils stand in relationship to these criteria? Your use of an instrument such as that shown in the figure will help you to determine this. Similarly, it is important that you identify and study the processes relevant to the other subjects you teach. Knowing these, it is then a relatively simple matter to devise evaluation instruments, such as that shown in Figure 8-15, with which to assess your pupils' understanding and application of the processes.

Keep in mind as you devise your assessment procedures that your pupils are the most important figures in your program of evaluation. Therefore, it is essential that they also participate in the assessment of their academic, social, and emotional growth. Encourage their self-evaluation of their behavior and performance. You can adapt some of the instruments illustrated thus far for this purpose. The section that follows will also help you to formulate still other instruments for use in your program of evaluation.

PUPIL SELF-EVALUATION
OF LEARNING EXPERIENCES

There is little question that your pupils' processes of self-evaluation have been initiated long before they have entered school, usually in the form of the many questions that occur to them. Upon entering school, their questions persist. Will I like school? Will the classwork be too hard? Will I be separated from my friends? Will I make new friends? Will my teacher like me? Your listening and responding to the questions your pupils ask is a necessary beginning point in making them conscious of the importance of self-evaluation. Urge them to follow their natural inclinations. Ask them what they would like to learn. Question them as to whether or not they would like to have certain learning experiences continued, modified, or done away with. Encourage them to make many of the classroom decisions. In this way, the self-evaluation process will make their own behavior clear to them.

This very significant component of the learning-centered classroom bears directly on the pupils' experiences throughout their lives:

> To be critically and appreciatively aware of one's own immediate environment is to provide oneself with a criterion against which to judge the everyday incidents which make up life ... to be able to record one's own feelings, one's own thoughts and imagination, is to possess the key to the door of mankind's total experience.[6]

FIGURE 8-15   *Evaluation Criteria for Science*

Pupil's Name_____ Date Beginning_____ Date Ending_____ BEHAVIORAL CHARACTERISTICS	Almost Always	Much of the Time	Some of the Time	Almost Never
1. Sensitizes self to problems in need of solution.				
2. Devises experiments needed to solve problems.				
3. Sensitizes self to factors that must be controlled.				
4. Selects appropriate data.				
5. Establishes appropriate controls.				
6. Secures information and source materials appropriate to the problem under study.				
7. Uses appropriate instruments to secure desired data.				
8. Devises instruments for measuring when needed.				
9. Observes accurately.				
10. Understands the degree of accuracy involved in obtaining data.				
11. Determines causes for discrepancies in data.				
12. Uses wide samples to obtain greater accuracy.				
13. Presents findings objectively.				

It is important that you invite your pupils' participation in the development of the procedures and instruments to be used in the evaluation of their progress. Keep in mind, however, that there is no single sequence of learning experiences for all of your pupils. All learning centers, therefore, will not appeal to all of them. Thus, in establishing your centers, you need to take into account the varied attitudes your pupils have about school and the different ways they prefer to learn. Figure 8-16 illustrates one instrument that may be used for this purpose.

FIGURE 8-16   *Criteria for Pupils' Self-Assessment of Their Attitudes*

PUPIL CHARACTERISTICS	YES	NO
I...		
1. Like to do things on my own.		
2. Don't like a noisy classroom.		
3. Like to stick to a job once I've started it.		
4. Rather be told what to do and how to do it.		
5. Prefer to select my own activities.		
6. Find most school work easy.		
7. Don't like to disagree with my classmates.		
8. Have trouble keeping up with school work.		
9. Don't like to think a lot about things.		
10. Wish I were more of a leader.		
11. Don't like to talk about what I feel.		
12. Like to lead group activities.		
13. Always try to finish activities I start.		
14. Have difficulty in expressing my ideas clearly.		
15. Like to initiate projects.		
16. Don't like to be picked to do things.		
17. Usually get along with my classmates.		
18. Feel there is one best way to solve a problem.		
19. Do not enjoy new and unusual situations.		
20. Don't like to check my work once it is done.		

Along with their evaluation of their attitudes, it is also important to have your pupils evaluate their work habits. To accomplish this, you will need to utilize a rating scale such as that illustrated in Figure 8-17.

FIGURE 8-17   Self-Rating Scale for Pupils' Self-Assessment of Their Work Habits

Pupil _____ Period Beginning___ Period Ending___ WORK HABITS	Almost Always	Much of the Time	Some of the Time	Almost Never
I . . .				
1. Listen attentively.				
2. Follow directions carefully.				
3. Seek clarification when I don't understand something.				
4. Approach my work with originality, where appropriate.				
5. Select and use source materials carefully.				
6. Organize material logically and clearly.				
7. Check my work for errors.				
8. Contribute ideas for learning centers.				
9. Go beyond minimum requirements.				
10. Ask relevant questions.				
11. Use more than one reference in constructing reports.				
12. Make good use of my time.				
13. Etc.				

Logs, diaries, inventories, "goal books," and videotapes are other tools by which your pupils may assess their own progress. Note, however, that the form or vehicle used for their self-evaluation is not necessarily the important factor. More important is that the instrument used makes visible to your pupils their input into classroom activities, their ability to initiate personal growth and group actions, their capacity to work independently, their degree of creativity, the extent and quality of their questioning, and the other processes ascribed to open education. Questions they may use as guidelines for this self-evaluation might assume the following pattern:

1. What did I initiate today?
2. What did I contribute to someone in the class or to the class as a whole?

3. What did I enjoy most today? Why?
4. With whom did I enjoy working? Why?
5. What did I feel were my most important experiences? Why?
6. What did I do most effectively? Why?
7. What did I not accomplish that I might have? Why?
8. What did I find the most difficult today? Why?
9. Where do I need help?
10. What suggestions do I have for following up my learning experience?

Consider, also, the importance of having your pupils assess each other's attitudes and work habits as well as their own. In this chapter are a variety of evaluation instruments that you may, with modifications, use for this purpose. Similarly, you may develop evaluation instruments for the purpose of having your pupils assess, for example, the extent to which each contributes and listens to others' ideas, supports and works with others, explains and demonstrates things to others, and carries on various other responsibilities associated with open learning. In encouraging this procedure, you will be taking a most important step in helping your pupils to make the transition to communicating openly and freely with each other.

The extent of open communication between you and your pupils and among your pupils is often revealed in class meetings. Therefore, some time should be spent at the end of each day assessing your pupils' progress. Ask them: How did the day go? Were you able to meet your goals? If so, how? Tell us about some of your successful procedures. If not, why not? Tell us about the problems you faced. What can we do to help you? What learning centers did you like or not like? What are your ideas?

Your role in assisting your pupils to make the transition to open learning is, without question, a pivotal one. How ready are you for this role? Let me now try to help you assess the extent of your readiness.

ASSESSMENT OF TEACHING PRACTICES

I am sometimes asked if there is a particular kind of teacher who functions best in an open classroom environment. This is a difficult question to answer. For just as open classrooms vary in form and direction, so do the characteristics, dispositions, and value systems of teachers who perform effectively in them. The discussion in Chapter 5 of your readiness to open up your classroom suggested that to evaluate the extent of your readiness, it is necessary that you go beyond your feelings about open learning to what you actually practice or intend to practice in your classroom.

Assessment of your teaching practices may take a variety of forms. These include a number of standardized instruments, such as the *Flanders System of*

Interaction Analysis[7] and *The Teaching Evaluation Record,*[8] both of which are designed to evaluate teacher behavior patterns in the classroom. In keeping with the thesis of this book, however, I feel you should turn to more immediate procedures for assessing your teaching practices.

SELF-ASSESSMENT OF TEACHING

Rarely, if ever, have teachers been called upon to assess their own teaching practices. This is unfortunate. As self-evaluation by pupils is a necessary process for opening them up to the best possible learning experiences, self-assessment by teachers is also necessary to open them up to the best possible teaching practices. Figure 8-18 is presented for your use in assessing your own individual practices in the classroom.

Note the dual purpose of Figure 8-18. Those of you who are now teaching are invited to assess your teaching practices; those of you who are preparing to teach can make your assessment on the basis of the teaching practices you think you would prefer. To use the figure, simply check each item you practice in the appropriate column. On completion of your self-assessment, it is then necessary to identify which of the teaching practices you have checked are considered to be open and which are thought of as being closed. Figure 8-19 will assist you in making this identification. Which do you practice more, open or closed teaching? Which would you like to practice more? Study the figure to find out.

In examining Figure 8-19 and comparing its components with the results of the assessment of your teaching practices (Figure 8-18), you will undoubtedly find that you practice both open and closed teaching in your classroom. To find out precisely where each is taking place, examine your teaching practices more closely. What is there about a certain practice that invites you to be more open or more closed? How might you change your closed teaching practices so that they become more open? Perhaps Figure 8-18 will lead you to raise questions about your closed teaching practices and encourage you to seek measures for changing them.

As you take steps to move towards more open learning experiences for your pupils, you should start with one teaching practice that you feel confident about and are capable of changing. For example, if all of your pupils are presently reading from one basal reader, an initial step might be to make a second basal reader of a different reading level available to those pupils who would benefit from this opportunity. Gradually build on this procedure by extending the range and variety of reading materials to the point where you subsequently establish a personalized reading program for your pupils. (See Chapter 4.) In time, as you achieve more and more success in making the gradual transition from closed to open teaching practices, you will feel increasingly confident in taking on the more difficult challenges listed in Figure 8-18.

FIGURE 8-18   Self-Assessment of Selected Teaching Practices

The following statements are representative of teaching practices in the classroom. To help you think about your present practices and perhaps guide you to practices you would like to implement in your classroom, place a check (✓) to the right of each statement under the category which you feel best indicates your current practices (I . . .) or your preferences (I'd like to . . .).

	I . . .				I'd like to . . .			
TEACHING PRACTICES	Almost always	Much of the time	Some of the time	Almost never	Almost always	Much of the time	Some of the time	Almost never
1. Make my pupils the center of attention.								
2. Stimulate my pupils through cooperation.								
3. Discourage my pupils' self-expression.								
4. Reward my pupils by arousing their curiosity and interest.								
5. Confer with my pupils.								
6. Expect my pupils to know answers.								
7. Involve my pupils in problems that challenge them.								
8. Invite differences of opinion and argument among my pupils.								
9. Place all my pupils at the same point on learning continuums.								
10. Tell my pupils what and how to do things.								
11. Require equal amounts of work from each of my pupils.								
12. Vary my expectations and standards in evaluating the progress of my pupils.								
13. Permit free movement of my pupils in their activities.								
14. Have all my pupils work on similar objectives.								
15. Listen more than I talk to my pupils.								
16. Use a set standard for assessing my pupils' progress.								
17. Accept stereotyped answers from my pupils.								
18. Assume arbitrary stances with my pupils.								

FIGURE 8-18—Continued

	I . . .				I'd like to . . .			
	Almost always	Much of the time	Some of the time	Almost never	Almost always	Much of the time	Some of the time	Almost never
19. Differentiate instruction, content, and materials for my pupils as needed.								
20. Make myself the center of attention in my classroom.								
21. Participate in my pupils' activities.								
22. Deviate from planned schedules of activity when beneficial to my pupils.								
23. Provide no or few options for my pupils.								
24. Have my pupils listen, watch, and wait during the greater part of each day.								
25. Ask my pupils to evaluate much of their own work.								
26. Use the results of diagnosis to place my pupils on learning continuums.								
27. Provide my pupils with opinions, detailed facts, and information constantly.								
28. Allow my pupils to leave their desks only with permission.								
29. Prevent my pupils from testing unrecognized data.								
30. Expand subject matter to include experiences of my pupils, flexibly implemented by me.								
31. Reward my pupils with grades and privileges.								
32. Plan the learning experiences of the classroom with my pupils.								
33. Require that my pupils accept courses of action prescribed by me.								
34. Ignore pupil misconceptions and over-generalizations.								
35. Allow my pupils to work individually in pairs, or in small groups.								
36. Ask my pupils to substantiate their responses where appropriate.								
37. Solicit ideas and strategies from my pupils for accomplishing tasks.								

	I . . .					I'd like to . . .			
	Almost always	Much of the time	Some of the time	Almost never		Almost always	Much of the time	Some of the time	Almost never
38. Vary the objectives of my pupils according to diagnostic findings.									
39. Predetermine my pupils' learning experiences.									
40. Detach myself from my pupils' learning experiences.									
41. Encourage my pupils to search out opinions, facts, and answers.									
42. Evaluate all the work of my pupils.									
43. Dissuade my pupils from perplexing problems.									
44. Vary the amount of work from pupil to pupil.									
45. Ask my pupils questions that are not readily answerable.									
46. Have all my pupils work on the same task with the same materials at the same time.									
47. Organize the experiences of the classroom on the basis of questions and interests expressed by my pupils.									
48. See that my pupils work apart from each other.									
49. Provide my pupils with multiple opportunities to freely select their learning experiences.									
50. Rely heavily on textbooks as sources of information.									
51. Encourage my pupils to hypothesize answers and make predictions.									
52. Encourage my pupils to test far-fetched ideas.									
53. Probe misconceptions and unwarranted conclusions derived by my pupils.									
54. Emphasize reward and punishment to maintain order in my classroom.									
55. Invite and act on my pupils' suggestions and ideas.									
56. Provide time for my pupils to reflect when they are confused and puzzled.									

FIGURE 8-18—Continued

	I . . .				I'd like to . . .			
	Almost always	Much of the time	Some of the time	Almost never	Almost always	Much of the time	Some of the time	Almost never
57. Organize the experiences of the classroom on questions and interests I formulate.								
58. Reduce subject matter to cut-and-dried material, routinely implemented by me.								
59. Use natural and logical consequences of behavior to maintain order in the classroom.								
60. Encourage my pupils to weigh merits of alternative courses of action in making decisions.								
61. Stick to scheduled activities.								
62. Make a wide, diversified range of informative materials available.								
63. Stimulate my pupils with answers every time they are confused and puzzled.								
64. Ask my pupils questions they can easily answer.								
65. Supply my pupils with questions every time they are confused and puzzled.								
66. Undertake frequent ongoing conferences with my pupils.								

FIGURE 8-19   *Categorization of Selected Teaching Practices Ascribable to Open and Closed Teachers*

TEACHING PRACTICES OF THE OPEN TEACHER	TEACHING PRACTICES OF THE CLOSED TEACHER
The open teacher . . .	The closed teacher . . .
Makes pupils the center of attention.	Makes self the center of attention.
Diagnoses pupils' entry point on learning continuum.	Places all pupils at same point on learning continuum.
Varies pupil objectives as result of diagnosis.	Has all pupils work on same objective.
Listens more than talks to pupils.	Has pupils listening, watching, waiting.
Stimulates pupils through cooperation.	Stimulates pupils through competition.
Invites and acts on pupils' suggestions and ideas.	Discourages pupils' self-expression.
Plans learning experiences with pupils.	Predetermines pupils' learning experiences.
Varies the amount of work from pupil to pupil.	Requires equal amounts of work from each pupil.
Permits free movement of pupils in their activities.	Allows pupils to leave desks only with permission.
Participates in pupils' activities.	Detaches self from pupils' activities.
Organizes learning around questions posed by pupils.	Organizes learning around questions posed by self.
Involves pupils in problems that challenge.	Dissuades pupils from perplexing problems.
Deviates from planned schedule of activities.	Sticks to scheduled activities.
Allows pupils to work in pairs or small groups.	Sees that pupils work apart from each other.
Makes a wide range of informative materials available.	Relies heavily on textbook as source of information.
Provides pupil options via self-selected experiences.	Provides no options for pupils.
Differentiates instruction, content and materials as needed.	Has all pupils work on same task with same materials at same time.
Expands subject matter to include experiences of pupils, flexibly implemented.	Reduces subject matter to cut-and-dried material, routinely implemented.
Solicits pupil strategies for accomplishing tasks.	Tells pupils what and how to do things.
Asks pupils questions that are not readily answerable.	Asks pupils questions easily answered.
Encourages pupils to hypothesize answers.	Expects pupils to know answers.
Asks pupils to substantiate answers.	Accepts stereotyped answers.
Probes pupil misconceptions and unwarranted conclusions.	Ignores pupil misconceptions and overgeneralizations.
Encourages pupils to search out opinions, facts information.	Provides pupils with opinions, detailed facts and information.
Encourages pupils to test far-fetched ideas.	Prevents pupils from testing unrecognized ideas.
Provides time for pupils to reflect when confused and puzzled.	Supplies answers to pupils when confused and puzzled.
Asks pupils to evaluate own work.	Evaluates all the work of pupils.
Varies standards for evaluating pupil progress.	Uses a set standard for assessing pupil progress.
Uses natural and logical consequences of behavior for classroom management.	Emphasizes reward and punishment to maintain order in the classroom.
Rewards pupils by arousing their curiosity and interest.	Rewards pupils with grades and privileges.
Encourages pupils to weigh merits of alternative courses of action before making decisions.	Requires that pupils accept prescribed course of action.
Invites differences of opinion and argument among pupils.	Assumes arbitrary stance with pupils.

To further assess your teaching practices, turn once again to Figure 1-2 (Chapter 1) for guidelines. Examine its operational components. Is your foremost instructional target the individual pupil? Is your teaching diagnostic? How do you react to the work accomplished by your pupils? Choose one of the following:

1. Insist they can do better.
2. Praise them undeservedly. ("Billy, that's the best _____I have ever seen!")
3. Point out what they have done well. ("Susan, your ideas have been expressed with sensitivity." "Henry, I'm looking forward to more imaginative paintings like this one from you.")
4. Ignore their work.

In making the transition to open learning experiences for your pupils, how will you get them to participate in the learning centers you establish? Choose one of the following practices:

1. Require their participation for a grade.
2. Encourage them to freely select the centers in which to work.
3. Lead them to the centers you think they should work in.
4. Emphasize order and discipline.

Assessing your teaching in this way will help you to look with greater insight into what you practice.

To derive further insight into your teaching, devise an evaluation instrument by which your pupils assess your attitudes and behavior. This is very important to the process of opening up your classroom. In fact, your pupils are apt to provide you with greater insight into your teaching practices and the way you relate to them than will your supervisory personnel. You can use a rating scale to have your pupils assess your manner, the degree to which you recognize their suggestions and contributions, the extent of interesting materials and experiences you provide them, the way you organize and implement their activities, the degree of your knowledge, your evaluation of their work, and the various other practices that constitute your teaching.

I am sure you will agree that kids are usually honest and forthright. When given the opportunity, they will probably reveal some things about you that you may not realize. You will see your degree of fairness, your sense of humor, speech, handwriting, appearance, and other characteristics through their eyes. They will let you know what they like best and what they like least about you. Put their assessment of your teaching practices to work. The first thing you know, you'll be doing things in your classroom that interest them, rather than those that interest you.

Most teachers have not ever seen themselves in action or perhaps have not heard themselves interacting with their pupils. Consider, then, using a videotape or a tape recorder as media for assessing your teaching practices. Seeing or hearing yourself for the first time may be startling to some of you. However, what a videotape and tape recorder reveal is the real you. The chances are that what they reveal will result in your taking a closer look at your teaching practices and will give you a greater incentive to maximize your strengths and minimize your weaknesses in teaching.

EFFECTIVENESS OF OPEN EDUCATION

How effective is open education? A definitive conclusion has not yet been reached. However, on a national level, the relatively few studies undertaken to measure its effectiveness show some promising trends in its favor. Thorough interpretations of the findings are dependent upon further analysis of the data and on future longitudinal studies. Most of the present research findings, moreover, have resulted from studies of open-plan or open-space schools, rather than those of the individual open classrooms that are the focus of this book.

Among the very few prominent studies undertaken to evaluate process outcomes in the open classroom is the research conducted within classrooms that have implemented the Tucson Early Education Model.[9] The results of this research indicate that children in the open classrooms exhibited more appropriate behavior than did those in the more traditional classrooms. In another significant study that may be of interest to you, the findings indicate that teachers in open schools were more satisfied with their jobs, felt more autonomous, and reported more influence in decision-making.[10] With respect to children's self-esteem, one study showed that pupils in the open space school gained in self-esteem, whereas those in self-contained classrooms demonstrated a loss.[11]

The Journal of Educational Research reports a few studies on the effectiveness of open education. A study by F. S. Wilson, R. Langevin, and T. Stuckey is of particular interest.[12] Their research shows the following encouraging results for the open education philosophy: (1) pupils in the open-plan schools surveyed displayed better attitudes than those in traditional schools due to higher levels of productive thinking, pupil interaction, and peer tutoring; (2) pupils demonstrated self-discipline, maturity, and absorption in their activities; (3) pupils displayed respect for each other, and problem children were rare.

A study in the *Journal of Experimental Education* shows that pupils in the open classroom, when compared with those in the closed classroom, exhibited less "casual exchange" behavior, had more interaction that led to other activities, and sought information oriented toward finding solutions to problems, whereas pupils in the closed settings tended to ask for answers to problems. The study also suggests that open settings are more conducive to learning than are closed settings.[13]

With respect to achievement by pupils in open classrooms, as reported by the National Education Association, findings were that:

> .... research conducted to date suggests that student achievement as measured by standardized tests is comparable to that attained through more traditional approaches ... observational and experiential accounts overwhelmingly attest to the dramatic increase of motivation, enthusiasm, and independence among students and teachers.[14]

Also, in regards to achievement, the book *Children Teach Children* documents astonishing gains in learning achieved when children instruct other children, a process that was discussed earlier in this book.[15]

Empirical evidence, gathered from six comprehensive studies conducted at the University of Houston, supports the claimed advantages of the open classroom over the traditional classroom.[16]

As encouraging as these research findings may be, even more encouraging are the views held by pupils and teachers who are undergoing open learning experiences. For example, eleven-year-old Cecelia evaluates her experiences:

> I know I have change since the beginning of school. First, when I came to this class, I was used of being in a room with desk and having the teacher go to the front of the class and telling us to read this page and that page. Now I can do things for myself and take care of my own problems. I don't have to go to the teacher so much. I really can do things for myself.

Sharon Meier, whom I have previously cited, expresses the dramatic changes that have taken place in her pupils as follows:

> They [the pupils] have become beautifully aware of each other. They're just different people now. They cope well with different situations, work harder, and are capable of working independently where formerly they were not. They've learned to take care of things and to seek each other out when they need help. They are, I feel, capable of making wise decisions.[17]

In making the transition to more open learning experiences for her pupils, Sandra Abernathy, a second grade teacher previously mentioned, noted the following behavioral changes in them:

1. More self-confident
2. More able to take care of themselves
3. More task-oriented
4. More able to work through a task
5. Discussed problems freely with each other
6. Learned to work together
7. Asked for help without feeling inferior
8. Gave help without showing superiority
9. Performed as if the classroom was their workshop
10. Aimless, random movement virtually disappeared

11. Deliberate, distracting activities were infrequent[18]

Other teachers report similar results. However, enthusiastic and positive accounts of the benefits of open education by pupils and teachers often do not serve to placate administrators, parents, and others who are in positions of authority. Although you and I might agree that this ignores the people who really count—teachers and pupils—the reality is that you are increasingly being held accountable for the academic progress of your pupils. I feel, therefore, that those of you who are contemplating or are practicing open education in your classrooms must establish the communication necessary to insure its continuance.

Among the formal, pertinent steps you need to consider are: (1) the continuance of your day-to-day, ongoing evaluation of your pupils' progress; (2) the use of those portions of standardized tests appropriate to the evaluation of open learning experiences; (3) the use of various instruments, such as those developed by Torrance, MacKinnon, and Guilford (previously cited) to measure the creative behavior of your pupils; (4) the use of interaction types of procedures, such as the Flander's System of Interactional Analysis (previously cited) to assess your interaction with your pupils and the interaction between them; (5) the use of various standardized observation scales, such as the Classroom Observation Rating Scale developed by TDR Associates, Inc. of Newton, Massachusetts; (6) the use of teacher-constructed instruments such as those presented in this chapter; and (7) your own pupils' assessment of their progress. Systematic and thorough procedures of assessment such as these are necessary if the effectiveness of open education is to be clearly evaluated and communicated.

This book has attempted to identify and illustrate the necessary processes for opening up your classroom. Your challenge is to use these processes to the extent that both you and your pupils are able to function openly and freely in your classroom. How, then, will you know when this is taking place? I suggest that you look to your pupils for the answer.

POINTS TO REMEMBER

- Central to the evaluation of pupils' academic progress and personal growth is how they feel about themselves and view others.
- New means of evaluation are required to communicate the effectiveness of open education.
- Establishment of criteria unique to open education is a necessary first step in evaluating the open learning experiences of pupils.
- Self-assessments by teachers and pupils are necessary processes in making the transition to open education practices.
- Systematic and thorough procedures of assessment are needed to evaluate the effectiveness of open education in the classroom.

NOTES

1. Adapted and modified from *Notes from the RMSEIMC Roadrunner,* State of New Mexico Department of Education, Division of Special Education, 121 State Educational Building, Santa Fe, New Mexico 87501, p. 122.

2. Adapted and modified from a paper submitted by Page Hubbard, a student teacher in my teaching laboratory class, New Mexico State University, College of Education, April 1972.

3. Adapted and modified from "Teaching and Evaluation," *Evaluation as Feedback and Guide.* Prepared by the ASCD 1967 Yearbook Committee, Association for Supervision and Curriculum Development, N.E.A., 1201 Sixteenth Street, N.W., Washington, D.C. 20036, pp. 97–98.

4. I draw upon the studies of MacKinnon, Torrance, and Guilford in formulating the behavioral characteristics shown in this figure.

   D. W. MacKinnon, "Personality and the Realization of Creative Potential," *American Psychologist* (1965), pp. 273–281.

   E. P. Torrance, *Gifted Children in the Classroom* (New York: Macmillan Co., 1965).

   J. P. Guilford, "Basic Problems in Teaching for Creativity" in C. W. Taylor and F. E. Williams, eds., *Instructional Media and Creativity* (New York: John Wiley and Sons, Inc., 1966), pp. 71–103.

5. John A. R. Wilson, Mildred C. Robeck, and William B. Michael, *Psychological Foundations of Learning and Teaching* (New York: McGraw-Hill Book Co., 1974), p. 196.

6. Sybil Marshall, *An Experiment in Education* (London: Cambridge University Press, paperback ed., 1966), p. 136.

7. Considerable research, along with an excellent bibliography of related research has been reported by Ned Flanders in *Analyzing Teaching Behavior* (Reading, Mass.: Addison-Wesley Publishing Co., Inc., 1970).

8. Dwight E. Beecher, *The Teaching Evaluation Record* (Buffalo, N.Y.: Educators Publishing Co., 1956).

9. Robert K. Rentfrow, Ocea Goldupp, and Maure Hurt, Jr., "Situational Task Methodology for the Evaluation of Process Outcomes in the Open Classroom." (A paper presented at the 1973 Annual Meeting of the American Educational Research Association, New Orleans, La., February 25–March 1, 1973.)

10. John Meyer et al., *The Impact of the Open-Space School Upon Teacher Influence and Autonomy: The Effects of an Organizational Innovation,* Technical Report No. 21, Stanford Center of Research and Development in Teaching, Stanford University, October 1971.

11. Norman L. Heimgartner, *A Comparative Study of Self-Concept: Open Space Versus Self-Contained Classrooms,* Research Study No. 4, University of Northern Colorado, 1972.

12. F. S. Wilson, R. Langevin, and T. Stuckey, "Are Pupils in the Open Plan School Different?," *The Journal of Educational Research* 66: 3 (November 1972): 115–118.

13. Robert B. Innes, "Environmental Forces in Open and Closed Classroom Settings," *Journal of Experimental Education* 41 (Summer 1973): 38–42.

14. National Education Association, *Briefing,* Instruction and Professional Development 2 (February 1973): 2.

15. Cited in *Openness—the New Kick in Education* (A Ford Foundation reprint of a lecture by Harold Howe II, Yale University, February 7, 1972).

16. Stanley G. Sanders and Jean P. Wren, "Open-Space Schools Are Effective," *Phi Delta Kappan* (January 1975): 366.

17. Excerpted from a talk given to members of the Student National Education Association at New Mexico State University by Sharon Meier, Spring 1972.

18. Excerpted from a paper by Sandra Abernathy, University Hills School, Las Cruces, New Mexico.

Final Note

You need only one small child who comes to class unwillingly, then reluctantly, then with half-interest, until one day he places a small hand within yours and grins to make you realize that your efforts are worthwhile.

—Romayne L. Thomas

Selected References

In addition to the references I have footnoted in the text, I include the following selections to help you extend your knowledge of open education. Although the relationship between the British Infant Schools and the open classroom movement in the United States has not been discussed, selected texts by British and American authors are included to assist you in noting this relationship. A more extensive reading list might also have included books and resource materials on nongrading, team teaching, team learning, and individualizing instruction, for all of these are closely interwoven with open learning experiences in the classroom.

BOOKS, MONOGRAPHS, AND PAPERS

American Association of School Administrators. Commission on Open Space Schools. *Open Space Schools: Report.* American Association of School Administrators, 1971.

Barth, Roland S. *Open Education and the American School.* New York: Agathon Press, 1972.

_____. "Open Education." Ph.D. dissertation, Harvard University Graduate School of Education, 1970.

Barth, Roland S., and Rathbone, Charles H. *A Bibliography of Open Education.* Newton, Mass.: Education Development Center, 1971.

Bassett, G. W. *Innovation in Primary Education.* New York: Wiley-Interscience, 1970.

Blackie, John. *Inside the Primary School.* American ed. New York: Schocken Books, 1971.

Blitz, Barbara. *The Open Classroom: Making It Work.* Boston: Allyn and Bacon, 1973.

Boulding, Elise. *New Approaches to Learning: Alternative Education and Open Schools.* Washington, D.C.: U.S. Department of Health, Education, and Welfare, Office of Education, 1971.

Bremer, Anne, and Bremer, John. *Open Education: A Beginning.* New York: Holt, Rinehart, and Winston, 1974.

The British Infant School. Institute for Development of Educational Activities. I.D.E.A., Box 446, Melborne, Fla.

Carswell, Evelyn M., and Roubinek, Darrell L. *Open Sesame: A Primer in Open Education.* Pacific Palisades, Calif.: Goodyear Publishing Co., 1974.

Chittenden, Edward A. et al. *Analysis of an Approach to Open Education.* Princeton, N.J.: Educational Testing Service, 1970.

Classroom Learning Centers. Belmont, Calif.: Fearon Publishers, 1973.

Clegg, Sir Alec. *Revolution in the British Primary Schools.* Washington, D.C.: National Association of Elementary School Principals, 1971.

Cohen, Monroe D., ed. *Learning Centers.* Washington, D.C.: The Association for Childhood Educational International, 1970.

DeBruin, Jerome E. "A Descriptive Analysis of Experience of Five First-Year Teachers Attempting Open Education." Ph. D. dissertation, University of Illinois, 1972.

Dennison, George. *The Lives of Children.* New York: Random House, 1969.

Featherstone, Joseph. *Schools Where Children Learn.* New York: Liveright, 1971.

Fisk, Lori, and Lindgren, Henry C. *Learning Centers.* Glen Ridge, N.J.: Exceptional Press, 1974.

Forte, Imogene, and Joy Mackenzie. *Nooks, Crannies and Corners.* Nashville: Incentive Publications, 1972.

Furth, Hans G. *Piaget for Teachers.* Englewood Cliffs, N.J.: Prentice-Hall, 1970.

Frazier, Alexander. *Open Schools for Children.* Washington, D.C.: Association for Supervision and Curriculum Development, 1972.

Gartner, Alan; Kohler, Mary; and Riesman, Frank. *Children Teach Children.* New York: Harper and Row, 1971.

Gattegno, Caleb. *What We Owe Children: The Subordination of Teaching to Learning.* New York: Outerbridge and Dienstfrey, 1970.

Giacquinta, Joseph B. *An Attempt to Implement a Major Organizational Innovation: A Case Study of an Elementary School.* Cambridge, Mass.: Harvard Graduate School of Education (unpublished doctoral thesis), 1968.

Gingell, Lesley. *The ABC's of the Open Classroom.* Homewood, Ill.: ETC Publications, 1973.

Glasser, William. *The Effect of School Failure on the Life of a Child.* Washington, D.C.: NAESP, 1971.

———. *Schools Without Failure.* New York: Harper and Row, 1969.

Graubard, Allen. *Free the Children: Radical Reform and the Free School Movement.* New York: Pantheon Books, 1973.

Gross, Ronald, and Gross, Beatrice, eds. *Radical School Reform.* New York: Simon and Schuster. A Clarion Book, 1971.

Guenther, Annette R. *Open Education Bibliography.* Washington, D.C.: American Association of Elementary-Kindergarten-Nursery Educators.

Hart, Harold H., ed. *Summerhill: For and Against.* New York: Hart Publishing Co., 1970.

Hassett, Joseph D., and Weisberg, Arline. *Open Education, Alternatives Within our Tradition.* Englewood Cliffs, N.J.: Prentice-Hall, 1972.

Hearn, D. Dwain; Burdin, Joel; and Katz, Lilian. *Current Research and Perspectives in Open Education.* Washington, D.C.: American Association of Elementary-Kindergarten-Nursery Educators.

Hertzberg, Alvin, and Stone, Edward F. *Schools Are For Children: An American Approach to the Open Classroom.* New York: Schocken Books, 1971.

Heyman, Mark. *Learning from the British Primary.* Englewood Cliffs, N.J.: Prentice-Hall, 1970.

Horton, Lowell, and Horton, Phyllis. *The Learning Center: Heart of the School.* Minneapolis: T. S. Denison and Co.

Howe, Harold II. *Openness—the New Kick in Education.* A Ford Foundation Reprint adapted from the 1972 Frank Ellsworth Spaulding Lecture on Education, Yale University, February 7, 1972.

Howes, Virgil M. *Informal Teaching in the Open Classroom.* Riverside, N.J.: Macmillan, 1974.

Hull, Bill. *Leicestershire Revisited.* Occasional paper. Educational Development Center, 55 Chapel Street, Newton, Mass. 02160.

I.C.E.D. *Children in the Open Classroom.* Encino, Calif.: International Center for Educational Development, 16161 Ventura Boulevard, 1973.

Infant School. Educational Development Center, Newton, Mass. Booklet prepared by Adeline Naiman with the permission of Courtney B. Cazden.

Isaacs, Susan. *The Children We Teach: Seven to Eleven Years.* London: University Press, Ltd., 1932, 1967.

Kahl, David H., and Gast, Barbara J. *Learning Centers in the Open Classroom.* Encino, Calif.: International Center for Educational Development, 1971.

Kaplan, Sandra Nina; Kaplan, Jo Ann Butom; Madsen, Sheila Kunishima; and Taylor, Bette K. *Change for Children: Ideas and Activities for Individualizing Learning.* Pacific Palisades, Calif.: Goodyear Publishing Co., 1973.

Kohl, Herbert R. *The Open Classroom.* New York: A New York Review Book, 1969.

Lawrence, Evelyn. *Friedrich Froebel and English Education.* London: Routledge and Kegan Paul, 1952, 1969.

Legant, Jean; Collie, Blanche K.; and DeLayo, Leonard J. *Things On a Ring.* New Mexico Department of Education, January 1972.

Leonard, George B. *Education and Ecstasy.* New York: The Delacorte Press, 1968.

Mann, Beatrice F. *Learning Through Creative Work (The Under 8's in School).* London: National Froebel Foundation, 2 Manchester Square, W.1., 1962 (revised 1966).

Marsh, Leonard. *Alongside the Child in the Primary School.* London: A&C Black, Ltd., 1970.

Marshall, Sybil. *Adventure in Creative Education.* London: Pergamon Press, Ltd., 1968. Available in this country through offices at: 44-01 21st Street, Long Island City, N.Y. 11101.

_____. *An Experiment in Education.* Cambridge: Cambridge University Press, 1963 (paper, 1966). Available in this country at: 32 East 57th Street, New York, N.Y., 10022.

McGavack, John, and LaSalle, Donald P. *Guppies, Bubbles and Vibrating Objects.* New York: John Day Co., 1969.

McPartland, James, and Epstein, Joyce L. *Interim Report: School Organization and Student Outcomes: A Study of the Effects of Open-Environment Schools.* Johns Hopkins University Center for Social Organization of Schools, Report No. 166, December 1973.

McPartland, James; Epstein, Joyce L.; and McDill, Edward L. *Student Reactions to the Transition from Open Elementary School to Junior High School: A Case Study.* Johns Hopkins University Center for Social Organization of Schools, Report No. 139, October 1972.

Mercer, Pat, and Beamer, Charles. *Learning Centers: Toward Individualized Instruction in Elementary Schools.* Austin, Texas: Austin Writers Group.

Murrow, Casey, and Murrow, Lisa. *Children Come First.* New York: American Heritage Press, 1971.

Myers, Donald A., and Myers, Lillian, eds. *Open Education Re-examined.* Lexington, Mass.: D. C. Heath, 1973.

National Elementary Principal. *Perspectives on Open Education.* Washington, D.C.: NAESP, November 1972.

National School Public Relations Association. *Informal Education: "Open Classroom" Provider Change, Controversy.* Arlington, Va.: National School Public Relations Association, 1972.

New School of Behavioral Studies in Education. *Insights.* University of North Dakota: Grand Forks, N.D. 58201.

Notes from Workshop Center for Open Education. New York: Workshop for Open Education, City College, Convent Avenue and 140th Street, 10031.

Nyquist, Ewald B., and Hawes, Gene R., eds. *Open Education: A Source Book for Parents and Teachers.* New York: Bantam Books, 1972.

The Open Classroom Environmental Education Project. Monograph. Encino, Calif.: International Center for Educational Development, 16161 Ventura Blvd., September 1973.

Open Door: Informal Education in Two New York City Public Schools. New York: Center for Urban Education, 1970.

Open Education. A special reprint of *The California Journal for Instructional Improvement.* Encino, California: International Center for Educational Development, vol. 14, no. 2, May 1971.

The Open Plan School: Report of a National Seminar. Cosponsored by Educational Facilities Laboratories, Inc. and I.D.E.A., Melbourne, Florida, 1970. (I.D.E.A. occasional paper.)

The Open Pre School. An early education handbook prepared by the editors of *Teacher Magazine,* November 1973.

Perrone, Vito. *Open Education: Promise and Problems.* Bloomington, Ind.: Phi Delta Kappa Education Foundation, 1972.

Plowden, Lady Bridget, et al. *Children and Their Primary Schools: A Report of the Central Advisory Council for Education.* London: Her Majesty's Stationery Office, 1966.

Program Reference Service. *Open Door.* New York: Center for Urban Education, 1971.

Rance, Peter. *Record Keeping in the Progressive Primary School.* London: Ward Lock Educational Co., Ltd., 1971.

Rapport, Virginia. *Learning Centers: Children on Their Own.* Washington, D.C.: The Association for Childhood Education International, 1970.

Rathbone, Charles H., ed. *Open Education: The Informal Classroom.* New York: Citation Press, 1971.

Rogers, Carl. *Freedom to Learn.* Columbus, Ohio: Charles E. Merrill, 1969 (paperback).

Rogers, Vincent R. *Teaching in the British Primary School.* New York: Macmillan, 1970.

Sargent, Betsye. *The Integrated Day in an American School.* Boston: National Association of Independent Schools, 1970.

Saxe, Richard W. *Opening the Schools.* Berkeley, Calif.: McCutchan Publishing Co.

Silberman, Charles E. *Crisis in the Classroom.* New York: Vintage Books, 1970.

———, ed. *The Open Classroom Reader.* New York: Vintage Books, 1973.

Silberman, Melvin; Allender, Jerome S.; and Yanoff, Jay M., eds. *The Psychology of Open Teaching and Learning, An Inquiry Approach.* Boston: Little, Brown, 1972.

Spodek, Bernard, and Walberg, Herbert J. *Studies in Open Education.* New York: Agathon Press.

Stephens, Lillian S. *The Teacher's Guide to Open Education.* New York: Holt, Rinehart and Winston, 1974.

Taylor, Joy. *Organizing the Open Classroom: A Teacher's Guide to the Integrated Day.* New York: Schocken Books, 1972.

Thackray, John; Chaudhry, Juanita; and Grine, Dorothea (program analysts). *Open Door.* New York: Center for Urban Education, 105 Madison Avenue, 10016.

Utsinger, Mary; Martin, Mavis; Belden, Bernard; and Atkinson, Laura. *Experience Centers in Primary Classrooms.* Albuquerque, N.M.: Southwestern Cooperative Educational Laboratory, Inc., 117 Richmond Drive, N.E., Summer 1970.

Vermont State Department of Education. *Vermont Design for Education.* Montpelier: State Department of Education, May 1968. Single copies available (free) from: Office of the Commissioner of Education, Montpelier, Vt., 05602.

Voight, Ralph C. *Invitation to Learning: The Learning Center Handbook.* Washington, D.C.: Acropolis Books Ltd., 1971.

Volkmer, Clara B.; Langstaff, Anne L.; and Higgins, Marilyn. *Structuring the Classroom for Success.* Columbus, Ohio: Charles E. Merrill Publishing Co., 1974.

Walters, Elsa H. *Activity and Experience in the Infant School.* London: National Froebel Foundation, 1951.

Weinstein, Gerald, and Fantini, Mario D. *Toward Humanistic Education—A Curriculum of Affect.* New York: Praeger, 1970.

Weber, Lillian. *The English Infant School and Informal Education.* Englewood Cliffs, N.J.: Prentice-Hall, 1971.

FILMS AND FILMSTRIPS

Films and filmstrips available from I.D.E.A. (Institute for the Development of Educational Activities), P.O. Box 446, Melbourne, Florida 32901 include the following:

Learning How to Learn—The Open Classroom in America. Film rental: $8.00.

Learning How to Learn—A British Junior Classroom. Film rental: $10.00.

Primary Education in England. Film rental: $10.00.

The Open Classroom—Organization and Arrangement. Filmstrip purchase: $12.00.

Films distributed by EDC (Educational Development Center), Inc., 55 Chapel Street, Newton, Massachusetts 02160 include:

Another Way to Learn. Film rental: $10.00.

Battling Brook Primary School. Film rental: $15.00.

Choosing to Learn. Film rental: $20.00.

The First Day. Film rental: $20.00.

I Am Here Today. Film rental: $20.00.

Infants School. Film rental: $15.00.

Medbourne Primary School. Film rental: $10.00.

They Can Do It. Film rental: $15.00.

Westfield Infant School. Film rental: $10.00.

Other films on open education may be obtained from the following sources:

Open Classroom. Sherwin Rubin, 4532 Newton Street, Torrance, Calif. 90505.

Living and Learning in the Open Classroom. International Center for Educational Development, 16161 Ventura Blvd., Encino, Calif. 91316.

The Informal Classroom. Educational Coordinates, 432 S. Pastoria Ave., Sunnyvale, Calif. 94086.

The British Infant School—Southern Style. Promethean Films South, P.O. Box 26363, Birmingham, Ala. 35226.

Index

Activities
artistic, 101–102, 238
choice in, 43–44
confidence-building, 174–175
creativity-encouraging, 23–27
diversity of, 7, 14, 17, 113, 126
formality of, 17
in history, 93–96
inquiry-fostering, 62–66
in invention center, 76–77
in language arts, 125–127, 238–239
with maps, 105–112
in mathematics, 143–144, 238, 282
motivational, 50–55
with natural objects, 194–197
noise level of, 17
optional and required, 125–126,
    137–138, 141–142
problem-solving, 66–69
pupil interests, basis for, 59–62
in reading, 155, 238
for reading readiness, 159–164
in science, 120–125, 238
for single-object centers, 84–87, 89–90
for skill development, 75–76, 213–214
in social studies, 91–93, 115–117, 239
sources of ideas for, 24, 188–190
for theme center, 69–75
in theme-centered classroom, 248
transitional, 238–239, 241
with visual aids, 97–100
Art
center, activities for, 101–102, 238
center, construction of, 101
center, guidelines for establishing,
    102–103
center, materials for, 101–103, 242–243
skills, 100, 103

Community, local
activities related to, 205–206
contact, from source materials, 93
Construction center, 17
Contract, learning
development of, 275
flexibility in, 282
forms of, 275–281
personal interest, 280
primary school, 277–278
for pupil-determined grades, 281

system, disadvantages of, 282
teacher and pupil input into, 274
upper grade, 278–279
varying activities for, 282
Curriculum (see Activities)

Diagnostic learning center, 51–52 (see also
    Diagnostic teaching)
Diagnostic teaching
contracts used for, 273–282
through diagnostic learning centers,
    51–52
formal and informal procedures for, 52
and guiding pupil choice, 45–46
implementation sequence for, 14–15
and implementing prescription, 52–53
of mathematics, 133–141
through observation of pupils' activities,
    51, 284–291
pupil needs and interests assessed for, 14,
    47–48, 268, 270–273, 282–283
of reading, 145–155
of reading readiness, 161–165
Disadvantaged pupils
difficulties of, with open classroom,
    211–213
modifying open classroom for, 213
skill-developing activities for, 213–214

Educational objectives, 249–251
Enrichment center, 54–55
as transition to open classroom, 231–232
Environment (see Physical environment)
Evaluation
through class meetings, 295
through conferences, 148–149
importance of, to continuance of open
    education, 305
and improvement of teaching practices,
    295–302
of learning centers, 266–267
through observation of pupils, 283–291
of openness of teaching practices,
    267–268
of pupil behavior, 288
of pupil creativity, 285–288
through pupil diaries, 282–283
pupil input into procedures for, 292
of pupils' academic progress, 290–292
by pupils of each other, 295

Evaluation *(continued)*
  by pupils of selves, mechanisms for,
    270–274, 292–295
  by pupils of selves, teacher encourage-
    ment of, 35, 270–271
  by pupils of teacher, 302
  of readiness for open learning, 266–268
  and recording of pupil behavior,
    288–289
  written by teacher, 149–150

Free activity period
  as transition to open classroom, 233–235

Implementation of open classroom *(see also*
    Transition to open classroom)
  choosing approach to, 229
  development of pupil readiness for,
    131–132, 208, 210–212
  establishment of climate for, 172–175,
    201
  evaluation of classroom readiness for,
    266–268
  gaining support for, 201, 225
  gradual approach to, 230–237
  guidelines for, 3, 112, 203, 208–209
  importance of physical decentralization
    to, 182
  and institutional requirements, 222–225
  moderate approach to, 237–241
  in one grade level, 224–225
  parent involvement in, 225
  pupil needs and interests assessed for,
    268, 270–273
  pupil participation in, 39–40, 176,
    179–180, 203–205, 230, 233
  pupil-teachers in, 177–178
  role of independent learning in, 174,
    176–177
  role of teacher-pupil relationship in,
    171–174, 176
Independent learning
  benefits to pupils of, 10–11, 31, 174–175
  conditions favorable to, 10
  with diagnostic teaching, 174
  gradual initiation of, 31–32
  in implementing open classroom,
    176–177
  through materials, 11–12, 32–34
  necessity of, 7, 11
  pupil capability for, 11
  for pupils age nine to eleven, 28–30
  for pupils age six to eight, 28, 30
  and self-pacing, 27–31
  training for, 31–32
Inquiry center, 62–66
Interest center
  pupil interests assessed for, 22
  and skills development, 59–61

transition to, from subject center,
    260–261
Invention center, 23–24, 76–77

Language arts *(see also* Reading; Reading
    Readiness)
  center, activities for, 125–127, 238–239
  center, materials for, 244
  center, subdivided, 58
  grammar, 75
  literature, 69
  visual aids as teaching tool for, 98–99
  vocabulary, 34
  writing, 53, 75–76, 104–105
Learning centers *(see also* Implementation
    of open classroom)
  advantages of, 41
  categories of, 49–56
  defined, 56
  guidelines for planning, 41–42
  providing for choice in, 43–44
  pupils' experiences the basis for, 42
Learning disabilities *(see* Disadvantaged
    pupils; Remedial learning center)

Materials *(see also* Multisensory materials;
    Sources of materials)
  antique, for studying history, 88–89,
    93–94
  for art activities, 101–102 242–243
  diversity of, 7, 12, 30, 43, 183, 193, 215
  for language arts, 244
  for mathematics, 141, 243–244
  motivational, 51–52
  natural objects as, 193–194
  prescriptive, 53
  for pupil constructions, 77
  for reading, 165–166, 215
  for reading readiness, 160–162
  for remedial skill development, 213–214
  for science, 245
  self-instructional, 7
  for single-object center, 82–83
  for skill development, 76
  for social studies, 88–89, 91–94, 114–115,
    244
  for storage, 192–193, 245–246
  traditional, 131–132, 137–138, 224
Mathematics
  activities in, 59, 238, 246–247, 282
  job sheets for team learning in, 136–139
  materials for, 141, 243–244
  multilevel approach to, 138, 140–141
  pretesting in, 133, 135, 140
  procedures for diagnostic teaching of,
    133–137
  pupil choice in learning, 44–45, 138
  skills, sequence approach to, 138,
    140–141

team learning in, 134–137
textbooks in, used flexibly, 131–134,
    137–138
Mobility (see Pupil movement)
Motivational learning center, 50–51
Multiexperience learning center
    advantages of, 114
    construction of, 157
    organization of, 157–158
    in pupil specialties, 156–157
    rock center, 194–197
    and skills development, 119, 157
Multisensory materials
    discovery box, 62–63
    importance of variety of, 7, 12, 91
    as sensory-motor aids, 12–13
    shell center, 89–90

Open classroom (see also Implementation of
        open classroom)
    assessments of effectiveness of, 303–304
    characteristics of, 4–5
    misunderstanding about, 2
    pupil behavioral changes from, 303–304
Operational guidelines (see Rules)

Parent involvement, 225, 278–279
Peer teaching (see Pupils as teachers)
Physical environment of open classroom
    construction of equipment for, 17–18,
        107, 137, 218
    equipment for, 6
    flexibility of, 6, 246
    floor use in, 218–219
    importance of, 183, 208, 210
    possible arrangement of, 6, 219, 221
    pupil input into use of, 19
    space use in, 2, 6, 217–222
    transitional arrangements of, 231–232,
        234–235
    use of existing equipment in, 219–221
Pupil input
    determining extent of, 181, 284
    into development of evaluation pro-
        cedures, 292
    into establishment of educational objec-
        tives, 249–250
    and evaluation of teaching, 302
    into implementation of open classroom,
        39–40, 176, 179–180, 203–205,
        230, 233, 236
    importance of, 204–205
    mechanisms for obtaining, 46–47, 75,
        270–275, 292–295
    into rule-setting, 179, 205–208
    ways of encouraging, 34–35
Pupil movement, 251–255, 258–259
Pupils as teachers
    advantages of, 8, 22–23

competency of, 23
    in implementing open classroom, 177–178
    in informal interactions, 21
    through partnership learning, 21
    in reading, 146–155
    training of, 23, 178
Pupil specialty center, 156–158

Reading (see also Reading readiness)
    activities in, 155–157, 166, 238
    as basis for interpretative skills, 55, 70–71
    center, establishment of, 144–145
    center, subdivided, 58
    diagnosis of ability in, 52, 149–152
    difficulties with, 158–159
    focused, 156–157
    materials for, 32–33, 145, 165–166
    through pupil interests, 29, 145–146,
        156–157, 165–167
    pupil-teacher program in
        advantages and disadvantages of,
            153–154
        guidelines for, 152
        preparation for, 146, 148
        procedures for, 148–152
        record-keeping for, 148–149, 154
        skills development through, 149,
            154–155
    skills in, developed informally in learning
        centers, 123, 144, 158
    taught through visual aids, 104
Reading readiness
    activities for, 159–164, 213–214
    center, for expanding pupil interest,
        215–216
    center, sequence of learning in, 216
    diagnostic program for, 161–165
    materials for, 160–162, 164–165, 215
    prerequisite skills for, 160–161
    pupil difficulties with, 158–159
    remedial, 213–214
Record-keeping (see also Evaluation)
    instruments for, 142, 256–259
    minimizing, 154
    and redirection of activity, 143
Remedial learning center, 213–214
Rules
    about completion of activities, 260–262
    criteria for, 206
    enforced by natural consequences of
        behavior, 179
    positively stated, 207
    about pupil movement, 251
    pupil role in formulating, 179, 205–208

Science
    activities in, 73–74, 120–125, 238
    center, construction of, 113
    chemistry, 44

Science *(continued)*
  evaluation of progress in, 291–292
  materials for, 120, 188–189, 245
  and space center, 124–125
Self-correction materials, 112
Self-directed learning *(see* Independent
    learning)
Single-object center, 82–89
Skills center, 75–76
Social studies
  activities in, 72–73, 239
  anthropology, 115
  archaeology, 116–119
  cultural history, 87–89, 91–94, 97–98
  current events, 54–55, 93
  economics, 67–69
  history, 93–96, 114
  through maps, 105–112
  materials for, 244
Sources of materials, 183–192
  in community, 93
  free, 83, 183–188
  ideas for, 188
  from pupils, 83, 190–192
  for reading, 165–166
  for science, 120, 245
  for social studies, 88, 91–93, 114, 116
Subject center *(see also* specific subjects)
  approach, disadvantages of, 247–248
  diversification of activities in, 58–59,
    246–248
  possible physical arrangements for, 6, 58

Teacher-pupil relationship

forms of, in open classroom, 8
  in implementing open classroom, 171–174
  improved by open classroom, 9, 10
  teacher's responsibility in, 27
Teacher's role
  discussion of, with pupils, 208
  in encouraging creativity, 26–27
  extent of, in planning, 202
  self-evaluation of, 296–302
  and values, importance of, 180–182,
    202–203
Team learning, 132, 134–137 *(see also*
    Pupils as teachers)
Textbooks, 131–134, 137–138
  required, integrating in open classroom,
    224
Theme center, 69–75
Transition to open classroom *(see also*
    Implementation of open classroom)
  combination of formal and informal
    learning as, 240–241
  through enrichment center, 231–232
  through free activity period, 233–235
  through interest activity period, 236
  one-day-a-week approach to, 237–240
  possible physical arrangements for,
    231–232, 234–235
  through skills development period,
    235–236
  starting with one learning center, 230–232
  starting with small number of pupils,
    236–237
  starting with traditional methods,
    131–132